In Pursuit *of* Democracy

Praise for the book

Dr Najma Heptulla's autobiography is a compelling read that highlights her distinguished career as a stateswoman and an unwavering advocate of democracy. Her sharp intellect and engaging, witty writing style bring to life the pivotal moments that shaped both her personal journey and the nation's history. As one of India's longest-serving parliamentarians and presiding officers, her autobiography is a testament to her remarkable contributions. I have seen her excellent performance as Governor under my tenure as President of India. This book is an invaluable addition to any collection, offering deep insights into the life of a true stalwart of democracy.

Ram Nath Kovind, Former President of India

In *In Pursuit of Democracy*, Dr Najma Heptulla reveals the human side of politics—a world where triumphs are hard-won, and challenges are met with staunch determination. Her autobiography brings to light her lifelong dedication to championing the cause of women. In various capacities, she has consistently advocated for women's rights and empowerment while also working tirelessly to advance their interests.

This book is not just a recounting of a life lived with purpose but also a guidebook for those who seek to make a difference in the world.

Nirmala Sitharaman, Union Minister, Finance and Corporate Affairs

Dr Najma Heptulla's autobiography is not just about her life in politics, but also a celebration of women's potential, underscoring the author's belief that women can achieve anything. Her narrative is enriched with personal anecdotes and emotional events, reflecting her philosophy of giving one hundred per cent to every task. The book is a treasure trove of lighter moments, world travels, and her deft handling of Arab state heads and diplomacy, which reveal her multifaceted personality.

Dr Heptulla stands as a symbol of unity in diversity, making this work an exhibit of her legacy and a must-read for anyone interested in the complexities of India's political and cultural heritage.

Nitin Gadkari, Union Minister, Road Transport and Highways

I have had the distinct privilege of witnessing Dr Najma Heptulla's remarkable journey in the Rajya Sabha. This book stands as a testament to her extraordinary career. As the longest-serving Deputy Chairperson of the Rajya Sabha, she managed the House of Elders with unparalleled grace and efficiency. Her autobiography offers an intimate glimpse into her advocacy for minority rights and social justice, and her contributions to diplomacy, cultural preservation, and women's rights. Her influential role as President of the Inter- Parliamentary Union highlights her international stature, while her tenure as Minister of Minority Affairs underscores her commitment to public service.

Ghulam Nabi Azad, Former Union Minister, Former Leader of Opposition, Rajya Sabha, and Former Chief Minister, Jammu and Kashmir

Growing up, we were always hearing stories of Najma-pijaan's trips abroad, meeting world leaders on behalf of our country. We knew her as an honest politician, but we had little idea of the full extent of her achievements. She earned her PhD at just 22, turned down a NASA job to care for her family, and eventually embarked on a political career that changed Indian politics for the better.

What truly stands out, though, is the humility and grace with which she reflects on her incredible journey. Her autobiography, *In Pursuit of Democracy*, is as remarkable as her life. It makes me proud to be her nephew.

Aamir Khan, Actor and Filmmaker

Few politicians have had a ringside view to Indian politics over such an extended period quite like Dr Najma Heptulla. She has a vivid memory that brings to life many a twist and turn in Indian politics. Hers is the story of an India old and new.

Rajdeep Sardesai, Senior Journalist, Bestselling Author

In Pursuit *of* Democracy
Beyond Party Lines

NAJMA HEPTULLA

First published by
Rupa Publications India Pvt. Ltd 2024
7/16, Ansari Road, Daryaganj
New Delhi 110002

Sales Centres:

Prayagraj Bengaluru Chennai
Hyderabad Jaipur Kathmandu
Kolkata Mumbai

Copyright © Najma Heptulla 2024

The views and opinions expressed in this book are the author's own and the facts are as reported by her to the best of her knowledge/memory and which have been verified to the extent possible, without any intention to cause harm, injury or damage. The publishers are not in any way liable for the same.

All rights reserved.
No part of this publication may be reproduced, transmitted,
or stored in a retrieval system, in any form or by any means,
electronic, mechanical, photocopying, recording or otherwise,
without the prior permission of the publisher.

P-ISBN: 978-93-6156-937-1
E-ISBN: 978-93-6156-381-2

First impression 2024

10 9 8 7 6 5 4 3 2 1

The moral right of the author has been asserted.

Printed in India

This book is sold subject to the condition that it shall not,
by way of trade or otherwise, be lent, resold, hired out, or otherwise
circulated, without the publisher's prior consent, in any form of binding
or cover other than that in which it is published.

My Mother and Father: Fatima and Syed Yousuf Ali
My Aunt: Aysha Ansari
My Husband: Akbar Ali Adamji Heptulla

CONTENTS

Foreword ix
Prologue xi

SECTION I: THE FORMATIVE YEARS

1. The Inheritance of History 3
2. A Woman of Substance 24
3. Training for Democracy 39

SECTION II: CHASING THE IMPOSSIBLE

4. In Indira's India 55
5. Party Work and Party Talk 81
6. A True Parliamentarian 97
7. Politics in Transition 125
8. A New Innings 144

SECTION III: ECHOES IN TIME

9. A Women's Woman 163
10. The World as My Family 182

Epilogue: An Ode to Chhipkalis and Mendaks 205
Acknowledgements 209
Annexure 212
Index 215

FOREWORD

I am deeply honoured to write this foreword for *In Pursuit of Democracy: Across Party Lines,* the autobiography of Dr Najma Heptulla, an esteemed leader and a remarkable individual whose impact on Indian politics and society has been profound and enduring. I have had the privilege of knowing Dr Heptulla both as a professional colleague and a close friend of my family for nearly four decades, since she began her political career in the early 1980s.

Throughout her journey, I have closely observed Dr Heptulla's ascent from her early days as a member of Parliament representing Maharashtra, to her significant contributions on both national and international stages. Her career, spanning over thirty-six years in the Rajya Sabha, has been characterized by her unwavering commitment to public service, her impartiality, and her dedication to upholding the dignity of the parliamentary process.

Dr Heptulla's work has consistently championed the empowerment of marginalized communities and women from all walks of life. Her efforts to promote their inclusion in mainstream society have been exemplary. Her tenure as Minister of Minority Affairs in the Narendra Modi-led government is a testament to her dedication to these causes.

From 1999 to 2002, Dr Heptulla served as President of the Inter-Parliamentary Union (IPU). I had the opportunity to participate in some of the conferences of the IPU where I could witness her deliberations with international delegates and dialogue with prominent world leaders. She demonstrated her diplomatic acumen and her ability to foster dialogue among nations.

Even at the national level, Dr Heptulla made her mark. On the backdrop of today's situation in Manipur, I recall her efforts to engage with various stakeholders in Manipur, which were instrumental in addressing some of the complex issues facing the state.

Dr Heptulla's autobiography is a reflection of her life's work, which has left an indelible mark on India's political and social fabric. Even after stepping down from active politics, she remains an influential figure, admired for her intellect, integrity, and unwavering commitment to public service. Her life continues to inspire many, making her a true icon in Indian politics and beyond.

I am proud to call Dr Najma Heptulla a friend and a colleague, and I believe her autobiography will serve as an inspiration for future generations, particularly for women who seek to enter the political arena. I wish her all the best as she shares her remarkable journey with the world.

Sharad Pawar
Former Chief Minister of Maharashtra &
Founder, Nationalist Congress Party
Mumbai, 20 August 2024

PROLOGUE

How does one revisit one's past? T.S. Eliot, one of my favourite poets, believed that the past is best captured in objects: 'It is only in the world of objects that we have time and space and selves.'*
I am immediately reminded of the fabulous radio series and book *A History of the World in 100 Objects,* curated by BBC Radio 4 and the British Museum to map two million years of human history. So far, while my own journey may have been a bit over eight decades, to me it resembles an outsized multimedia installation, filled with faces, ideas, events, people, words, sounds and colours—some blurred, others extremely vivid, a few rose-tinted, and yet others sepia-toned. Guided by Eliot's words, I would like to curate the 'objects' in my mind that have made me who I am, that have shaped my lived and experienced reality.

I never shied away from dreaming big, no matter how unrealistic it may have seemed. This has been true since my childhood. In 1947, as a seven-year-old in Bhopal when I learned about the United Nations (UN), I immediately dreamt of digging a tunnel to New York to work with them and help make the world a better place. This is the story of a girl who dreamed big.

At the same time, it traces the journey of India, the nation, in a geopolitical age. Many of my recollections are about moments in the life-story of modern India—during its calmer times as well as in its turbulent hours—and of its leaders who made or broke the system. It also chronicles issues I have been deeply concerned

---

*Eliot, T.S., in Roberts, Sam, 'Object Lessons in History', *The New York Times*, 27 September 2014, https://tinyurl.com/75mks3ev. Accessed on 16 July 2024.

about all through my life—women must get their fair share in life and in the national agenda; the environment must be preserved as an essential dimension of the nation's well-being; minorities must get priority in the political system, simply because they will never have a say in a non-consensus voting system; and finally, isolated communities, states and people must be treated with equal importance as everyone else in the national agenda.

In 1980, 33 years after digging my imaginary tunnel to the UN, I set foot in the Parliament in New Delhi, as a young parliamentarian. In the Central Hall was a life-size portrait of my Dada Abba, Maulana Abul Kalam Azad, scholar, freedom fighter and the first minister of education of independent India. The painting by K.K. Hebbar showed him with a book in one hand, a walking stick in the other, and a rose graciously pinned to his lapel. I stood in front of it for a while. As I stared at the portrait, I knew that my life was about to take a dramatic turn. I did not know that the thrill I felt that day would lead to a book one day, but I was truly inspired by the thought that my ancestor loved this country, fought for it, and gave back to it through public service. Even today, I remember that moment clearly.

Over the years, as I witnessed democracy at work, I realized that my experience in governance could well culminate in a book. *In Pursuit of Democracy: Beyond Party Lines* is a summation of the odyssey that has been my life.

The story starts with my formative years in a Muslim family helmed by strong women, in the princely state of Bhopal—the City of Lakes—in Central India, where I was born, and which had been ruled by generations of powerful Muslim women rulers. Growing up, I was made to understand that studies were important for both men and women, as both play equally important roles in advancing our society. I studied hard and aced in science and math. Although discouraged to study medicine as a girl, I brooked no argument when it came to studying science, albeit as the only girl in that section. I, however, outperformed the boys, topped the university,

Prologue

earned my doctorate, and started to teach at the young age of 22.

The events after marriage and motherhood altered my horizons. Heptulla Park, my husband's ancestral home in Mumbai, was inundated with a constant flow of politicians. I hardly realized when I started gravitating towards social work and politics under the gentle influence of my gregarious husband.

From Mumbai, the story moved to the massive circular building complex, the old Parliament, at the heart of New Delhi, where I spent most of my work life. At the relatively young age of 40, I became a parliamentarian at the benign insistence of Indira Gandhi, India's first woman prime minister and also a family friend. I learnt politics on the ground as a general secretary of the Indian National Congress as well as at the temple of democracy—the Parliament, where I served from 1980 till 2016.

During my political career, I came across people who inspired me and taught me the ropes of politics. I also saw people corrupted by excessive power, greed, ambition and sycophancy. For 17 years of my four decades as a parliamentarian, I was Deputy Chairperson of the Rajya Sabha—the longest-serving presiding officer of a Parliament anywhere in the world. I worked with almost all prime ministers of modern India, engaged with political leaders of all stripes, and fought tooth and nail to protect the dignity of the Upper House. While my reputation as a principled parliamentarian gained in stature, what remained hidden was my complex and steep learning curve: how to practise the art of persuasion and patience, listen to all views and polarized rhetoric, remain above party interest, maintain a fine balance between cooperation and conflict, and not become cynical or lose my sense of humour.

Call it kismet, destiny or luck, my childhood dream came true. Successive prime ministers of India sent me out to countries across the world—sometimes to deliver their messages to world leaders and international audiences, and at other times on goodwill missions. I was also assigned to work with global parliamentary organizations, especially the UN and its agencies, all of which gave me the opportunity to watch parliamentary practices in other countries up-close, as well as travel to places rarely visited by tourists. So intense and creative was my participation in the Inter-Parliamentary Union (IPU)—a world organization of Parliaments of 180 countries working in close collaboration with the UN—that in 1999 I was elected its first woman president. It was indeed a historic first in the IPU's 110-year history and a great honour for India.

The year 2004 marked a major turning point that ushered in the next chapter of my life. I left the Congress, and joined the Bharatiya Janata Party (BJP) under the inclusive and reflective guidance of its leader Atal Bihari Vajpayee. For years, my decision was dogged by controversy, with various news outlets probing for details. Undeterred, I carried on with my work as a vice president of the BJP, as a member of its national executive, as a cabinet minister under Prime Minister Narendra Modi, and finally as Governor of Manipur.

In many ways, my journey has been lonesome. There have been few women role models to emulate, or women in leadership positions to serve as mentors. Surprisingly, decades later, the situation has not changed. The percentage of women in India's newly-elected Parliament remains as dismal as it was during my time. In 2024, a year marked by elections in over 60 countries, there are very few women in the electoral race. Gender equality in the highest positions of power is clearly a distant dream. This can make my journey—a woman's journey—in a man's world relevant for many readers. I would like them to judge for themselves if I have managed to break the glass ceiling.

I have been quite certain, even before I picked up the pen, that my autobiography had to have the entertaining sweep of a good novel. Simply because I have never had a dull moment in my long life and career. I am reminded of American novelist Truman Capote's *In Cold Blood* (1965), a non-fiction novel that employs all the techniques of fiction but is immaculately factual. My aim has been to follow that captivating narrative form. So my memoir is not a journalistic narrative. And there is no criminal investigation in it, though I have lived through assassinations, tragedies and crimes against humanity. And yet, if the reader finds the story of my life a lively page-turner based on truth, real events and people, my purpose will have been served.

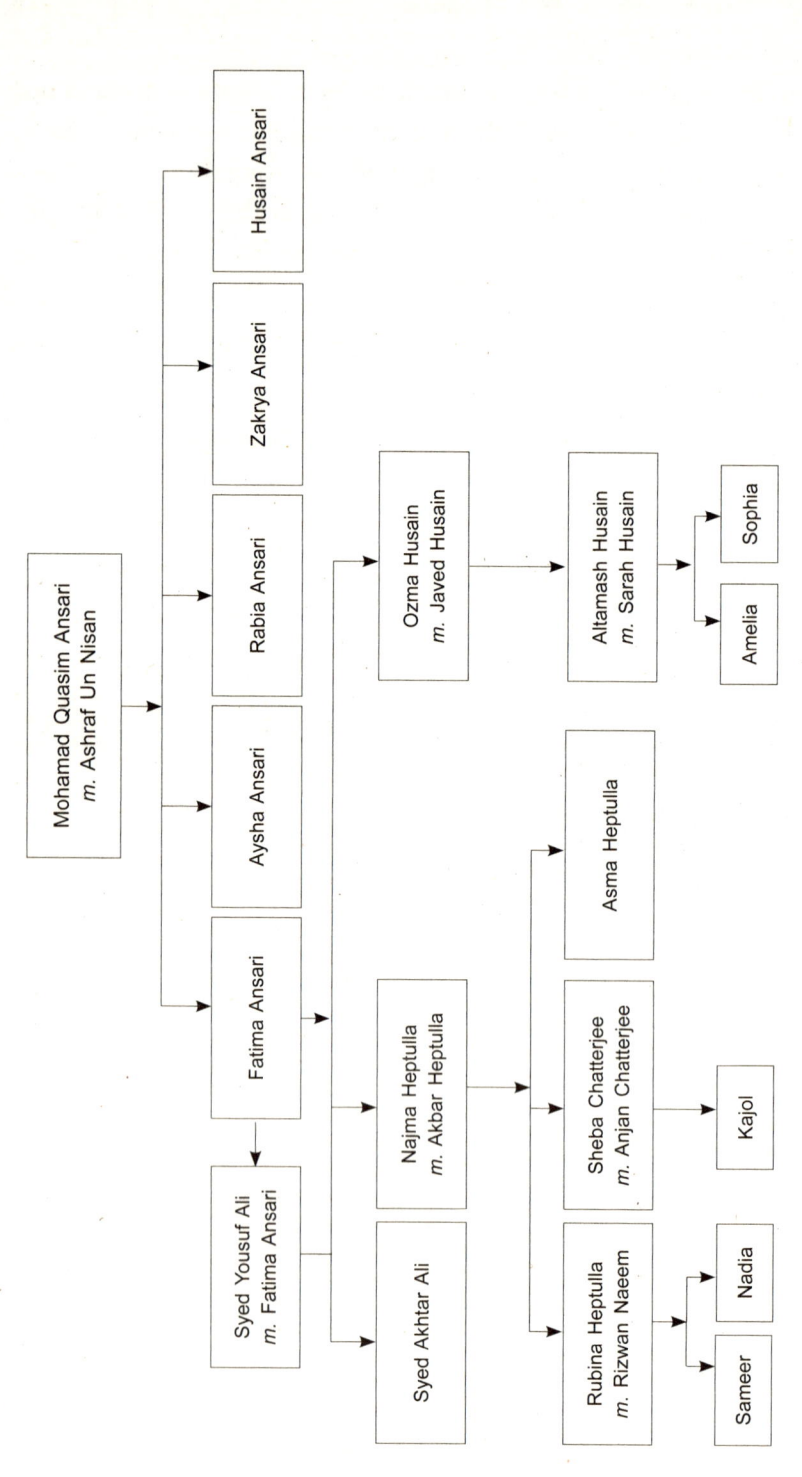

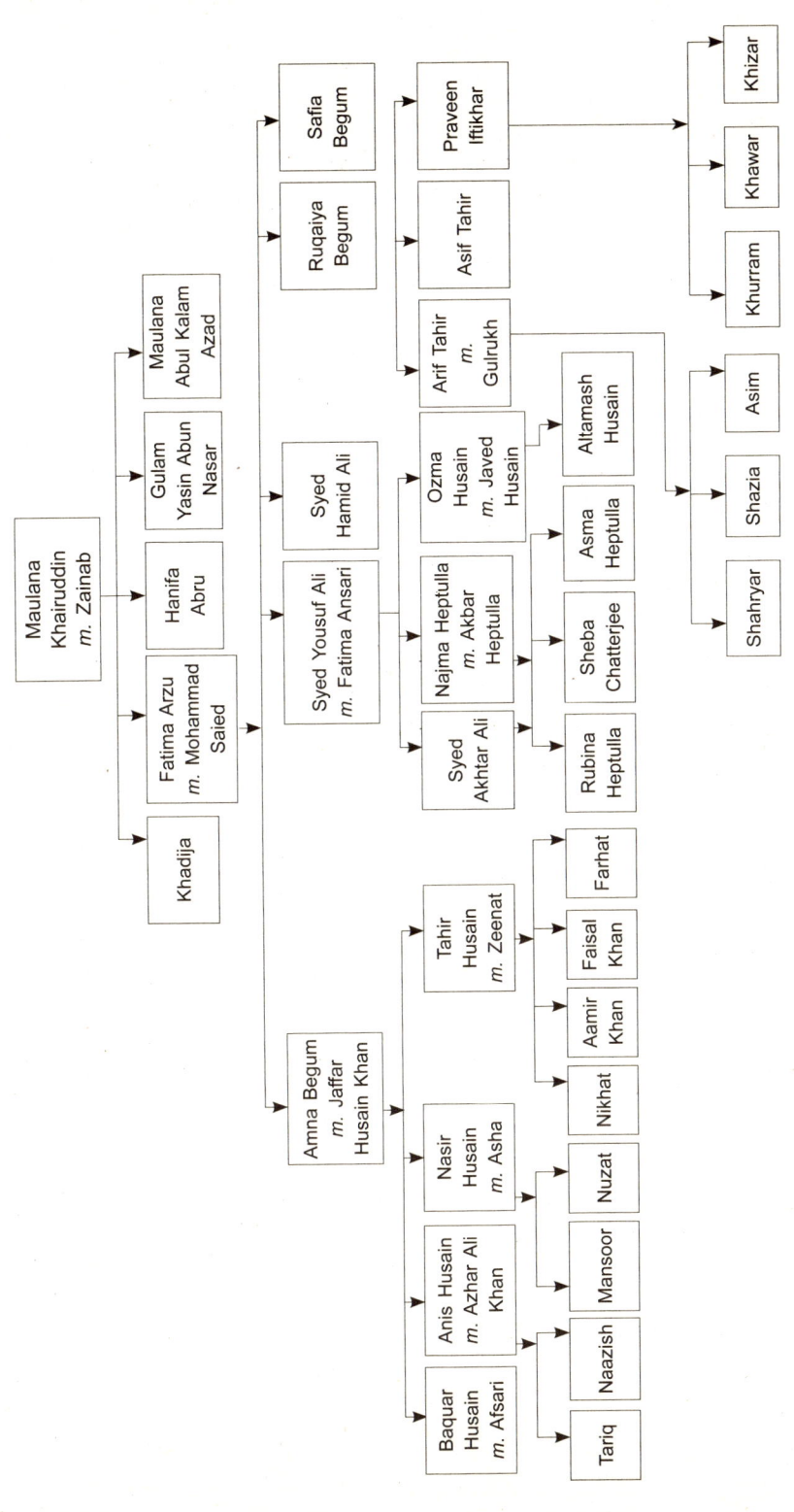

SECTION I

The Formative Years

1
THE INHERITANCE OF HISTORY

It was the night of 13 October 1989, my eldest daughter's birthday. She had just turned 22 and I had been unable to spend time with her—one more special day missed like many others before it, for a calling larger than life. I still remember exactly where I was, what I was doing, and why my work mattered on that day.

It was past midnight. The Rajya Sabha, or the Upper House of the Indian Parliament, was in turmoil over a Bill; if passed, the 64th Constitutional Amendment Bill proposing one-third reservation in favour of women at the lowest rungs of democracy—Panchayati Raj—could create history. As Deputy Chairperson of the Rajya Sabha, I had been presiding over the deliberations without a break for over six hours, although I had allowed the members to go out for coffee or to grab a bite.

Earlier that year, Prime Minister Rajiv Gandhi's announcement about including women in the governance of grassroots institutions like the Panchayati Raj had sparked a fierce war of words. His government enjoyed an extraordinary majority in the Lok Sabha, or Lower House, and the Bill had sailed through. The Rajya Sabha was another story since he did not have sufficient numbers there. I was tired but very hopeful that the Bill would be passed, and lead to the much-needed empowerment of women at the grassroots.

Heated arguments and counters flew thick and fast between the members of the ruling party seated to the right of the chairperson and those of the Opposition seated to the left. After the voice vote, the Opposition asked for a division (actual counting) by an automatic vote recorder. The galleries were cleared, the quorum bell was rung to summon back all the members, and entrances to the inner lobby of Parliament were closed. In front of each member was a voting console with three buttons—green for 'Aye', red for 'No' and yellow for 'Abstain'. When the results showed up on the electronic display boards on either side of the presiding officer's seat, I was dismayed—the Bill had been defeated by only three votes.[1]

I adjourned the House. By the time I reached home, 4 Akbar Road, in the heart of Delhi, I had tears in my eyes. With a heavy heart, I called up the prime minister. His secretary Vincent George picked up the phone and put me through instantly. I was so inconsolable that I blurted out, 'Sir, I am crying.'

He said, 'But why are you crying?'

'It was such a significant Bill; it would have changed the lives of millions of women. They stopped it from becoming a law,' I added.

'Don't cry,' he said. 'We will reintroduce it and we will pass it the next time.'

On that upbeat response, I calmed myself that night.

Destiny had its own plans. Rajiv Gandhi would never be able to reintroduce that Bill. A week later, the Congress Party lost its mandate. Within two years, on 21 May 1991, he was assassinated at Sriperumbudur in Tamil Nadu.

The Bill, however, could not be put down easily. Across the country, women had started demanding their democratic right to be recognized, heard and included in the political system. Soon, it became an election issue. The Congress Party was voted back to power the year Rajiv died. Prime Minister P.V. Narasimha Rao reintroduced the Bill. This time around, it was passed by both Houses of Parliament. One-third reservation for women

---

[1]Rajya Sabha Secretariat.

representatives in local self-governments was ensured. I presided again when the Bill became an Act of Parliament in December 1992.

Reservation of seats for women allowed them to learn the ropes of governance at the grassroots, get trained in collective deliberation, develop confidence, and compete for positions in the higher echelons of our tiered democracy—a predominantly male preserve for long. Mamata Banerjee, Chief Minister of West Bengal, and Mayawati, former Chief Minister of Uttar Pradesh, were two among a million-strong grassroots women who had built themselves and their parties from ground up over time, to become prominent leaders.

NOT THE SECOND SEX

My story is not one of personal achievement in isolation. When a society talks of women, words like 'women's empowerment' do the rounds, but nobody empowers women. They never have—not in England, which was the cradle of modern democracy, not in the United States, the first constitutional republic, not in modern Saudi Arabia, with its deep-rooted patriarchal patronizing of women. Women have always stood up and fought for their rights—the right to vote, the right to be heard, and the right to equal opportunity. And they have always stood on the shoulders of oft-overlooked, unspoken and uncelebrated giants.

The 'giants' in my world were strong and inspiring women—in my family and in the state of Bhopal, where I was born. The first 'feminists' I encountered were right in our house—educated women, who chose to work outside home, and garnered respect as educationists, authors, orators and administrators in those days. My lifelong commitment to women's issues was imbibed from them. Thanks to them, I just knew as I grew up—a bit of a 'tomboy' really, climbing trees, riding my pony, or playing cricket with my brother—that women had to study, they had to go out into the world and work, just as men did, for self-esteem, for social recognition, and for self-sufficiency.

Amma, my paternal grandmother, had an enormous influence on me. Her name was Fatima Begum, but she went by the epithet, Fatima Arzu Begum, styled after the genre of Urdu Arzu poetry that reflects universal human yearnings, hopes and aspirations. Her innate optimism and unwavering hope allowed her to fight off challenges and raise five children single-handedly, as my grandfather passed away when she was still carrying her youngest daughter. And she did a fine job of raising them, sending them to good schools and educating them to be confident citizens of tomorrow.

Born in the late nineteenth century, Amma and her younger sister, my Chhoti Amma, Hanifa Abru, or Abru Begum, had a highly academic upbringing. They were educated at home by their father alongside their brothers, without prejudice or difference. Extremely learned and dynamic, their lifelong concern was to uplift the condition of women. As members of the All-India Muslim Women's Conference, they travelled far and wide—Aligarh, Lahore, Hyderabad—attending and addressing women's conferences. They belonged to the first generation of 'new Muslim women' of India, who stepped out of their homes into the larger sphere of public life—something unthinkable until then.

My earliest memory of my grandmother was of her seated at her desk. Every morning, I woke up to see her reading official documents and signing papers presented to her by her secretary. Besides being Director of Girls' Education in Bhopal, she was also in charge of the technical training institution set up by the Bhopal royals—a groundbreaking effort to teach women high-quality arts and crafts, *zari*, *zardozi* and *karchobi* work as well as other equally sophisticated techniques of embroidery, and different types of handicrafts, including cane and bamboo—to enhance their skills and earning capabilities. The handicrafts they created were in great demand, giving many of them a strong foundation in entrepreneurship.

Grand Aunt Abru Begum was in charge of a progressive social

club for women—the Princess of Wales Ladies' Club, set up by the British royals. She and her secretary would often discuss work at the club. The purpose of the club was to provide a platform to elite women for learning, philanthropy and activism. Every year, Abru Begum would organize a month-long event called Numaish (exhibition), which was handled and attended exclusively by women. Women from all parts of the country convened to sell their handmade artefacts, accessories and cuisines here. For the women of Bhopal, Numaish was a source of great excitement.

Every morning, I watched as my grandmothers got ready and went out to work—school visits, inspections, supervision, or to take classes. For me as a child, they exuded confidence, authority and purpose. Their appearance, choice of clothing, and fluency in multiple languages set them apart as women. The typical Bhopali dress for women of the time consisted of a *kurta* with *churidar* or *pajama*, and a long *dupatta* (knee-length or long shirt with tight or loose pants, and a scarf). For the women in my family, however, it was always the saree, worn in the formal style even at home. They did not wear demure, full-sleeved blouses but half-sleeved puffed ones. And they donned a type of burqa only when they went out, never at home.

My grandmother and grandaunt, both polyglots, could easily switch from Urdu to Persian to Arabic and back again. I, however, felt that they spoke in Arabic when they wanted to hide something from us children. I remember how excited I was one day, when someone sent us boxes of laddu. I, however, was not well that day, so the elders decided to store those someplace where I could not find them easily. They spoke to each other in colloquial Arabic, 'Haza gattu' (Hide it). All ears and misconstruing the words, I piped up, 'Adha laddu' (Give me half a laddu). Everyone burst out laughing.

Another great influence in my life was my mother's sister, Aysha Ansari—Chhoti Khalajan to me. A much-esteemed teacher of Urdu, she had a Master's degree in those days, when few women went in for advanced degrees. She taught at Cambridge School, Bhopal's oldest English-medium, co-educational school. She never married and took me under her wing. She taught me all that she knew, from appreciating books and poetry to knitting, embroidery and crochet. She did not know how to cook, so I did not learn cooking until I got married—that, too, because my husband was fond of food. The confidence I gained, thanks to her, helped me blossom in all spheres of my life.

Chhoti Khalajan made me the person I am today, because she instilled in me some of the most important values I live by to date. I was sent to a co-ed school and college because she insisted on it. She told me, 'You have to be familiar with boys and treat them as you treat girls.' I grew to be comfortable with boys—a valuable experience indeed, as I worked mostly with men throughout my career. In the Indian Parliament, there were few women. Internationally, too, I dealt largely with men. I never thought of men as any different from women; to me they were just people.

Chhoti Khalajan was also a perfectionist and taught me to be one. I remember when my sister Ozma was born, one day Khalajan asked me to knit socks for the baby—not an easy thing to do when you are just a seven-year-old and new to knitting. Our home overlooked the massive Bhopal Lake called the Bada Talab. It was raining and I sat on a window sill, knitting, but distracted by the rainy ripples on the lake. I did not realize that I had skipped a few stitches. Khalajan flung the needles and ball of wool through the window and then asked me to fetch everything back and start all over again. That day, I learnt an invaluable lesson—to give cent per cent of myself to the task at hand. It would eventually become a way of life for me. Over time, I became a master knitter, embroiderer, crocheter, and a perfectionist.

The window sill in Khalajan's room was my favourite retreat. I went to school with her, came back and then sat there for hours, reading. I remember the first day she took me to school. I took a test and was sent to upper kindergarten, although I was younger than the other students. The teacher gave me a book—*The Radiant Reader*—and an exercise book to write in. I came back home, sat at the window sill and finished the book and the assignment. The next day, I asked the teacher for more. She was surprised that I had already finished reading the book, since it was meant to be studied over the year. That became a recurring pattern throughout my academic career, and eventually enabled me to obtain my PhD when I was just 22 years old. It was Khalajan's attention to detail and her home lessons that made me intellectually more mature than my age.

TRADITION OF LEARNING

For centuries, my family had distinguished itself in the pursuit of knowledge. My forefathers came to India from Herat in Afghanistan during the Mughal era and settled down in Delhi, excelling as scholars, jurists and religious teachers. The last of the line in imperial service was Maulana Munawaruddin, who was in charge of all the educational institutions of the Mughal Empire. A holy man, and a Sufi *pir* (spiritual guide), he had a number of followers across India.

By the eighteenth century, the Mughal Empire had begun spiralling into decline. Maulana Munawaruddin became frustrated with the moral degeneration of the Mughal court and decided to migrate to the Hejaz region of Saudi Arabia—home to Muslim holy cities—then under the Turkish Ottoman Empire. On his way, Maulana Munawaruddin passed through Bombay, where he had many followers, and eventually died in Mecca circa 1857–59. His grandson, Maulana Khairuddin, was highly enlightened and lived in the company of scholars and divine souls in Mecca.

One of Maulana Khairuddin's life's works was to restore the 20-km-long Zubaida Canal in Mecca. Built in the ninth century at the behest of Queen Zubaida, wife of the legendary Caliph Harun al-Rashid, to provide water to Hajj pilgrims, the canal had shrunk to a trickle in the course of a thousand years. A Sufi pir too, Maulana Khairuddin used to travel between India, Turkey and Indonesia to meet his followers and also to trade. Over these sojourns, he collected a large sum of money and donated it to the sharif, the Turkish representative in Mecca, to rebuild the canal. For this good work, he was honoured by the Sultan of Turkey. Years later, I managed to track down and unite with the descendants of the family who had donated to the project, both in Saudi Arabia and India.

Maulana Khairuddin married Zainab, the niece of Sheikh Mohammad bin Zahire Watri, the *mufti* (in this context, governor) of the city of Medina, and had five children—three daughters: Khadija Begum, Fatima Abru Begum, and Hanifa Arzu Begum, and two sons: Gulam Yasin Abun Nasar and Abul Kalam. Abul Kalam, who came to be known as Maulana Azad, became one of the greatest freedom fighters and founding fathers when India won Independence. A scholar, writer, poet and journalist, like his ancestors over the centuries, he was also the first minister of education of independent India.

Around the 1890s, when Maulana Khairuddin visited India with his family, his wife passed away in Calcutta (now Kolkata), then the capital of India. He had a large number of disciples in the city and settled down there. He educated his children at home; the same education was given to both boys and girls. In those days, women were engaged at an early age to be married to men from within the family. My grandmother, Fatima Arzu Begum, was engaged to her cousin while still in Saudi Arabia. When her fiancé, Mohammad Sayed, came to Calcutta for the wedding, Maulana Khairuddin convinced him to stay back and work in the city.

A Muslim scholar who had authored over ten books, Maulana Khairuddin was a very influential and respected figure among the larger Muslim population. Due to his stature, even his children were treated with reverence. His son, Abul Kalam, however, did not like the excessive adulation of his father's followers and refused to carry forward his father's legacy. My grandmother used to say that her brother Abul Kalam was different even as a child. He was the intellectual, the enlightened one, a *maulana* (learned Muslim scholar). His father had once foretold that as a man, Abul Kalam or Maulana Azad would either lead millions towards light or lead them astray into darkness. He did the former. A brilliant student, he developed an independent and enlightened view on life. Open to Western knowledge systems, he experimented with atheism and the teachings of Sri Aurobindo. His path as a leader was clear to him.

By the early decades of the twentieth century, Maulana Azad's political persona was rapidly evolving. Calcutta was the hotbed of revolutionary nationalism against colonial rule. He joined the movement, launching his own Urdu journals—*Al-Hilal* and *Al-Balagh*—for young Muslims. Through these, he openly attacked British policies and encouraged young Muslims to fight for Hindu-Muslim unity, and for India's independence. The tremendous popularity of these journals disturbed the British government. The journals were banned, his home was repeatedly raided and ransacked, and the punitive Defence of India Act, 1915, was invoked against him. Calcutta became dangerous for the family. In 1916, he was arrested. It was around this time that the family found a new and unexpected safe haven—Bhopal.

A HOME CALLED BHOPAL

Surrounded by the formidable Vindhyachal Mountains, the undulating volcanic landscape of the Malwa Plateau and the mighty Narmada River, Bhopal was a small princely state in Central India. Its breathtaking terrain was replete with lakes and hillocks, lush greenery and waterfalls, forts and palaces, monuments and sculptures. Of the numerous lakes, the massive Bada Talab dated back a thousand years, while the smaller Chhota Talab was created in the eighteenth century.

Bhopal was ruled by four generations of strong women—Nawab

Begums—belonging to an Afghan dynasty of Jalalabad. Between 1819 and 1926, they survived murder plots and forceful seizure of power. Known for their relentless diplomacy with the British, they experimented with tradition and modernity, to build a rich legacy.[2] They ruled with a strong hand and under their enlightened rule, Bhopal developed a singular culture that was syncretic and inclusive. It also became a significant centre of innovative social reforms, especially in women's education and health. The rulers gave refuge to progressive women of all communities, who, in turn, influenced the reformist development of the state through their service.

The Nawab Begums were known for leading armies into battle and indulging in the male-dominated pastimes such as polo (Bhopal royals played polo on cycles), archery, lancing and tiger-hunting. The last woman ruler of Bhopal, Nawab Sultan Jahan Begum, who ruled between 1901 and 1926, promoted innumerable women's schools and training institutes, founded women's clubs and hospitals, and developed schemes for underprivileged women. She also undertook extensive vaccination drives and improved sanitation, hygiene and water supply. Sultan Jahan Begum considered learning martial arts, marksmanship, swimming, and riding essential for the girls of the royal family. In the 1930s and '40s, her two youngest daughters, Princess Sajida and Princess Rabia, joined a glamorous circle of Indian princes who were fond of sports. Nawab Hamidullah Khan, who ascended the throne in 1926, was President of the Board of Control for Cricket in India. His daughters played cricket and Princess Sajida married cricketer Iftikhar Ali Khan, Nawab of Pataudi. Their son, Mansur Ali Khan Pataudi, was one of the finest batsmen and captains of India.[3]

---

[2]Hurley, Siobhan Lambert, 'Contesting Seclusion: The Political Emergence of Muslim Women in Bhopal, 1901–1930', *ProQuest LLC* (2017), May 1998, https://tinyurl.com/mssphezv. Accessed on 16 July 2024.

[3]Mandal, Prasanta Kumar, 'Administration under Begums with Special Reference to Princely State of Bhopal', *International Journal of Research in Social Sciences*, Vol. 9, No. 3, March 2019, https://tinyurl.com/2fsk7ac5. Accessed on 16 July 2024.

Nawab Sultan Jahan Begum was one of the leading lights of Aligarh Muslim University and its first chancellor. She met my grandmother Fatima Arzu Begum and grandaunt Abru Begum at some conference and was impressed by their erudition and their work in the uplift of Indian women. She invited them to settle down in Bhopal and bestowed positions of honour to the members of the family.[4]

A MELTING POT

Life in Bhopal was cosmopolitan in outlook. The city was multi-ethnic and multinational, comprising people from all over the country and the world. This made Bhopal unique in many ways. The royal family led by example. Due to our close association with the royal family, we would be invited to the palace on birthdays and other occasions. Raja Awadh Narain Bisariya, then Prime Minister of Bhopal, was a Hindu; Dr Barkley, a Christian, was in charge of the Sultania Hospital founded by the royal family, and Dr Bose, our family physician, was a Bengali. That Bhopal society was inclusive was amply reflected in the urban landscape too. At Chowk Bazar, in the heart of the city, shops around the Jama Masjid belonged to Hindus. Some of India's finest makers of *kundan* jewellery—a special technique of setting stones or gems in gold—were from Bhopal, especially the famous Madanlal.

One of my classmates and close friends was Sheila Bourbon, a French girl with freckles who spoke fluent Urdu. At the time, I did not know that she was a descendant of the royal House of Bourbon of France. During the French Revolution of 1789, one of her ancestors had fled and found shelter in Bhopal under Mamola Bai, Bhopal's first woman ruler.[5] The family was bestowed a grand

---

[4]Special Collections, SOAS Library, *Women's History Month 2020: Sikandar Begum, Nawab of Bhopal*, 8 March 2020, https://tinyurl.com/4z2ff7yr. Accessed on 16 July 2024.
[5]Iyengar, Indira, 'Bourbons and Begums: How the descendants of French royals

mansion and settled down in Bhopal. Since then, they played a key role in the development of Bhopal under the Nawab Begums, who trusted them. Known for their bravery and administrative acumen, they defended Bhopal as generals in the army and mediated between the Begums and the East India Company as prime ministers of the state. They were given Muslim names, wore Muslim attires, spoke fluent Urdu, and celebrated both Hindu and Muslim festivals. Years later, the French ambassador to India traced back the family in Bhopal.[6]

A PICTURESQUE CHILDHOOD

In the beautiful city of Bhopal, Maulana Azad's family breathed a sigh of relief. After Calcutta, their home was a haven of peace—a small bungalow in the Ahmedabad locality near the scenic Bada Talab, surrounded by tall trees, a dense forest where panthers prowled at night, and the gentle peaks of the Shyamala Hills in the distance. Communities lived in harmony in Bhopal. The rulers were sensible and celebrated every festival in the palace, be it Holi, Eid or Christmas. My family developed deep friendships with people from all communities.

Sultan Jahan Begum played an important role in my parents' wedding. My father, Syed Yousuf Ali, an agro-horticulturalist and an alumnus of the Pune College of Agriculture, was in charge of the state gardens of Bhopal. My mother, Fatima, belonged to a family of *jagirdar*s (landowners) close to the royal family. One of her father's aunts used to teach the royal children and lived in the palace.

I was born in Bhopal on 13 April 1940, the second child of my parents, four years junior to my brother Akhtar and seven years

---

played a vital role in Bhopal's history', Scroll.in, 7 September 2018, https://tinyurl.com/2v4xkhpj. Accessed on 17 July 2024.
[6]Khan, Shaharyar M., *The Begums of Bhopal: A History of the Princely State of Bhopal*, I.B. Taurus, 2000; Iyengar, Indira, *Bourbons and the Begums of Bhopal: The Forgotten History*, Niyogi Books, 2018.

senior to my sister, Ozma. We called our father Papa and mother Ammi.

My father enjoyed having people share meals with us. He and my grandmother believed that we should feed someone every day, or send food to a mosque for the needy. So, ours was a welcoming home, always filled with family and friends. My father was very respected in the community and had many friends who came to visit us from far and near. The kettle was always on the boil, ready for an extra pot of tea for anyone who might drop by. My mother, a very loving person, took care of everyone. She was a gifted cook and rustled up the best of Bhopali dishes—from *pasanda, khichra* and *kofta* to biriyani.

In every way, my big brother was my first teacher. He had endless tools in his pocket and tricks up his sleeve. Playful and joyous, he had mastered the mechanics of a fishing reel and taught me to rough-and-tumble, climb trees and swing on branches, ride, swim, build things, and play cricket—with three sticks for each end—and bounce the ball. If he was leading an imaginary team through the woods, I was right there with him. Thanks to him, I grew up to do the things boys did, flouting the unwritten rules of 'girlhood' and 'femininity'.

At home, my father laid down a grass lawn and planted plenty of trees—guava, orange, and mango, among others. We never bought fruits, except for apples. In our farm at a village called Kolukheri, we grew wheat and pulses and also had an orchard. We got milk from our cows and buffaloes, eggs from hens, and played with cats and dogs. They never bothered each other but a rooster ruled over them all—he screamed so much that the dog would curl up and shut his eyes, the cat would retreat to a corner and the hens would go back to pecking the ground. We also had a horse, which I learnt to ride when I was about eight years old.

Near our home was a forest of custard apple trees. We used to play hide-and-seek amidst the enormous trunks and buttress roots of the trees. The fruits ripened in summer, filling the air with their sweet fragrance. As children, we had no clue that the government auctioned off the right to the fruits to the highest bidder. We felt we had as much right to have them as the birds, animals and village people. We used to wake up early in the morning and quietly troop down to the forest, to pick up fruits and bring these home.

Once, however, we got caught by the man who had bought the rights to the fruits. As we ran home, he followed us shouting, and complained to my father. Papa was very angry and said, 'If you want to eat custard apples, I'll buy them for you. Why do you steal?' I stood up to him and said, 'We were not stealing. It's not his garden. They are just wild fruits. They don't belong to him.' The colonial policy of diverting India's forest wealth for profit continued even after Independence. The symbiotic relationship between forests and forest-dwelling communities found legal recognition for the first time in the National Forest Policy of 1988.

There used to be a *chilbil* (elm) tree near our home. For some reason, we used to call it *chudail ka ped*, or the haunted tree. It was a big tree with strong branches. Much to our annoyance, people from the village often crept up after dark to chop its branches. My brother and I used to sit vigil on our terrace, and the moment we saw any movement or heard sounds, we shone a torch and shouted, 'Don't cut the tree; it belongs to all of us.' I was very keen on protecting trees. Perhaps I got it from my father, who had a passion for nature. Or, perhaps, because trees were our everyday friends—we climbed them, played around them, swung from their branches and sat in their shade.

The terrace was the family's refuge, especially in summer. In peak summer, with temperatures hovering at around 40°C, we used to sleep on the terrace. The other family passion was the radio—a very big Pye with a fluorescent green 'magic' eye as the tuning indicator. The whole family used to sit around it for news. My brother and I were asked to join in. On 15 August 1947, when India gained freedom at midnight, my father woke us up, saying, 'Don't sleep, it's a great moment.' We sat around the radio and listened to the famous speech of Pandit Jawaharlal Nehru, Prime Minister of the newly independent India: 'Long years ago, we made a tryst with destiny...' My friends knew how important the radio was to my family and were suitably impressed to know that we were invited to listen to news with the adults at home.

The liberal atmosphere at home was reinforced by the broad-minded changes Sultan Jahan Begum introduced in Bhopal. Under her patronage, the 'new' women of Bhopal left behind the world of strict purdah, attended schools, lived in boarding houses, socialized with women from all over India, were introduced to modern medicine, professional training, outdoor sports, and political issues, worked for the poor, organized meetings and gained employment. This synergy allowed me to grow up freely. I engaged in all activities without facing any discrimination on the basis of my gender.

My father taught me how to handle guns as I started going with him on shikar (hunting for sport). During summer holidays, my father would engage a retired policeman to teach us physical fitness. Every day, he would show us how to exercise, keep our body tuned up, walk with our backs straight, chin up, so that we could be like the *Angrezi bachcha* (English children). The man used to carry a whip and swung it menacingly to get our attention.

Much thought went into which school I should attend, when and why. So, I studied at both Cambridge School and Sultania Girls School founded by Begum Sultan Jahan. I was a bit of a teacher's pet everywhere, because of my high scores in maths and English—subjects that had most girls of my class in tears. My favourite subject, however, was geography, especially the books written by British geographer Laurence Dudley Stamp. Much to my joy, Maulana Azad's nephew, Nuruddin, who looked after the former's massive library in Delhi, gifted me subscriptions to two magazines—*National Geographic* and *Woman and Home*. The latter carried a new genre of fiction, featuring ambitious, intellectual girls, who were also physically active.

At home, Khalajan subscribed to the popular Urdu children's

magazine *Khilauna* for us. Khalajan was a poet and used the pen-name Zulfi (tresses). Urdu poet Jigar Moradabadi, recognized among the greatest ghazal writers of the twentieth century, was her mentor. She used to send her poems to him for review. When I was in Class 10, she introduced me to the classical Urdu poetry of Ghalib, Mir, Iqbal and Faiz. I spent hours on her window sill, lost in poetry, mesmerized by words, sentences and rhythms. She also exposed me to the world of Urdu poets. Many of them were her friends and colleagues and used to visit our home. Very soon, I started experimenting with poetry—both Urdu and English.

As an important centre of Urdu literature, Bhopal frequently organized *mushaira*s (poetry recitals). I was very young but remember seeing renowned poets at home, especially Jan Nisar Akhtar, his wife Safiya and her brother, the romantic rebel Majaz Lakhnawi, who penned the Aligarh University anthem, 'Ye Mera Chaman Hai' (This is my garden). It was much later, during a chance conversation with poet and activist Javed Akhtar in Parliament, that I discovered how closely his family and mine were interlinked, thanks to Khalajan and the culture of Urdu poetry in Bhopal.

Music was woven into the fabric of our family. My father used to play the sitar. A student of sitar maestro Ustad Hafiz Ali Khan (Ustad Amjad Ali Khan's father), when he played at night, we used to listen spellbound as the music flowed through the house with a life of its own. We were all taught Hindustani classical vocals. My brother learnt to play the tabla, but I was secretly fascinated by my father's sitar. During summer vacations when he left for office, I quietly took the instrument and tried to play the ragas. The sitar being a big instrument was difficult for me to hold, and I did not know which note was where. So I just played as I heard my father play.

One day, he came home early while I was playing. I thought he would be annoyed, but he looked at me quietly and said, 'Do you wish to learn?' I said, 'Yes.' He asked me to play something and I played Raga Khamaj and Raga Jaijaiwanti. He said, 'Where is *sa* (the first of seven notes)?' I said, 'I don't know.' He then took me under his wing and taught me *sargam*—the successive steps of the octave. My musical journey received another boost when Khalajan employed someone to teach me the harmonium. I was a left-handed player, because my initiation was with the sitar where the fingers of the left hand are used to play the notes. Then I learnt to play the banjo and often played the old American song, 'I come from Alabama with my banjo on my knee, Oh, Susanna,' with great gusto.

I have so many other memories as well from my childhood. During summer vacation, my two phuphis or paternal aunts who lived in Bombay and Lucknow often came to stay with us. With them around, our house would be filled with joy, fun, and laughter. My father's eldest sister Aamna Begum was widowed at a young age, with three sons and two daughters to look after. My father decided to bring them over to live with us. They had their own kitchen, but we all lived in the same house. Two of her sons, Nasir Hussain and Tahir Hussain, became famous film directors and producers of Hindi cinema in Bombay film industry. They made many classics like *Teesri Manzil* (1966), *Hum Kisise Kum Naheen* (1977) and *Qayamat Se Qayamat Tak* (1988). It was hardly surprising that Tahir bhai's son, Aamir Khan, went on to become one of the leading actors and voices of Indian cinema, and Nasir Bhai's son, Mansoor, became one of the most creative directors and producers of Hindi films. As a tribute to and in memory of great grandfather Maulana Azad, Aamir named his younger son Azad Rao Khan.

A BEACON OF INSPIRATION

Maulana Azad—Dada Abba to me—had a larger-than-life presence in our lives. He appeared in every family conversation, every family gathering, every decision the family took. Yet, the unspoken tragedy was that he could not be with us. With his fiery political activism, he was continuously in and out of jails. The princely states had aligned with the British Empire to safeguard their own interests. So Dada Abba was banned from entering Bhopal. I remember how anxiously Amma used to wait for any communication from, or on, him: 'Bring all letters to me when the postman comes,' she would say, although she knew all communication from jail was banned by the British.

Being very young and not really understanding the reason for his absence, I used to constantly pester Amma, much to her annoyance: 'Where is Dada Abba? Why don't we meet him? Why doesn't he come to see me?' Then she would calm down and patiently explain that he was in jail because he was asking the British, who were ruling us, for freedom of this country. The complexities of the reasons for his incarceration were beyond my childish mind. There was no direct influence of the British in Bhopal—it was an independent state. I did, however, understand that Dada Abba could not come to Bhopal because of the British. Freedom was not an easy concept to comprehend, but I did understand that he was asking for something momentous.

The family endured painfully long periods of separation from Dada Abba. When Chhoti Amma, Abru Begum, fell seriously ill, she desperately wanted to see her beloved brother. She sent him a letter with a few lines of a couplet by Persian Sufi poet Amir Khusrau:

Balabam raseed jaanam fabiya ki zindah maanam;
Pas azan ki man na-maanam bacha kar khuahi aaamad.

(My soul has come on my lips (I am on the verge of expiring);
Come so that I may remain alive—
After I am no longer—for what purpose will you come?)[7]

---

[7]Khusrau, Amir, 'Khabaram Raseed Imshab', All Poetry, https://tinyurl.com/dkx6vepv. Accessed on 16 July 2024.

Yet, he was not allowed to enter Bhopal even to visit his dying sister. Before she passed away, her last note was a line from Khusrau:

Ba-janazah gar nayai ba-mazaar khuahi aamad.

(Should you not come to my funeral, you'll definitely come to my grave.)

This loss was a sadness he carried with him all his life.

∞

Around the time I was born, Maulana Azad was President of the Indian National Congress. A prominent leader of the Quit India movement, he was the head of Congress-led delegations to crucial meetings. And intermittently he was incarcerated, sometimes at Naini Jail in Allahabad (now Prayagraj), or in Ahmednagar Jail in Maharashtra, among others. When his wife was breathing her last from tuberculosis, he requested the British permission to visit his wife one last time. The British said he could, but only on condition that he bent his knees to the empire, which he did not. As she passed away, he started his prison notes, *Ghubar-e-Khatir* (The Dust of Memories). He wrote that he conversed with his friends in his imagination. We did the same with him in his absence.

Being a child of the two World Wars and the violence of the colonial rule, Maulana Azad believed in the power of institutions and diplomacy in advocating education, culture, plurality and democracy. Even before Independence, he was one of the founders of Jamia Millia Islamia (1920), one of India's best universities. He laid the institutional foundations of India's higher education and culture: Indian Institute of Technology (IIT Kharagpur), All India Council for Technical Education (AICTE), University Grants Commission (UGC), Sahitya Akademi, Sangeet Natak Akademi, Lalit Kala Akademi, Indian Council for Historical Research (ICHR), and Indian Council of Cultural Relations (ICCR). He was a very close friend of Pandit Nehru, who stood by him in all his efforts and inaugurated each institution he set up. He was the only Muslim leader of his stature who at that time vehemently opposed the partition of India.

Dada Abba was the spiritual guide in my evolution and growth as a public person. His life and work, his character and sincerity, his astute and compassionate insights—all had a profound effect on me. In October 1984, when Prime Minister Indira Gandhi sent me to Pakistan to attend a conference on women, reporters asked me a pointed question: 'You are Maulana Azad's grandniece. He was against the partition of India and the birth of Pakistan. What are your views?' I told them, 'Pakistan is a reality and my views have no meaning. But for whatever reasons Maulana Azad was against Partition, if they were true then, they are true now. Because religion does not unite or divide people, it is the culture which unites and divides people, and as he predicted that the two-nation theory will not last the test of 25 years, East Pakistan separated from West Pakistan and became Bangladesh in exactly 25 years.'

Maulana Azad was against Partition because he believed you cannot divide people who are geographically, economically, linguistically and culturally joined. In the twentieth century, a number of countries were created on the basis of religion and politics, but none of them have been peaceful. The creation of Bangladesh proved him right—shared history and experience of life was greater than religious and political polarization. 'I have nothing in common with a Muslim from Chechnya or Bosnia, except that we are co-religionists.' I added, 'He gave me the force of conviction to pronounce that I am a Muslim, and that I am equally proud of the fact that I am an Indian. And for this, I will always be grateful to him.'

The day I first took oath of office as a newly elected Member of Parliament (MP) in 1980, I was led to the historic Central Hall. Iconic upside-down fans arose from the ground. A plaque read: 'The Constituent Assembly of India Met in This Hall.' Life-size images of the stalwarts of India's freedom struggle stared down from the circular walls. I came face to face with the portrait of Dada Abba. It took me back to my days at Sultania Girls School in Bhopal, where standing under his portrait, I used to tell my friends, 'I pray and hope that God gives me at least an iota of the brilliance and memory that He has given Dada Abba.'

While I felt a surge of pride, staring at my ancestor and being reminded of the personal sacrifices of my family, and of so many others who had made it possible for me to be here, I also had a strange sense of misgiving. The hallowed hall was redolent with the aroma of Indian spices and delicacies, as new MPs were welcomed and veteran politicians mingled all around us. With a jolt, I realized that this was the reality, the way of Delhi—the hurly-burly of national politics, the wheeling and dealing, the gossip and rumours, the place of true bipartisanship, where the actual business of governing the nation was conducted. I whispered a little prayer to Dada Abba: 'Please be my guardian angel.'

2
A WOMAN OF SUBSTANCE

What would it be like to meet myself at the cusp of adolescence and adulthood? With four decades of hard work behind me, what letter of inspiration could I write to my younger self? I could write that she had passion, enthusiasm, confidence, believed in equal respect for all, at home and outside. And she was proud of her ancestry, although she believed in forging her own path. A touch of reality would also help—she was lucky. Her successes were not wholly her own. There were many who kept a supportive hand on her shoulder, enabled her to move ahead with their empathy, encouragement and, when necessary, practical help.

I must have been doing something right as a young adult for Pandit Jawaharlal Nehru, first Prime Minister of India, to be impressed with me. I still remember the day when his daughter and late Prime Minister of India, Indira Gandhi, told me that Pandit Nehru was very fond of me: 'He wants informed and educated women for a "new India"—women like you.' These words have always inspired me. And I continue to believe in his famous words: 'You can tell the condition of a nation by looking at the status of its women.'[8]

Maulana Azad and Pandit Nehru were close friends and comrades, as much in the struggle against colonialism as in the

---

[8] 'Essay on Status of Women in India for Students and Teacher', toppr from BYJU's, https://tinyurl.com/msa57vvv. Accessed on 17 July 2024.

building of a new nation. Whenever Pandit Nehru came to Bhopal, he dropped by at our home to meet my grandmother, even after Dada Abba was gone. He also invited us to come and stay at his prime-ministerial residence at Teen Murti Bhavan in New Delhi.

We visited him several times. In fact, I met Mrs Gandhi during one such visit to Teen Murti. She was taking care of her father, while her sons, Rajiv and Sanjay, were studying at The Doon School in Dehradun. Every morning, a large number of children used to come to Teen Murti to meet Pandit Nehru. The gates were always kept open.

Pandit Nehru was another person who influenced me from afar. After Dada Abba died in 1958, I used to write to Pandit Nehru. For his birthday on November 14, I always sent him a gift—something I made myself. Thanks to Khalajan, I was an ace with needles. I would embroider or knit a scarf and send it to him. Once I spun cotton yarns on the *charkha*, or spinning wheel—the quintessential symbol of Mahatma Gandhi and of India's freedom struggle. The local Khadi Bhandar wove a piece of *khaddar* (coarse homespun cotton cloth) out of my yarns, and I sent it to Pandit Nehru as a birthday gift. He always acknowledged my letters and gifts graciously.

A SCIENTIFIC MIND

At school, apart from maths and English, I was also very good in science. When I finished intermediate, I wanted to study medicine at Lady Hardinge Medical College in Delhi. Dada Abba, then Minister of Education, was living in Delhi. When my father informed him that I wanted to be a doctor, he wrote back: 'She will have to do public service. That is the commitment of a doctor. She should be able to fulfil that obligation even after marriage. Are you ready for that?' Although I was his favourite grandchild, he raised that question because of his absolute impartiality and unimpeachable integrity. What if I could not keep up with the commitment of being a doctor and a precious medical seat was wasted? The problem, however, was resolved in an unusual way: I could not study medicine because I was underage, thanks to a double promotion at school. I was 17, a year short of the official age required for medical school.

So I enrolled at Hamidia College, one of the oldest colleges in Bhopal, housed in a majestic building and surrounded by serene lakes. The Department of Science—the Motilal Vigyan Mahavidyalaya, inaugurated by Pandit Nehru, with state-of-the-art labs and eminent professors—however, came up in 1956, on the southern bank of the Chhota Talab. While girls enrolled at Maharani Laxmi Bai Girls College, my aunt wanted me to study in a co-educational college, to be more in step with the modern world, and to be more career-oriented than most girl students. I was, however, discouraged by the college authorities. Science is very difficult, they said, one has to study very hard. I still went ahead and took up zoology, with botany, physics and chemistry. Needless to say, I was the only girl in my class.

After graduation, I enrolled for a Master's in zoology at Vikram University in Ujjain. During the first year of my Master's, Pandit Nehru came for the convocation ceremony at our university. As students in colourful graduation gowns and mortarboard caps lined up on the stage, he presented the degrees and awards, urging them towards a new future. I was thrilled, especially by the crimson gowns of research doctorates. I made up my mind, then and there, to top my batch next year, enrol for a PhD, and wear that crimson gown one day.

After the ceremony, as I met Pandit Nehru with my family, I told him, 'If you come next year, I will get a gold medal, which you will give me.' 'You are making a promise a year in advance,' he exclaimed. 'I will keep it,' I said.

In my first year, I scored more than 75 per cent and was given the chance to submit a dissertation on any topic of my choice. I chose 'The Origin and Conduction of Heartbeats in Birds'.

The subject involved the study of certain cells and tissues in the hearts of birds that initiate the process. It was a challenging topic, because the hearts of birds are fast-pulsating. I was working under Professor Ravi Prakash Mathur, Head of Department of Zoology, and Professor S.P. Bhatnagar, faculty member at the department.

It was not just my promise to Pandit Nehru, but also a challenge that goaded me towards the gold medal. A fellow student had approached me with the strangest request I had ever received: 'Can you please not top the university?' He went so far as to offer me money for this. I was stunned. 'You are a girl. It doesn't matter if you top.' he added. As a boy, if he topped, his dowry would increase manifold, he explained. I was so angry I told him, 'Now that you have mentioned dowry, I will not let you top under any circumstances.' It was not that dowry is prohibited in Islam, marriage being a mutual contract, but his unabashed impudence and greed had overwhelmed me. I was determined to top my batch, come what may.

And I did keep my promise. In addition to the exams, I submitted my dissertation, and topped the university, securing a gold medal. I was all of 20 then. When I wrote to Pandit Nehru, he expressed great satisfaction. However, with his deteriorating health and Sino-Indian relations under strain in the early 1960s, I did not get the opportunity to receive my degree and medal from him.

LIFE AS IT REALLY IS

Ever since our childhood years, my Bhaijaan was my hero. Everything he did, I wanted to do too. He and I went to the same college. He and his friends were naughty and mischievous. They played pranks on their classmates and even on their teachers. The classrooms had fixed furniture, arranged like a gallery. And their favourite prank was to tie bicycle bells under their tables and ring those on and off or in unison, especially in physics professor Dr Nene's class. One day, Bhaijaan even carried a bell on his crown, hidden under his Turkish fez—the official headgear for men on special days—so that he could touch his fez covertly and ring the bell without anyone suspecting anything. That is how he was, my Bhaijaan.

At 26, Bhaijaan started working at Bharat Heavy Electricals Limited in Bhopal after finishing his engineering degree. He was young, in love, and about to be married. Fate, however, had other plans for our family. The day after my convocation was Holi. Bhaijaan loved the festival of colours and was out with his friends participating in the festivities. On his way back home, he decided to stop and wash up in the Narmada River. He was a champion swimmer, but that day, the currents were so strong that he could not fight them and was claimed by the rising tides.

Shock and grief overwhelmed my family. My father had a heart attack that nearly killed him. My sister Ozma was still in school, and had to deal with grief of the magnitude no child should have to. With this tragedy, the family dynamics changed. The loss made me feel utterly lonely and the only thought that could comfort me was that this wound needed to be healed and these people needed to be taken care of. I decided to dedicate myself to looking after my family, just as my brother would have.

Around this time, I had started receiving a fellowship. With Pandit Nehru's encouragement, I had written to Professor M.S. Thakkar, Director-General, Council of Scientific & Industrial Research (CSIR), and received a Junior Research Fellowship for a PhD of ₹250 per month. I would give the money to my parents. Meanwhile, I also took up another job to take care of sundry expenses.

I finished my PhD under Professor Ravi Prakash within two years—the minimum time before which one could not submit a thesis—and proudly received my degree in a crimson convocation attire. After my PhD, I was offered the job of Assistant Professor in my college for ₹275 a month. Along with teaching, I continued to do research.

The University of Newcastle upon Tyne in the UK offered me another fellowship right after my PhD. Unfortunately, I was underage and overqualified for what they were offering. I was just 22 at that time, so I regretfully declined. The American space agency NASA had also offered me a research position, but I had to decline that too due to the family tragedy. I was unable to attend an anatomical conference in New York around this time, as my father did not allow me, but my paper was read at the conference.

I applied for a Senior Research Fellowship, which was more remunerative than my college job. As I received the post-doc fellowship, I took leave from this job and started research at the same college. I also undertook voluntary teaching sessions there.

My post-doctorate was on a topic that was considered cutting-edge then: 'How the Heartbeat is Initiated and How Blood is Pumped from One Side of the Body to Another.' Around then, I was published for the first time in a peer-reviewed journal. I had sent my paper to the esteemed *Anatomical Record* in Philadelphia. They sent it back a month later, with the editor explaining that my paper was one of the best they had received that year, but wanted me to replace the British spelling style I had followed with the American style they used. I was delighted. I corrected those and sent in the paper with microscopic photographs of avian hearts I had learnt to take. My other articles were published in *The American Heart Journal*, another peer-reviewed, leading medical journal covering all aspects of cardiology.

My family and friends were most proud of me and my educational achievements. Academics, however, was just one of the many activities I was engaged in. There were several other priorities in my life—from taking care of the household and helping aged and ailing family members, to running errands and paying bills, apart from entertaining the incessant stream of relatives, friends and neighbours who stood by us through thick and thin. What stood by me also was the family car. Just as my brother drove, I too started driving.

The liberating force of being a woman at the wheel at a time when very few women drove, was a heady experience. As I zipped past, people would stop on the streets and exclaim: *Ladki gadi chala rahi hain* (A girl is driving a car). Not surprising, for the motor age for women the world over started only with the World Wars. On the wings of my new-found freedom, I decided that I liked being single. As I told myself 'I will never get married,' fate must have been smiling down upon me and smiling indulgently.

∞

Many people came to my father, Syed Yousuf Ali, for help. He knew several top players in the government, personally and professionally. And he liked to help people by always doing his best for them. He also had a large circle of friends, who continued to engage with him until his last days. One of his closest friends since school was Shankar Dayal Sharma, a legal luminary who had served not just as President of the Indian National Congress but also as Chief Minister of the princely state of Bhopal, and later on as a union minister of India, the eighth Vice President and the ninth President of India.[9] He had always maintained a very close friendship with my father, and our families were very close, meeting every week. When he became a union minister, I would go and stay with his family in Delhi.

Around this time, I became engaged to the eldest son of my aunt who lived in Bombay (now Mumbai). She had told my father, 'I want to get your daughter married to Arif.' My father was very fond of them, but said, 'It is up to her.' We got engaged and communicated through letters. I had big dreams about my research, of going abroad for higher studies, of continuing to work in Bombay. I had already heard of Salim Ali, one of India's greatest ornithologists and naturalists, who lived and worked in

---

[9]India Today Web Desk, 'Remembering Shankar Dayal Sharma, the President of India who believed in shaming offenders with acts of kindness', *India Today*, 26 December 2018, https://tinyurl.com/3zhexuj2. Accessed on 17 July 2024.

Bombay. I expressed my fervent hope of working with him.

However, Arif, an engineer, had very different ideas. He wanted me to learn shorthand and typing, so I could work in his office. That's not what I wanted to do with my life. We clearly had very different ways of looking at things. My grandmother called up my aunt and said, 'Najma will not be happy in this relationship.' The engagement was called off and the rings returned. However, there were no hard feelings between us. He moved on to marry a wonderful lady, Gulrukh, who belonged to the royal family of Rampur. Over time, Gul became one of my closest friends.

THE TURNING POINT

The turning point in my life came through Kalay Khan, one of my father's friends. An extremely prosperous beedi industrialist, he used to drop by every morning to meet my father, sit for a while, have a cup of tea and leave. Our families became very close. For his daughter's wedding, a number of their friends and family members came over to Bhopal. Around the same time, Dadi, Maulana Azad's elder sister, passed away. After Bhaijaan's death, most responsibilities of managing guests for weddings or funerals fell to me since my father and Ammi had lost interest in such things, and Ozma was too young. Guests were streaming in and out to pay their respects to Dadi. One such guest was Akbar Ali Adamji Heptulla, a friend of Mohammad Hanif, the eldest son of Kalay Khan.

Akbar belonged to the denomination of Bohra Shia Muslims, renowned for their culinary culture, business ethics and the high status their women enjoyed. He was the largest importer of tissue paper in India for making beedi wrappers that he printed at his own factory. He lived at Heptulla Park in Santa Cruz West, Bombay. Hanif had spoken of me to Akbar in glowing terms.

When Akbar and I saw each other for the first time at the funeral, I honestly did not look my best. I was dressed in an ordinary white salwar kameez as was customary on such occasions, and my eyes were swollen and red from crying. That did not stop Akbar from being, as he said later, 'smitten'. Hesitatingly, he sought my permission to visit my college and see me work. At the time, I did not think much of it. I agreed. He came, visited my lab, saw the microscopic photographs I had taken, and was very interested in the details of my work, which by no means was for the faint-hearted, literally and figuratively.

Several months later, he returned to Bhopal with Ismail Bhai Fanaswalla, a friend who had travelled with him from Bombay. They stayed at Hotel Imperial Sabre, the only five-star hotel at the time that was near our house. When they came home to meet my father, I was running around barefoot, playing a game of seven tiles with the neighbourhood kids at home. That day Akbar asked Papa, Ammi and Khalajaan if he could marry me. Khalajaan said, 'Our daughter is independent, she is highly educated and has her career. We don't force anything on her. If she agrees, we will agree.' So, he decided to bite the bullet and asked me.

By that time, while engaged in my post-doctoral research and family responsibilities, I had a fair idea of what I wanted, and did not want, in a life partner. I wanted somebody who was kind, gracious, generous and generally decent. I wanted somebody who would respect me, who would accept my choices—whether I wanted to be a stay-at-home mother or a working woman. I also knew that he had to respect my family, and my responsibilities towards my family.

In Akbar I saw all of that and much more. At the time he proposed to me, I was very honest with him and laid down three conditions before accepting his proposal: one, that I could come to Bhopal on and off after marriage and continue to support my family; two, that he would never stop me from doing whatever work I wished to do; and three, that he would not be miserly, that he would not ask me for what I needed money or how I spent it. He agreed to all three conditions and he respected and honoured his commitment for 40 years of our marriage, till his death in 2007.

TO LOVE AND TO CHERISH

We got married on 7 December 1966 in Bhopal. I was 26 years old and he was 37. Unfortunately, Akbar was not able to convince his family about his choice of life partner. They belonged to the highly close-knit and inward-looking Bohra community, with strict rules to keep outsiders separate from their private world, especially in marriage. When Akbar told his family about his intention to marry me, his mother and seven sisters objected, though not his brother. He told them, 'I am going to marry her. If you happily attend our marriage, you are welcome.'

He came alone with his friend. His mother and one sister came to Bhopal later, but did not want to participate in the wedding. In Bhopal, the tradition was to hold *nikah* (marriage) ceremonies at a mosque—for both the rich and the poor. We decided to go with handmade paper wedding cards and an open invitation for all. All my friends, professors and classmates came forward to help with the wedding preparations. Santosh Kumar, my college friend and *rakhi* brother, did all the running around and everything else Bhaijaan would have done had he been around.

My father held a reception that was attended by a large number of guests, including Begum Maimoona Sultan and Shankar Dayal Sharma. At the reception, I refused to sit like a coy and demure Indian bride and moved around, interacting with guests in the courtyard. This was unexpected in those times. Many guests went inside the house looking for me. On finding the newly married daughter-in-law of one of my father's friends sitting there quietly—more in keeping with the demeanour expected of brides—they started giving her the wedding presents. A humorous memory that had my friends and family in splits for years to come.

Right after the wedding, we set off on a road trip for our honeymoon. Akbar owned a 1950 black Morris Minor and we decided that since we both loved to drive, we would motor through the heart of India. We travelled, passing by green valleys, rugged mountains and cascading waterfalls, and made memories. We stopped at the historic site of Sanchi, one of India's oldest Buddhist monuments built in the 3rd century BCE by the Mauryan emperor Ashoka, and which houses the ashes of Sariputta and Moggallana, disciples of the Buddha.

On our return to Bhopal, Akbar left for Bombay. I stayed back. I had to settle things and make arrangements for my family before moving permanently to Bombay. By that time, the age of the telephone had arrived in India. Akbar booked calls and we spoke many times every day, a habit that continued for 40 years of our marriage, no matter where I was or where he was, no matter what time of the day it was for him or me.

Akbar wanted to introduce me to many of his clients who could not make it to our wedding. We took to the roads again for 20 days, visiting the big beedi manufacturers. For the first time, I saw people's lives and homes up close across a huge swathe of Central and North India: Indore, Sagar, Jabalpur, Bareilly, Allahabad and Lucknow. I also understood how much leaf-rolled cigarettes dominated the smoking market of India, the range of brands that existed, and the extent of the phenomenal wealth of beedi barons. We then went to Delhi to meet Mrs Gandhi and I introduced her to my husband.

NEW HOME, NEW CITY

Progressive, urbanized, secular and cosmopolitan, Bombay became my home. It saw the birth of my three daughters, gave me my first lessons in social and political work, and also bequeathed me numerous friends and a few precious mentors. Bombay was also my identity as a 'Member of Rajya Sabha from Maharashtra' for a very long time—from 1980 to 2004. Despite the official name change in 1995 to Mumbai, the city is still Bombay to me.

Our home in Bombay was a sprawling two-storeyed, 12-bedroom bungalow, with lawns, gardens, a fountain, verandas and quarters for the domestic staff. Akbar's paper-printing factory and offices were located in the same area as the bungalow—in the western suburbs, about 20 kilometres from downtown Bombay, at Heptulla Park, named after his grandfather. It was a pristine, scenic neighbourhood, with lush dense gardens and soaring Gothic towers of Catholic churches and convents, in the midst of the homes of the Goan Catholic community. We lived on the first floor with the rest of the family.

Good relationships, however, were not forged overnight. To begin with, my in-laws did not find it in their heart to accept me. Due to the awkwardness and the increasingly strained relationships, it was decided that in the best interest of our marriage and our family, Akbar and I would separate from the rest of his family. We decided to move to the ground floor of the bungalow, which was until then the common area with a few guest rooms. I was already pregnant with my first baby. Slowly, I settled down and took care of my grandmother-in-law, who moved in with us. My daughter Rubina was born on 13 October 1967.

Bombay was not completely alien to me. We used to visit my phuphi Aamna Begum in Bombay after she moved out of Bhopal to live with her sons who had moved there, Nasir and Tahir. When I went to Bombay, Nasir Bhai and Tahir Bhai had already found success in the film industry, and were living in Pali Hill, the Beverly Hills of Bombay. Although a bit crowded now, Pali Hill was then one the most beautiful neighbourhoods, with sprawling white mansions, stretches of gardens, thick barked banyan trees with hanging roots that worked as sun shade for cigarette sellers plying their carts, bright canna flowers that bloomed on the sidewalks, while pink bougainvillea trailed over high walls and iron gates.

Nasir Bhai's lovely wife, Asha Bhabi, was a delight. She was the 'glue' that held the family together with her vivacious personality, inquiring mind, infectious smile, and a heart that was so large and generous that even if a universe was forced into it, there would still be infinite space to fill. Every Eid, Nasir Bhai's house was the gathering ground for the family. Asha Bhabi's prawn pulao was legendary, as was her sense of aesthetic décor. I can still remember the blue fairy lights she used to hang from trees. Celebrated film personalities like Shammi Kapoor, Asha Parekh, Neetu Singh, and Majrooh Sultanpuri, among others, would be in and out of their house. Nasir Bhai and Asha Bhabi were ever welcoming to all.

Asha Bhabi took me under her wing. She showed me around the city and introduced me to her friends. She also accompanied me to meet Professor Salim Ali. I had communicated with him previously through letters, but had never met him. When we both showed up, he mistook Asha Bhabi for me and launched into a lengthy, voluble discourse on bird anatomy and conservation of bird habitats. Twenty minutes into this lecture, Asha Bhabi looked at him calmly and said, 'You are talking to the wrong person, Professor. She is your audience. I have come with her.' Dr Ali, a shy man, was so embarrassed that he started apologizing profusely. He said that he could not fathom that a 26-year-old could be a PhD, with a post-doc and such extensive research.

Looking back, that meeting could have been a game-changer. Coming, as I did, from a research background, my interest was in working with Dr Ali, as my work was also on birds. I did not understand then that I was standing at the cusp of change: as a new mother, I was taking a much-needed break. At the same time, I was actively looking for a new career as a scientist. At the time, had anyone told me that in 10 years I would give up science and gravitate towards politics, I would have been astonished.

GRAVITATING TOWARDS POLITICS

Once I settled down in Bombay, my life became busy and full. As a new mother, my time was precious, my friends many, and my schedule was always in top gear. I was very satisfied with my life. Long before we came to know each other, Akbar was sympathetic to political activists and intellectuals of the Left-leaning ideology—a legacy of India's struggle for independence, when socialists and the Indian National Congress were 'fellow travellers' in a patriotic alliance.

Akbar had strong friendships with prominent progressive, liberal and Left leaders. There was Aruna Asaf Ali, the 'Queen of the 1942 Quit India Movement.' When she launched the *Patriot* newspaper in 1958, Akbar played an important role as its publisher. Then there were Rajni Patel, a top-flight barrister as well as a senior Congress leader; Balraj Sahni, Marxist intellectual, writer and 'the common man's hero' of Hindi cinema; Dilip Kumar, the ultimate method actor of the Bombay film industry, and also a vocal Nehruvian although he never joined electoral politics; Russy Karanjia, veteran journalist and editor of the fearless tabloid *Blitz*; and writer, thinker, journalist, filmmaker, screenplay writer and director Khwaja Ahmad Abbas, better known as K.A. Abbas, who attained celebrity status as a stalwart of neorealism in Indian cinema, with movies like *Dharti Ke Laal* (1946), *Awaara* (1951) and *Shree 420* (1955).

I also knew some of them through my own family connections. For instance, I had met Aruna Asaf Ali earlier. Her husband, barrister Asaf Ali, was a close compatriot of Dada Abba, Maulana Azad. Both were fundamentally committed to secularism. Both had fought against the two-nation theory promoted by Muhammad Ali Jinnah, the Pakistan Movement and the subsequent partition of India.

During our first trip to Delhi after marriage, Aruna Asaf Ali was delighted when we met her. She told me, 'I am so happy Akbar has married you. I knew Maulana Saab so well. We are relations from both sides.' She took us out for dinner to the iconic Karim's in Gali Kababian near Jama Masjid in Old Delhi, founded by one of the royal chefs of the last Mughals. That was the first time I visited Purani Dilli, the walled city set up by Mughal emperor Shah Jahan.[10]

---

[10]Safvi, Rana, 'A musical tale of an old Delhi', 20 April 2018, *Hindustan Times*, https://tinyurl.com/wmbwv79e. Accessed on 17 July 2024.

Akbar's connections had made Heptulla Park a hub of political activity years before we were married. In 1957, V.K. Krishna Menon, the brilliant Congress leader, and a close confidant of Pandit Nehru, was given a parliamentary ticket to contest the Lok Sabha elections from North West Bombay Constituency. It was suggested to Akbar that he allow Krishna Menon to use his home as the campaign headquarters, for its size and convenience, which he willingly did. Since then, Heptulla Park became the North West district headquarter of the Bombay Pradesh Congress Committee. When I came to Heptulla Park, I found the house abuzz with political activity and discourse. There was a constant flow of politicians. I used to take part in these meetings, though I was not interested in active politics.

Politics was not unusual or difficult for me. In fact, I found it very easy to get involved. Being the grandniece of Maulana Azad, political instincts came naturally to me. Growing up, the finer points of political action were absorbed in our household almost through an osmotic process. Nobody held forth on politics, nobody lectured us. It was just all around us. It was quite possible for us to bump into people like Pandit Nehru in our drawing room or find my father chatting with his friend Shankar Dayal Sharma. Gradually, I got involved in the work of my compatriots at Heptulla Park. Starting with baby steps, over time, my work led to my appointment as Vice President of the North West District Congress Committee. More than that, my Bombay years taught me incredibly valuable political lessons—both bottom-up as well as top-down.

3

TRAINING FOR DEMOCRACY

How do politicians mastermind their politics? Where does a political aspirant learn politics? What are the pathways that make a politician a great leader? Since the 1920s, Oxford PPE (philosophy, politics and economics) graduates—from David Cameron to Rishi Sunak—have led Britain. But is a heavy focus on philosophy and macroeconomics relevant in a world of climate change and pandemics? China invests heavily in imparting training in law, technology and Marxism at party schools. Internships in Washington and staff jobs at campaign headquarters are par for the course in the US.

In India, training camps have been organized for long by most national parties, to groom party cadres in policies, grassroot messaging, election management and propaganda countering. As citizens become more sensitive to performance, and more demanding of political institutions, what a candidate does, wears, or looks like have become just as important as what they say. Media training, public speaking, getting camera-ready and managing image are a reality in the world of politics, globally. Courses in political leadership and political management are mushrooming everywhere.

There is, however, no curriculum or training camp that teaches an aspirant the dynamics of power. Since governing means exercising power, understanding power in politics—or the ability to have others do what one wants—is the key. During my long engagement with politics, I have seen that most politicians learn on the job. And if they are from a political family, they learn politics at home, around the family dinner table. I have, however, always believed that it takes a mentor to navigate the intriguing linkages between politics and power.

Coming from an academic background, mentoring has always mattered to me. In research, mentorships are the norm. In politics, however, mentors are hard to find. Hence, whenever a leader has not been in power, I have reached out to them. As a junior person, I have learnt a lot from their experience, wisdom and insight. On their part, they have had the time to spare and have been most willing to teach me. I must say, in my life I have been extremely fortunate in having some outstanding teachers as my mentors. They have taken interest in my work and encouraged me towards my goals and dreams.

GRIT, PASSION AND PERSEVERANCE

Before I could reach out to mentors, I had to prepare myself. My political work began at the grassroots. At Heptulla Park, my compatriots and I formed a gritty team—people who worked hard, had a strong sense of priorities and purpose—that would be resilient in the face of setbacks. We had to be plucky, yet sensitive, to work in some of the larger slums of Bombay— Golibar, Khetwadi, Jogeshwari. The Golibar slum, for instance, is spread across 140 acres of prime, albeit marshy, land in Central Bombay. Back then, most residents—more than 15,000–20,000 families— were poor migrants, who had flocked to the city from different parts of India, especially Uttar Pradesh and Bihar, in search of livelihood.[11,12] Their living environment was unhygienic and dire.

---

[11]Birkinshaw, Matt, 'The battle for Golibar: Urban splintering in Mumbai', *open Democracy*, 22 April 2013, https://tinyurl.com/29we55vc. Accessed on 17 July 2024.
[12]Singh, Simpreet, 'DEVELOPMENT, DISPOSSESSION AND ACCUMULATION: MUMBAI IN CONTEMPORARY TIMES', The Urban Design Research Institute, https://tinyurl.com/3vjbx3wx. Accessed on 17 July 2024.

Densely packed, makeshift, ragtag tenements, stacked on each other so closely that sunlight could hardly penetrate the maze of lanes so narrow that only one individual could walk through at a time. Plastic tarps served as roofs in most shanties, with the thinnest of walls separating one from the another, while storm drains clogged with silt, garbage and sewage coursed through the slum.

We started interacting with the residents closely to see what resonated with them. The interactive and immersive experience allowed us to identify common themes and ideas that came up from within the community, across ethnicities, gender and age. We realized that there were certain low-hanging fruits. Addressing these immediately and imaginatively could have a cascading effect on improving the life of the community. That would also show them that their voice mattered. Along with the local government and Youth Congress workers, we arranged to plant trees across the slums. This had the dual benefit of beautifying the slum and also giving the residents a semblance of the 'home' they had left behind in their ancestral villages. Working closely with Bombay Municipal Corporation and representatives of the local government, we also built a large number of toilets all across for hundreds of thousands of the poor slum dwellers to improve sanitation and provide facilities for washing.

When I started working, the term 'women's empowerment' had not become popular. Women's participation in the freedom struggle had given rise to a sense of women's emancipation, but from the 1950s, the focus was on women's 'uplift' through the limited perspective of legislation and education. From the 1970s, however, grassroots organizations for women's welfare, not affiliated to political parties or trade unions, had started coming up. They were largely involved with violence against women—from dowry to sexual exploitation. There was very little focus on women's ability to make a living, gain control over resources, or to have a voice in society.

During my experience of working in the slums, I was more interested in listening to and learning from women about what they wanted. I started collaborating with several grassroots women's groups in Bombay. One such group was the Shri Mahila Griha Udyog Lijjat Papad, started in 1959 by seven semi-literate Gujarati homemakers, who wanted to put their culinary expertise to use and earn some money to help their husbands run the household. They started making poppadoms, one of India's favourite healthy snacks, in lip-smacking flavours, with just a small capital of ₹80 (around ₹7,000 in today's value). When I started my political work, they registered as a cooperative society and received certification as a cottage industry.

The scheme was simple—needy women were given raw material and an assurance of income. Those who had the wherewithal to step out of home, kneaded the dough at the cooperative. Those who did not, could collect the dough and roll them into poppadoms at home. The women were trained in the importance of standardization and cleanliness, with maximum focus on quality. The products were then sold in the market by the cooperative. Over time, it became a big success story, touted by marketing gurus worldwide as a successful model in development economics. I was offered directorship on their board, which I held for several years, supporting and advising them.

∞

During this time, beyond my political work and running my home, I had another interest—the Indo-Arab Society. Founded by Rukmini Devi Arundale—famous dancer, theosophist, animal welfare activist, and first woman to be nominated to the Rajya Sabha—and inaugurated by Pandit Nehru in 1959, the society, housed in an Art Deco building on Marine Drive, was devoted to promoting greater understanding between India and the Arab world. Over time, it became an unexpected fount of political learning for me, particularly in the areas of foreign policy and international relations. It stood me in good stead later, as I worked with various prime ministers to develop India's relationship with the countries of West Asia—as Pandit Nehru preferred calling the region.

Initially, my participation was driven by my need for self-education or cultural immersion. Over the centuries, my family had moved between India and Saudi Arabia and I still had distant relatives in Saudi Arabia. The Indo-Arab Society, with its many programmes and speakers, allowed me to learn about a part of my cultural inheritance. I was also encouraged to participate by its president, the brilliant Dr Rafiq Zakaria. Barrister, scholar and Rajya Sabha MP, he had represented India in many global assemblies, including the UN. His first wife, Shehnaz Khan, was from a Bhopali aristocratic family. He came and stayed at our home in Bhopal on many occasions. He was also a close friend of one of my uncles in Bombay. One of his sons Farid Zakaria went on to become a well-known journalist, political commentator and author.

The Indo-Arab Society had a Nehruvian vision on foreign relations. In 1961, India initiated the Non-Aligned Movement (NAM) along with other leaders of newly independent countries of the so-called Third World, to safeguard their independence in the face of the complex geopolitical situation of the Cold War between the Soviet Union and the United States. NAM's policy was to not align with either superpower, and maintain its independent position to ensure peace and security of its member countries. With its humble beginnings as a movement around Pandit Nehru, Gamal-Abdel Nasser, then President of Egypt, and Josip Broz Tito (popularly known as Marshal Tito) of Yugoslavia, it became an attractive model for developing countries of Africa and Asia. The Indo-Arab Society recognized West Asia as an increasingly key area, because of the strategic significance of the Suez Canal and the abundance of oil in the region.

I worked with the Indo-Arab Society for long, coordinating

with the different Arab consulates and Arab diplomatic corps to organize cultural events to highlight shared values and interests of both cultures, and educating the public about this shared heritage. I became General-Secretary and eventually President of the Indo-Arab Society. This relationship lasted for nearly 25 years. I developed extremely good relations with all Arab countries. I came to know the people of the region very well, understood their attitude and thinking, and could foretell correctly the geopolitical environment—a quality that served well in furthering India's interests in times of crises, be it during the first Gulf War (1990–91) or the economic crises India faced in 1990.

BATTLE OF THE TITANS

In 1959, Mrs Gandhi had taken over as President of the Indian National Congress. Between 1964 and 1966, she served as Union Minister for Information and Broadcasting. When Lal Bahadur Shastri died suddenly in January 1966, she became the leader of the Congress Party by defeating Morarji Desai in the Congress Party parliamentary leadership election, and became Prime Minister[13]. I was not surprised by her rise, because I had already seen powerful and strong women like her, both in my family and in the princely state of Bhopal.

During my Bombay years, I was still a greenhorn in politics. It was a time of towering leaders and political power-play, both at the Centre and in my state of Maharashtra. Around Mrs Gandhi, however, was a powerful faction of non-Hindi-speaking leaders, led by the Tamil Nadu political stalwart Kumaraswami Kamaraj, popularly known as 'the Kingmaker'. They called themselves the Syndicate, and credited themselves with making Lal Bahadur Shastri as well as Indira Gandhi prime ministers (Ram Manohar

---

[13]The editors of Encyclopaedia Britannica, 'Indira Gandhi', 5 August 2024, Britannica, https://tinyurl.com/37erun75. Accessed on 17 July 2024.

Lohia had nicknamed her *Gungi Gudia*, or dumb doll)[14]. In return, they expected the prime ministers to be accountable to them. From 1967, however, Mrs Gandhi had started asserting her independence.[15]

They clashed over the appointment of the President of India after Dr Zakir Hussain's death in 1969. The Syndicate wanted Lok Sabha Speaker Neelam Sanjiva Reddy to be President, overriding Vice President Varahagiri Venkata Giri. Reluctant to give them so much power, Mrs Gandhi played a masterstroke—she refused to issue a 'whip' to Congress members[16], indicating that they could vote in the presidential election 'according to their conscience'. In other words, she did not support Reddy. When Giri was elected by a majority, the Syndicate accused her of stifling internal party democracy, fostering a personality cult, and expelled her from the party on 12 November 1969. This led to a split in the Congress, with 446 of the 705 members of All India Congress Committee (AICC) supporting her, and the formation of Congress (R), where 'R' stood for Requisitionists, that she led. Also, 220 of the party's Lok Sabha MPs went with Mrs Gandhi and 68 with the Syndicate.[17]

At this time, Maharashtra had an outstanding leader in Yashwantrao Balwantrao (Y.B.) Chavan. Born in 1913 in Satara District to a poor Maratha family, he had been a Congress activist since his student days. A lawyer by qualification, he actively took part in India's struggle for independence and was an acolyte of Mahatma Gandhi and Pandit Nehru. He had served in the cabinets of successive prime ministers, from Pandit Nehru to Charan Singh.

---

[14]Dutta, Prabhash K., 'Indira Gandhi, a goongi gudiya who went on to become Iron Lady', 19 November 2017, *India Today*, https://tinyurl.com/47ytjhec. Accessed on 17 July 2024.
[15]Chibber, Maneesh, 'K. Kamraj: The southern stalwart who gave India two PMs', 2 October 2018, *The Print*, https://tinyurl.com/5n936c8p. Accessed on 17 July 2024.
[16]A 'whip' is issued by the prime minister to inform members of the party line on parliamentary Bills.
[17]Chandra, Bipan, Mridula Mukherjee and Aditya Mukherjee, *India After Independence 1947–2000*, Penguin Books, 2000, p. 296.

Popularly known as 'Leader of Common People', he had mentored political stalwarts from Maharashtra, like Sharad Pawar who calls him his guru. Decades after his death, Y.B. continued to remain relevant in the state's politics.

As the first chief minister of Maharashtra, he was responsible for the landmark legislations that led to unprecedented growth and development of the agrarian sector in the state. He eventually joined Pandit Nehru's cabinet with prominent portfolios, and was especially remembered as Minister of Defence of India while it was fighting two significant wars—with China in 1962 and with Pakistan in 1965.

In 1969, Y.B. was opposed to the Congress split. He had voted for Sanjiva Reddy, even though he was Mrs Gandhi's supporter. As he told me later, he belonged to the old school of the Congress and tried to prevent a split in the Grand Old Party. Eventually, when he realized that the split was inevitable, he joined Mrs Gandhi's Congress (R). She welcomed him back and appointed him Minister of Finance in 1970.

To me, the battle of the titans epitomized how regional politics shape federal polity. It was a case study that allowed me to learn the finer nuances of centrifugal politics. To begin with, there was the rise of language politics as the vehicle of identity politics in Maharashtra. The state was created in 1960 (along with Gujarat) on linguistic grounds, with the standardized Marathi of Pune dominating over all the 42 Marathi dialects and 38 other languages spoken by the people.[18,19] The four main political regions of the state had distinct linguistic features—Konkani was spoken in coastal Konkan, Marathi by the Marathas of Western Maharashtra, with Pune as its epicentre, the Varhadi dialect in Vidharbha, with

---

[18]Deshpande, Prachi, 'Suddhalekhan: Orthography, Community and the Marathi Public Sphere', *Economic and Political Weekly*, Vol. 51, No. 6, pp. 70–82, February 2016, https://tinyurl.com/8vpvdyhd. Accessed on 17 July 2024.
[19]Pathak, A.S., ed., *Maharashtra: Land and Its People*. Maharashtra State Gazetteer, 2009, pp. 155–158, https://tinyurl.com/4h8mm7un. Accessed on 17 July 2024.

Nagpur as its biggest city, and Gujarati as the dominant language of Northern Maharashtra. The fact that Maratha caste- cluster accounted for more than one-third of the population made Maratha leaders the prime contenders of the state.[20] Although a Maratha icon, Y.B. always insisted on presiding over *Bahujan*, or the masses, and not just the Marathas.

Something else was at work—the sugar economy, which assumed phenomenal significance in Maharashtra politics. Modernization of this agrarian economy in Western Maharashtra was behind the rise of the powerful cooperative movement that came to influence regional and national politics—an interesting study of geography and topography driving politics.

It was Y.B. who had started the sugar cooperative movement from the 1950s, with the help of celebrated economist Dr D.R. Gadgil, to aid small farmers by giving them a fair price for their sugar crops. Over time, the system began to be controlled by unscrupulous cooperative bosses, who enriched themselves so much that they began to be called sugar barons, forming a key power bloc in the state. No other sector of the economy was as well represented in the government as the sugar sector. Over the decades, the control of sugar cooperatives became a means of acquiring political power for the rich peasant class, overwhelmingly the Marathas.

The prime reasons behind Y.B.'s grip over Maharashtra politics was that, first, he was a Maratha, which also strengthened his position in the power-play of Delhi politics; second, under his stewardship (and after him that of his protégé V.P. Naik), the combination of a range of land reforms, community development, new farm technologies, expansion of irrigation, cooperative institutions and rural governing bodies built up a formidable politico-economic framework that became a source of power for the Maratha leadership as well as for sugar barons, because

---

[20]Maharashtra State Gazetteers, *History of Maharashtra, Ancient Period*, Directorate of Government Printing, Stationery and Publications, Maharashtra State, 1967, Chapter 4, https://tinyurl.com/3d9uz3fv. Accessed on 17 July 2024.

the sugar cooperatives movement had flourished in Western Maharashtra. Not surprisingly, Y.B. had a tremendous hold over them.

This was something Mrs Gandhi, possibly, considered a threat. Although the dominance of the Congress Party in Maharashtra was largely due to Maratha hegemony, she decided to clip the wings of the sugar barons as well as the Chavan-Naik dominance in Maharashtra state politics. Did she think they could challenge her leadership? She replaced Naik with another Maratha loyalist, S.B. Chavan, who was known to be strongly opposed to Y.B. This was clearly a direct challenge to the leadership of Y.B. and, in turn, a challenge to the cooperative movement of rich farmers and sugar barons. A slew of measures was announced to undermine the cooperatives. This attempt to truncate the Maratha leadership led to intense factionalism and political instability in the state. It also turned Y.B. into her adversary.

In the 1977 elections, both Mrs Gandhi and her son, Sanjay Gandhi, lost their parliamentary seats and the Congress Party was nearly decimated. Y.B., however, retained his seat; he now became Leader of the Opposition in the Lok Sabha with the Janata Party coalition government, headed by Morarji Desai as the ruling party. The months that followed saw bickering and brinkmanship for party leadership. Mrs Gandhi was unsuccessful in her bid to become Congress President. In December 1977, she split the Congress once again, forming her own party, Congress (I). This time Y.B. opposed her, as he stated in Parliament, to 'counteract the propaganda that will be launched against us by unscrupulous elements,' and declared, 'we have full faith in our capacity to meet the challenge.'[21]

The non-Indira breakaway faction formed by D. Devaraj Urs, then Chief Minister of Karnataka, was renamed Congress (U).

---

[21]'Congress Party Ousts Mrs. Gandhi', *The New York Times*, 4 January 1978, https://tinyurl.com/3xhn862p. Accessed on 17 July 2024.

In mid-1979, after attempting and failing to form a coalition government in the wake of Desai's resignation, Y.B. accepted appointment as Deputy Prime Minister in a coalition government headed by Charan Singh, India's fifth Prime Minister. The government lasted only a few months—from 28 July 1979 till 14 January 1980. In the elections of 1980, Y.B. retained his seat from Maharashtra, but the government fell. Less than three years after her resounding defeat, Mrs Gandhi was voted back to power. She then systematically sidelined Maratha leadership, especially Y.B.

IT TAKES A MENTOR

That was when I met Y.B. Despite being an MP from Maharashtra, I had never met him in Bombay. Our first interaction took place in Delhi after I was elected to the Rajya Sabha. I had called him and introduced myself as a first-time MP from Maharashtra, and expressed the desire to meet him. Nearly 70 years old, and away from the limelight, the battle-scarred political warrior was happy to meet a young parliamentarian eager to learn politics.

Those days, I drove around in a blue Datsun, which Akbar and I had driven all the way from Bombay to Delhi. On the designated Sunday, I made my way to Y.B.'s residence at 1 Race Course Road, now a helipad within the prime-ministerial complex. Though a cabinet-designated bungalow, it had been allotted to him as a mark of respect for his seniority. I told him that I was not Marathi-speaking, but that I had worked in Bombay for years, and understood the intricacies of politics there. I would be very grateful if he could guide me, be my mentor, and enlighten me about Maharashtra politics. He graciously agreed.

Since then, I started spending Sunday afternoons with him, deep in discussion over steaming cups of tea. I started calling him 'Y.B.', as everyone did. He was extremely kind to me, but I noticed that after a lifetime dedicated to the service of the nation, all the din and bustle had disappeared from his life. His wife had passed away and he had no children or grandchildren to keep him company. An avid reader, he spent his spare time in his excellent library, crammed with thousands of books in Marathi and English.

From him, I learnt about his relationship with Pandit Nehru and Mrs Gandhi, his vision for Maharashtra, his belief that the real wealth and strength of the state were in its villages, how and why he worked to raise the standard of living of the people, not just around Western Maharashtra but the entire state. He had started his career inspired by Mahatma Gandhi's vision and had remained true to its core values. 'The rest was politics,' he used to laugh.

Mrs Gandhi was quite aware that Y.B. was the only person to hold all the four important portfolios—Home, External Affairs, Finance and Defence—at the Centre. What's more, he was one of the most effective troubleshooters whenever governments were in trouble. Not surprisingly, in 1982, when Y.B. rejoined the Congress (I), Mrs Gandhi appointed him Chairman of the Eighth Finance Commission.

The year 1984 was marked by Operation Blue Star, when the Indian Armed Forces stormed the Golden Temple in Amritsar, Punjab, from 1 June to 10 June, to remove Sikh militant and secessionist Jarnail Singh Bhindranwale and his followers, who were using it as a fortification. Soon after that, one day I met Mrs Gandhi in her South Block office. She looked troubled. I asked, 'Why do you look so worried, Madam?' She said, 'I am worried about the upcoming Maharashtra elections.' I knew that Sharad Pawar was not with her any longer, and that his party had made great strides in the interiors of the state. I said, 'Why don't you talk to YB? Nobody knows Maharashtra better than him.' She liked the idea and said, 'Why don't you bring him in?'

I drove down to Y.B.'s home and brought him over to Mrs Gandhi's office. She asked me to join their meeting. I declined, saying, 'I am too junior to participate. I will wait in Mr Dhawan's room.' R.K. Dhawan was Mrs Gandhi's personal secretary.

The meeting lasted about an hour—a long meeting given the

prime minister's busy schedule. When Y.B. came out of her office, he looked very happy and I drove him back home. On the way, he mentioned that the discussion had been very constructive. He said that she was concerned about Punjab, wanted him to visit the state and report back his observations to her.

She had also asked him about the upcoming elections in Maharashtra, and Y.B. had advised her on political strategy that had paid off time and again in Maharashtra. When we reached his home, I was delighted to notice a statue of the Hindu deity Ganesha near the entrance of his living room. The Ganesha was not styled in the usual manner, with the trunk turned towards the left. This statue had a straight trunk with a slight curve to the right. I told him, 'You know, they say, if a statue of Ganesha has a trunk that curves to the right or is straight, then you must put some flowers before it. This is a Siddhivinayaka Ganesha, so you have to take special care to please him.' He laughed and told his man Friday to put some flowers in front of the statue every day.

THE LAST MILE

Following Mrs Gandhi's assassination on 31 October 1984, I organized a condolence meeting in her memory at the Oberoi Towers in Bombay on 23 November. I requested Y.B. to be the chief guest and he agreed. On that day, as I prepared for the big event, I received a telephone call—Y.B. had suffered a massive heart attack and had been admitted to the hospital. On 25 November, he breathed his last. In less than a month, I had lost two very important people in my life—my mentors, who demystified politics for me, taught me politics by example, and encouraged me to give my best. Little did I know that this would not be the last such tragedy I would have to face.

SECTION II
Chasing the Impossible

4

IN INDIRA'S INDIA

How I wish that Indira Gandhi had written her autobiography. At a time when commanders across the world pick up a pen to share their story—sometimes as an essential part of election campaigns—future generations could draw nuanced mental pictures of the struggles, failures and achievements of one of India's most enigmatic women leaders, away from her speeches, interviews, photographs and film clips of orchestrated appearances, news reports or propaganda. For me, her time and her contributions echoed again and again in the life of the modern nation.

I had known Mrs Gandhi for years. For me, she was someone I greatly liked and admired, for our shared family history and for her strong, brave yet feminine and witty persona. She had once told me why she was fond of me: 'I like women who are educated, independent yet feminine.' For me, she epitomized courage, elegance, and tremendous fighting spirit. And I stood by her through thick and thin. What I did not foresee in those days was that her rise would also signal yet another turning point in my life—my entry into national and international politics and public affairs.

On several occasions, she asked me to stay with her at 1 Safdarjung Road, her residence. And I always met her in Bombay whenever she came to the city. However, my bond with her grew stronger when she was out of power in 1977. She was always very appreciative of me for being there for her at difficult times. I used to write to her, too, be it for her birthday or to send her festival greetings. But most of my letters were to inform her of what I was learning about the effect of her policies on a vast majority of people I came across in the course of my work at the grassroots level. I thought it was important that she heard some hard truths, away from the sycophants and aye-sayers who often surrounded her larger-than-life personality. Over time, we became close.

On one such occasion, I informed her about the anxiety farmers were experiencing with the radical food policy she had introduced in 1973. The government had announced that it would take over wheat distribution to keep the price of wheat low, and remove exploitative middlemen. Since my father was into farming and knew the local farmers, I had asked him for his opinion. He had told me that the farmers were very unhappy with this policy. The middlemen, according to the farmers, actually served a purpose—they would pick up crops from the village against an advance. The new policy forced farmers to carry their produce to the *mandi* (wholesale market) themselves, which they considered an unnecessary burden. This also exposed them to corrupt government officials who saw this as an opportunity to extort money from the poor, dependent farmers. Shortages began to develop while costs began to rise drastically, with rampant hoarding and black marketing. I was relieved when she cancelled the policy in 1974.

THE FIRST ENCOURAGEMENT

In 1975, Mrs Gandhi nominated me to a women's committee formed as part of the UN's International Women's Year celebrations, to foster equality, development and peace from women's perspective. Our objective was to highlight the issues women faced across sectors within four to five months and make recommendations to the government, which could then present the final resolutions to the UN. About 35 women, largely elderly, distinguished activists with enormous experience, were chosen. At 35 years, I was the youngest and the least experienced in the team. It was a fantastic opportunity, and I was thrilled.

One of my key ideas for the recommendations that were to go in the report came from the domestic workers in Bombay. And for that I am eternally grateful to them. These women did not wish to live with their employers, nor did they take up multiple chores around the house. They charged for jobs by specialization and by the hour. Professionally dressed, some handled cooking, others cleaned kitchen utensils, washed clothes, mopped floors, did the grocery shopping, ironed clothes, or looked after infants and the elderly. What mattered to me was that these women were great sources of news and views—from personal problems they faced with drunk husbands and lazy sons to politics. It was from them that I learnt about the textile mills.

Back then, you could not find a working-class person who wasn't somehow associated with textile mills. Dating back to 1854, when the Bombay Spinning and Weaving Company was set up, these mills were the bread and butter of the city. The heart of the city was dotted with textile mills, with workers living in chawls close by. They shared a common urban experience both at the workplace and in their personal space, had similar grievances, and needed to organize themselves for better working conditions and wages. This spurred the largest trade union movement in the country.

Established in 1887, the Rashtriya Mill Mazdoor Sangh (RMMS) Swadeshi was the first textile mill with an officially recognized union of about 2.5 lakh workers, primarily agitating over wages and bonuses. In 1982, led by Dr Datta Samant, RMMS spearheaded an indefinite strike that crippled Bombay's textile industry, leaving thousands jobless and forcing many mills to close down. This marked Bombay's transformation to Mumbai, shifting from manufacturing to financial and high-value services.[22]

I realized that RMMS was focused on the grievances of male workers. Women's needs were largely ignored in their negotiations. I approached the RMMS union and requested for any data they might have gathered on women workers. I was surprised to find that although about 25,000 women worked there, somehow their numbers were going down. That was because RMMS did not allow women to work in the third shift, at night. Not allowed to work on the spinning spools either, women worked mostly in the packing units. And when women asked for fringe benefits such as equal wages or maternity leave, mill owners surreptitiously reduced their numbers, by mechanizing the packing and disbursing department. Nobody could take them to task over ignoring women workers' demands.

I also decided to see how things were with women in rural Maharashtra. And I saw the same pattern unfolding—mechanization and modernization were not working in women's favour. Generally rural women work in weeding, tilling, seeding, sowing and harvesting. Several of these activities were being taken over by machines, with higher efficiency and precision. New tools were overwhelmingly entrusted to male workers, reducing both the opportunity and confidence of female workers. Hence, women were working on small road-building programmes in rural areas. I saw how children suffered as their mothers worked. The women had no water supplies or toilets, and nowhere to leave their children. I saw how the children were kept on road sides, how they ran around or played among piles of bricks and gravel, squatted in the dirt, or carried jerry cans of water to and fro. These were also not regular jobs and women did not get equal wages for the same amount of work done by men. Clearly, mechanization was working against the women.

---

[22]Chhachhi, Amrita, and Paul Kurian, 'New Phase in Textile Unionism?', *Economic and Political Weekly*, 1982, Vol. 17, No. 8, 20 February 1982, pp. 267–272, https://tinyurl.com/39ky9wmu. Accessed on 17 July 2024.

I presented my research at the committee meeting and pointed out that there should be equal wages for equal work, crèches in any workplace for women, state protection for women, and that there should not be any gender discrimination. I could see that the senior women were surprised. They did not expect the member with the least experience to be as thorough as I was. When our report was submitted to Mrs Gandhi, a high-ranking civil servant attached to the committee paid me a visit to understand my research and recommendations, which he was to take forward to respective ministries for further pursuance. After completion of its mandate, the committee was dissolved but the experience I gathered from it became a lifelong lesson.

THEN CAME THE EMERGENCY

The Emergency was a turning point for the country and me. Akbar and I were visiting Delhi and staying with Shankar Dayal Sharma, then Minister of Communications. It was 25 June 1975, a very hot and unusually dry day. We had travelled to the capital to participate in an advisory telecommunication committee that I was on. In the afternoon, Dr Sharma called us into his drawing room and informed us that an Emergency had been declared across the country by President Fakhruddin Ali Ahmed. He did not say much more but looked like he was in a state of shock and disbelief. We decided to leave for Bombay as soon as possible, which was the next day. My three young girls—eight, five and two years old at the time—were alone in Bombay with my mother and I was worried about the fallout of the Emergency.

In 1971, Mrs Gandhi had won the Lok Sabha election from Rae Bareli, defeating Raj Narain, who then accused her of electoral malpractice and of violating the Representation of the People Act, 1951, alleging misuse of government officials for her campaign. On 12 June 1975, the Allahabad High Court convicted Mrs Gandhi, disqualifying her from Parliament, and imposed a six-year ban on holding any elected post.[23]

A fortnight later, the Emergency was declared, suspending fundamental rights, censoring the media, and imprisoning dissenters, with the government citing national security threats, particularly the recent war with Pakistan. Despite discomfort within her party, Mrs Gandhi had strong support from key figures like Siddhartha Shankar Ray, then Chief Minister of West Bengal, and her son Sanjay Gandhi, both egging her on. The 1971 war with Pakistan had ended in victory but strained India's economy, with over eight million refugees to look after, and the cessation of US aid. Additionally, the global energy crisis led to soaring oil prices, rampant inflation, and sluggish industrial growth, prompting the government to believe that freezing government employee wages would help curb inflation.

With the declaration of the Emergency, the muzzling of the press had a chilling effect across the country and instilled fear in the hearts of the general public. I also noticed a sharp spike in public policing. I remember a person walking up to me randomly and asking me what I had done personally to further the government's 20-Point Programme to increase industrial and agricultural production, improve public services and fight poverty. In addition to this was also the Five-Point Programme, Sanjay Gandhi's brainchild, which included adult education, abolition of dowry, tree plantation, family planning (limiting to two children), and eradication of the caste system—all very enlightened and noble ideas if not considered in the context of the Emergency. It was alleged that during this period, incarcerations increased manifold as did police brutality. Misinformation peppered with propaganda and garnished with reality was rampant.

Despite the Emergency, I continued with my work at the local

---

[23]'State of U.P vs Raj Narain & Ors on 24 January, 1975', *Indian Kanoon*, https://tinyurl.com/5yefat8n. Accessed on 17 July 2024.

level. I would hear of men being picked up from their wedding *mandaps* (pavilions) and forcibly sterilized. This violation along with other excesses were committed on citizens, who were randomly picked up from places like the Bombay local trains, where public gatherings were still allowed. However, in my extensive work in Bombay's public sphere, I personally never came across any such incident of torture, murder or forcible sterilization.

While vasectomy camps were organized by the government, I did not find any abuse as often claimed. Another measure taken by the government during the Emergency was the clearing of the slums in parts of larger cities. Besides providing shelter to the migrant and the poor who flocked to cities for opportunities, slums were also a source of considerable influence for political powerbrokers who understood the importance of vote banks. One such mover and shaker was Maulana Syed Abdullah Bukhari, Shahi Imam of Delhi's Jama Masjid.

Back then, as it is true even now, votes were divided along caste and religious lines and anybody who could master the numbers game could manage to wield substantial power. Muslim voters were considered a voting bloc and they took their cue from the Shahi Imam.

With his open opposition to Mrs Gandhi, she lost a significant voting bloc. At the time, it was not easy to communicate with her. One could only go so far with one's honest thoughts through letters. She was a victim of poor advice from her advisors, and even poorer judgement. During that period, I saw very little of her and bringing up the Emergency was not a comfortable conversation.

Such was the opposition to her Emergency powers that it became impossible for her to continue to govern amidst such severe discontent. On 18 January 1977, she called for elections, and on 21 March 1977, she reversed the Emergency powers.[24] That

---

[24] ET Online, '1975 Emergency explained: A look back at India's "dark days of democracy"; Govt designates day as "Samvidhaan Hatya Diwas"', 12 July 2024, *The Economic Times*, https://tinyurl.com/y36xay36. Accessed on 18 July 2024.

year, the Janata Party alliance defeated Mrs Gandhi. Morarji Desai's government came to power winning 298 seats in the Lok Sabha, and with the support of political allies, added another 47 seats, thereby securing a majority. The ruling Congress Party and its allies (Communist Party of India 23 seats, All India Anna Dravida Munnetra Kazhagam 19 seats) obtained 189 seats. Mrs Gandhi lost her own seat in Rai Bareli to Raj Narain.[25]

All her privileges were withdrawn. The government focused its entire strength on tarnishing her image. Most people in her party and in the government believed her political career was over and shunned her. She moved out of the prime minister's residence on 1 Safdarjung Road to a modest bungalow at No. 12 Willingdon Crescent. She was asked to appear before commissions and courts. The commissions came up with absurd allegations, which had no basis in facts. One such allegation was that treasure troves were hidden underground in her private farm near Delhi. Another was that she had stolen six eggs and two chickens somewhere in the Northeast.[26]

Mrs Gandhi had a very strong character, but she was very hurt by such allegations. None of these could be proved. The Morarji government was literally led up the garden path by misinformation. The allegations became a public scandal. Meanwhile, she started visiting different parts of the country to acquaint herself with the difficulties and problems of common people and to rebuild her party. Also, the Morarji government itself was getting more and more unpopular due to its policies and management of the country. I never got a chance to discuss the Emergency with her, but I did get the impression that she regretted it deeply.

---

[25]Prasad, Ravi Visvesvaraya Sharada, 'How Morarji Desai Became Prime Minister in 1977', *OPEN*, 24 April 2022, https://tinyurl.com/yae95f26. Accessed on 18 July 2024.
[26]POI, 'Prime Minister Indira Gandhi: On No-Confidence Motion in the Council of Ministers (1981)', Parliament of India, Lok Sabha Digital Library, 17 September 1981, https://tinyurl.com/c5w5et26. Accessed on 18 July 2024.

In October 1977, Mrs Gandhi was arrested. She refused to post bail and insisted on being handcuffed but the police officers denied her request. There were two main charges against her. The first charge was of engaging in criminal conspiracy and misusing her position in order to get jeeps for her election campaign in several parliamentary constituencies, along with P.C. Sethi and five other individuals. The second charge was related to the agreement made by Oil and Natural Gas Corporation Ltd (ONGC) and French oil company Compagnie Française des Pétroles (CFP) to hire the latter as consultants for Phase III of the Bombay High offshore drilling activities which, according to the newly elected government, resulted in an overpayment. When she appeared before the magistrate, he was startled at the lack of evidence to support the arrest. Within 16 hours of her detention, she was freed but the suspicion of political corruption and bias lingered in the air.[27]

A FRIEND IN NEED

After her release, Mrs Gandhi came to Bombay like an ordinary citizen. Every time she visited Bombay, I made sure she did not stay anywhere else but my home. So I would fetch her from the airport and cook for her. Often, I used to make Gujarati dishes like *kadhi* and *khichhri* for her, which she loved.

One day, when she visited our house, she appeared exhausted. I offered to press her legs, despite her initial reluctance, explaining that doing so would make me happy. After a brief silence, she warned that the government would harass me for taking care of her and meeting her in public. I said, 'What can they do? At most, they can hang me. They are already harassing my husband, attacking his business. But I cannot be disloyal to you.' I told her I was sure

---

[27] 'Indira Gandhi's arrest seen as Janata Party's first major political blunder', *India Today*, 25 March 2015, https://tinyurl.com/bdhr4u8h. Accessed on 18 July 2024.

someday she would be back again at the helm of things: 'The very people who abandoned you will be back tomorrow. Unfortunately, I have a feeling they will be in and I will be out. But that thought does not really keep me up at night.'

My youngest daughter, Asma, was about three years old at the time. Mrs Gandhi was very fond of her. Asma was a confident, talkative child who loved to spend time with her. One day, she came in with a voter slip we had received. It had party symbols. Mrs Gandhi's breakaway faction, Congress (R), had opted for a cow with a suckling calf. In 1978, after the second split in the Congress, she had chosen the open palm symbol for her new outfit, the Congress (I) or Congress (Indira). Asma took the voter slip to her and said, 'You will milk the old cow with this new hand.' Mrs Gandhi was astonished: 'What is she saying?' I explained, 'She is saying that a hand is important even for milking a cow.' She started laughing. Mrs Gandhi was patient and gentle with my children. She was always respectful, no matter how young a person was or whether she understood their logic or not—a quality she certainly shared with her late father.

I still remember vividly one rain-soaked July day in 1977 in Delhi, when she gave me a lesson on surviving in a world where betrayal and trust, rise and fall were the norm. She was out of power then. When I arrived from Bombay to meet her, she was closing the drawing room door against the rain after bringing me inside. I had never seen her looking so tired. 'What has happened?' I exclaimed. She was quiet for a long time. I searched her face for clues. She did not smile or grimace, just sat still.

'I was Prime Minister, but I did not know the nuances of running a country,' she said. Bit by bit, she told me how people she had faith in—from her trusted bureaucrats and advisors to a Bengal politician and friend—tried to control her. When she began to break free from their shackles, and take her own decisions, they wanted to teach her a lesson. Their politics of patronage tipped her towards her downfall.

She came back, of course, but I always marvelled at how she had changed. This time around, she was tough, shrewd, ruthless and skilled in the use of power.

As part of my work at the Indo-Arab Society in Bombay, I had become well acquainted with different members of the Arab diplomatic community and managed to build amicable relations with them. I wanted to support Mrs Gandhi's campaign and garner support for her from the Indian Muslim diaspora for her campaign for the 1980 general elections. So I managed to convince Dr Mohammed Yousef Magarief, then Ambassador of Libya to India, to invite her for a reception. He did so, and she got an opportunity to meet and mingle with Muslim intellectuals from different parts of the country and present her side of the story to them.

I also convinced the Ambassador of Saudi Arabia to India to hold a reception for her. He was very close to the Shahi Imam of Delhi's Jama Masjid, and the most powerful Muslim religious figure in India back then. The reception was a colossal event held at The Ashok. At this meeting, Mrs Gandhi managed to convince the Shahi Imam to support her and cleared the misunderstandings that had turned him against her in the first place. His support was one of the main reasons why she got a large voting bloc in her favour.

During her election campaign, Khodabux Rustom Irani, the owner of the famous ice cream shop K-Rustam in Santa Cruz, contacted me. He informed me that there was a sadhu who had known Pandit Nehru when he was in Naini Jail in Allahabad in Uttar Pradesh back in 1934. The sadhu claimed that he was wrongly arrested by the British when he was returning from his meditations in the secluded Himalayan mountains. That was a time of great mistrust and suspicion, and the British government cracked down on any person even remotely linked to the struggle for independence. He claimed to have fallen prey to their suspicion and, consequently, thrown into jail.

For him, the silver lining of the wrongful arrest was that he became acquainted with Pandit Nehru and got to know him better. So, when his daughter Indira was campaigning for the 1980 general elections, he wanted to bless her. Despite her very busy campaign schedule, she agreed to fly down to Bombay. She asked me to accompany her, but I thought it would be best for her to meet him on her own. By this time, it was clear that Mrs Gandhi had regained her popularity and I wanted to ensure that my closeness to her was not seen by others as currying any favour. She agreed to visit him on her own. He blessed her, gave her an amulet for her protection, which she carried with her. He predicted that she would get re-elected. He was old and suffering from cancer and this was his last meeting with her, just before he passed away. She was re-elected and her party got a landslide victory in the 1980 general elections.

Even after such a victory Mrs Gandhi did not forget her friends and loyalists. Akbar and I decided to be in Delhi when the results were being announced. We wanted to partake in the jubilations and celebrations. Unfortunately, we were in such a rush to get there that neither of us realized it was winter. And Delhi winters are cold, unlike those of Bombay. We landed there with no woollens and were freezing to death. We went down to meet her at her bungalow. She was taken aback that we had both showed up in summer clothes. She left the room. We were not sure if she had left the room for good or she was planning to come back. So, conservatively we assumed the former and we left too. The next morning when we caught up again with her, she said that she had gone in to get a shawl for me and returned to find us gone. I was so touched by her thoughtfulness.

ENTREATED INTO HER WORLD

It was 1980, a June afternoon. At home, we were getting ready for our usual Sunday outing—lunch at Holiday Inn or Juhu Hotel, followed by coffee and treats at the Oberoi coffee shop.

The telephone trilled and I recognized Dr Rafiq Zakaria's voice. 'Congratulations,' he said. 'You have been selected for nomination to the Rajya Sabha by Shrimati Indira Gandhi.' My mind raced back to the day when Mrs Gandhi had asked me, 'Would you like to contest the elections?' I had said, 'No, Madam, I am not interested.' I realized then that she had not forgotten that day, nor had she accepted my answer.

Dr Zakaria said, 'You don't seem too excited. Others would have jumped at this opportunity.' I was in a bit of a bind—happy and proud, yet a little anxious and wary. 'I am elated and much obliged,' I said. 'But, as you know, I have a family and three little daughters, who are still in school. This will bring a lot of changes to my life. I will have to move to Delhi.' Akbar, my husband, was of the opinion that it would be an amazing opportunity for me and offered to shoulder the family responsibilities while I was away. We both thought that this would be a short stint, at the most six years, the term for a Rajya Sabha membership. At his behest and with his support, I accepted the offer.

The official intimation came a little later from the office of A.R. Antulay, Chief Minister of Maharashtra. The next morning, on June 23, I visited Sahyadri, his bungalow, to file the nomination papers. I went to meet the chief minister along with my husband and two young friends, Salim and Shamim Qureshi, from the Youth Congress. We expected a cheerful atmosphere. Instead, a hushed silence greeted us. 'What happened?' I asked. We were informed that Sanjay Gandhi, the younger son of Indira, had met with a terrible accident. His plane had crashed in New Delhi and he had not survived. I was stunned and overwhelmed with grief. I had known Sanjay for a very long time, in fact since he was in school. It was difficult to fill up the nomination form, but I had to—it was the last day to file the papers. We then delivered the completed forms to the Council Hall near Regal Cinema.

Next day, I flew to Delhi and went straight to 1 Safdarjung Road. A lot of people were sitting under a *shamiyana* (marquee).

I saw the urn in which Sanjay's ashes were kept. Priests were chanting mantras for the final rituals. I sat down on the grass. Soon the prime minister came out of her bungalow, noticed me and indicated a dhurrie. There was not a single dry eye amongst the people sitting there. Mrs Gandhi, however, stood like a statue. One could see pain and grief in her eyes, in the way she carried herself stiffly, but she did not cry.

After the rituals, she gestured me to come into the house. She took me into the dining room from a side door. I leaned on the table and started to cry. She attempted to console me and said in a hollow voice: 'You have arrived straight from the airport. Would you like a cup of tea?' At her generosity and kindness, I put my head down on the table and started sobbing. She brought a cup of tea for me. That made me cry even more. There she was in untold pain at the loss of a child, and she was trying to console me. I knew what losing a loved one meant; years ago, I had lost my beloved Bhaijaan. She sat next to me and said, 'I would like you to go back to Bombay and get elected, so that you can work with me.' That evening, I left for Bombay and was elected MP from Maharashtra to the Rajya Sabha.

Thus started my active political career which inadvertently lasted, even to my surprise, close to 40 years.

SELLING SCIENCE TO POLITICIANS

As children of independent India, many of us were inspired by Pandit Nehru's push towards a policy that underscored using science and technology for the betterment of society. His large projects had put India on the scientific map, and Mrs Gandhi had continued in his footsteps. Being a scientist myself, I was in complete agreement with them. If India was to succeed, it had to be a powerhouse in the field of research and application of the sciences. Back then, 70 per cent of India was still agrarian and large swathes of it illiterate. Most conversations or even policies centred on the urban middle classes. Plenty of research was being done but most seemed to miss a commercial connection. Confined to isolated pockets of urban university laboratories, the research was not being used effectively or efficiently to make policy choices. Above all, rural India seemed to be almost ignored in that research.

I had a twin advantage—I was a scientist and I came from a rural background. This allowed me some insight into what could help define a roadmap to achieve Pandit Nehru's vision, and thereby address the huge gap in policy. Progress would come from training villagers to think and approach problem-solving scientifically and seek solutions accordingly. It had to be in the fields for which they had a natural aptitude, or had learnt about through experience and wisdom passed down from one generation to the other. If we could use their knowledge and explain the science to them, then we would be able to convert them to a more logical form of problem-solving.

I wrote to Mrs Gandhi about an idea, which I called 'Lab to Land Policy'. It was to start with a pilot project, which entailed sending a group of young scientists with experience in soil management, environmental studies, and water management, and agriculturalists to a chosen district. By collaborating with each other and studying the current farming and resource management practices, this group could be used to make suggestions, which then could be implemented successfully. Besides adjusting current practices to meet the demands of a changing environment, the interaction of these scientists with the villagers would serve dual benefits. A scientific approach could impact the villagers, while the scientists could benefit from seeing how their theory could be put into practice by taking the laboratory outside of the four walls and into the open.

Mrs Gandhi was very excited about the idea and suggested that I put them to her very senior and trusted bureaucrat, P.N. Haksar. Haksar was a seasoned diplomat, one of the most powerful in Mrs Gandhi's office. Educated at the London School of Economics, he had Left leanings and admired the Fabians. He became Mrs Gandhi's key advisor, influencing India's support for the creation of Bangladesh. He championed the license raj and nationalization of banks and foreign-owned companies. As the mastermind behind the 1972 Shimla Agreement, he facilitated Pakistan's recognition of Bangladesh and established the Line of Control. The treaty aimed to resolve Indo-Pakistani disputes peacefully, without resorting to war. Eventually, he fell out of favour because of his dislike for Sanjay Gandhi, and refused to come back to Mrs Gandhi's office when she was back in power in 1980.[28]

I went to Delhi and met him. A well-built man, Haksar was about 60 years old, with a thick crop of greying hair, and black-framed spectacles. When I entered his office, he was sitting behind his desk. I said 'namaste'. He looked up from his papers but ignored my greeting. I handed over my recommendations. He read them and said they were good suggestions. Then, very patronizingly, he dismissed my suggestions by saying: 'Now, sell it to the politicians, young lady.' I was annoyed. I thought he was rude and insulting (back then, I was young and not very diplomatic). I too got up in a huff and retorted, 'I would rather not sell it to any politician but become one myself.' That was the end of that.

Somehow, Haksar's advice kept gnawing at me. When I went to the Rajya Sabha, I joined the Science and Technology Consultative Committee, headed by Mrs Gandhi, since that ministerial portfolio was under her.

As time went by, Haksar's words resonated more and more. I guess I had grown up. Looking back, perhaps, he was smarter and far more sagacious than I had given him credit for. Or perhaps the fire of my youthful arrogance had been quelled by the realities of life. Or maybe it was a bit of both. I realized that for me to be effective, it was important to convince the right stakeholders—

---

[28]P.N. Haksar Papers, Archives of Contemporary India, Ashoka University, https://tinyurl.com/3u2u8hxa. Accessed on 18 July 2024.

in my case, my compatriots and comrades in Parliament. It was important, as he said, to 'sell' an idea on how it could help them with their constituencies. I realized I had to involve 'the politicians' in the decision-making process. The lesson learnt on that day with Haksar helped me over the years, whether I was presiding over an unruly House or negotiating on behalf of India with foreign leaders.

The committee also became a good source of finding people who had similar views. One such person I came across was Digvijaysinh Jhala, Maharaja of Wankaner, who became a great friend and fellow accomplice in our attempt to influence policy related to science and technology. I fondly called him Wankuji because he was from Wankaner, a city in the Morbi District of Gujarat on the banks of the Machchhu River. Wankuji was a wonderful person and besides being interested in the sciences, his interest was focused on environment and resource management. We found a common ground and decided that our first task was to find like-minded members who could support us on our different policy recommendations.

We retrieved all the résumés of the members from the committee administrators (back then, it was not as easy as it is now—almost all information is available today at the click of a button) and approached them for their support. We thought we should keep it simple (but nothing is simple, of course). A simple agenda we thought would be convincing legislators and Mrs Gandhi of the importance of a colour television (remember this was still 1980 and the Asian Games were still a few years away). Mrs Gandhi always thought that investment in a colour television was a frivolous expenditure since it would take tremendous resources for the conversion. I had raised it with her several times earlier, and every time her eyes would glaze over and she would ignore what I was saying, which she did not do often.

We realized that we needed to make it attractive for Mrs Gandhi to even consider the proposal. The one thing that always caught her attention were the words 'benefit the farmers'. In those days, one of the main purposes of television was education of farmers. Farming and farm management programmes, like 'Krishi Darshan' in Hindi-speaking India, 'Amchi Mati Amchi Mansan' in Maharashtra and in all states in their own languages, were prime-time mainstays. I took my proposal to her once again and said that colour television could really help the farmers. I explained how, for instance, a black-and-white programme on leaf rust—a fungal disease of the wheat—could hardly help the farmers. They could relate to it easily if shown in colour. And it could also draw in the younger audience. She just looked at me in disbelief with a slight smile and a twinkle in her eyes at my perseverance. Finally she chuckled, 'You are so mischievous. You never give up, do you?'

In 1982, we finally tasted sweet victory. India was hosting the 9th Asian Games in November of that year. It was a proud moment for us. Games in black and white would not have the same effect as those broadcast in colour. Doordarshan was given 18 months to shift to colour technology, procure outdoor broadcasting (OB) vans, cameras and train its engineers. Doordarshan OB vans were stationed at three games venues to provide coverage in colour. In April 1982, the broadcaster started introducing and testing programmes in colour, and officially the games were telecast in colour. Mrs Gandhi was not yet convinced that India needed to move to all colour. So again, I armed myself with more benefits for 'Krishi Darshan' and suggested these to her since we had already invested in the OB vans and training. To my surprise, she seemed to agree and since then, colour television became a permanent feature across households in India. A very popular decision indeed, it met with great success nationally. And that felt good.

SOLVING ENVIRONMENTAL PROBLEMS

I realized that resource management would be key to India's development. The country's population was growing and our colonial history had left us with very lopsided development, primarily intended to support and cater to the needs of the British Empire. Everywhere, the countryside had been devastated by high rents with a focus on cash crops, like opium to be exported to China, and famines were rampant. Most of us even remotely linked with the agrarian world knew firsthand about the effects of the ravages wreaked by climate change, since we were witnessing these in our farms. Wankuji and I had discussed this at length.

I shared the report I had shown Haksar back in the early '70s. I had also started following the United Nations Environment Programme (UNEP) formed during the Stockholm Conference in 1972. We formed an environment forum of Parliament. We convinced the prime minister that it was critical to make a concerted effort, and set aside resources to address an impending disaster. Increase in famines and floods across the country had also convinced her that more certainly needed to be done.

In 1982, a second UNEP conference was held in Nairobi. Mrs Gandhi was the only head of state to attend it. It laid the groundwork to address environmental challenges globally. At our initiative, a Department of Environment was created and Wankuji was made the first Union Deputy Minister for Ecology and the Environment. He served from its initiation in 1982 till Mrs Gandhi's passing in 1984. Mrs Gandhi remained its cabinet minister until her death. At the time, she was the only head of state to talk about the environment politically.

※

I first travelled to Saudi Arabia back in 1972, when Akbar, my husband, and I had gone for Hajj. There we were introduced to T.T.P. Abdullah, Ambassador of India to Saudi Arabia. He had taken a great liking to us. I had talked at length about my interest in science and the cutting-edge research that was being done, thanks to my participation in the Council of Scientific and Industrial Research, of which I was an ardent supporter, a member, and a former fellow. Through the years, we kept in touch with T.T.P. In one such meeting, he mentioned that there was some amazing research being done in Saudi Arabia, especially related to energy and desalination. I was very interested. I asked him if it would be possible for me to visit. Due to his tenure in Saudi Arabia, he had a lot of friends and contacts there. He arranged for us to be invited by Dr Rida Obaid.

Dr Obaid was President of Saudi Arabian National Center for Science and Technology (SANCST), an autonomous government organization that promoted research in the sciences, and that was later renamed King Abdulaziz City of Science and Technology. We travelled to the kingdom and met with Dr Obaid. He showed me their solar energy project. It had parabolic troughs with reflectors and high-density oil pipes. As the parabolas moved with the sun, the oil supplied thermal energy and a turbine generator generated electricity. We were also taken to their desalination plant. The director-general of the plant was Abdullah Bin Omar Nasseef, whose mother happened to be Indian (he later became the Secretary-General of Muslim World League). At the plant, they were making steam out of salted water, then condensing the steam into saltless potable water and harnessing electricity as a by-product.

On my return to India, I wrote to the prime minister with details on the research and how solar energy could reduce India's dependence on imported oil as well as facilitate the electrification of rural India. I also suggested that a desalination plant in Tamil Nadu could help with the water scarcity problems the state faced. In 1982, when Mrs Gandhi visited Saudi Arabia, she invited me to be part of the delegation, and visited the desalination plant at Jeddah.

Around this time, she took a personal interest in India's first expedition to Antarctica under marine biologist Dr Syed Zahoor Qasim—a proud moment, when the world sat up and took note. I knew Dr Qasim from my Bhopal days. He had been my external examiner, when I had started teaching. He had come to our house and stayed for a while. Dr Qasim also led India's first successful expedition to explore deep-sea polymetallic nodules, covering vast areas of the Indian Ocean and containing significant amounts of critical metals. I made a statement in Parliament about his discovery. Mrs Gandhi greatly appreciated our efforts.

PREDICTING WEST ASIAN STRATEGY

I saw our Hajj pilgrimage in 1972 as an opportunity to assess the political situation in the region. Oil prices were rising sharply, increasing Arab purchasing power. On my return, I reported to Mrs Gandhi that a war was likely in the near future, with Arabs winning and the Suez Canal being liberated. When questioned about my predictions by a diplomat from the Ministry of External Affairs, I explained that Americans and Europeans would ensure an Arab victory to regain control of the Suez Canal—a crucial trade route.

The Suez Canal is a 193-kilometre waterway connecting the Mediterranean Sea to the Indian Ocean via the Red Sea, and providing a direct shipping route between Europe and Asia. Previously under British control, the Suez Canal was nationalized in 1956 under Gamal Abdel Nasser, then President of Egypt.

Nasser's nationalization and, more importantly, closure of the Straits of Tiran, a waterway linking Israel to the Red Sea, angered European powers. UN intervention ensuring access to all at the time prevented a full-blown war. However, the situation escalated in 1967 when Nasser ordered UN peacekeeping forces out of the Sinai Peninsula, leading to the Six-Day War with Israel. Israel emerged victorious, winning four times its original size in land and more importantly, gaining control of the Golan Heights and the Sinai Peninsula.

The canal's blockage halted trade as it separated mainland Egypt from Israeli-occupied Sinai. Israel built the Bar Lev Line, a massive sand wall with fortifications along the canal's eastern coast. In 1970, Egyptian President Anwar Sadat's attempts to recover Sinai were rejected by Israel.

I reasoned that while Sinai was less important to Israel, it could manage a peace agreement with Egypt and a win-win for Western nations which prioritized reopening the canal for trade with the Gulf states. Egypt would not allow this without recovering its lost lands. The logical solution was for Egypt to challenge Israel in war, and Egypt would find sympathizers in Washington. However, Israel would not relinquish the strategically important Golan Heights as a source of fresh water from the Sea of Galilee.

On 6 October 1973, during Yom Kippur, Arab armies breached the Bar Lev Line, catching Israel off guard. The Arab coalition, including Egypt, Syria, and Jordan, advanced 36 kilometres into the eastern bank. Richard Nixon, then President of the United States, delayed emergency military aid to Israel, signalling sympathy with the Arab states.

On 25 October, a ceasefire was declared between Egypt and Israel. Despite Egypt's loss, Sadat's leadership was bolstered. In 1975, he reopened the canal. The 1978 Camp David Accord, signed by Anwar Sadat, Jimmy Carter, and Menachem Begin, aimed to resolve regional conflicts. The agreements had a larger intent— withdrawal of Israel from Gaza and the West Bank, return of Golan Heights to Syria, and withdrawal of Israeli forces from Sinai. It only achieved withdrawal of Israeli forces from Sinai.

Sadat's agreement with Israel without securing the allies' interests was seen as a betrayal of the Arab cause. This made him unpopular in Egypt and the Arab world. On 22 November 1977, Egypt was voted out of the Arab League. On 6 October 1981, Sadat was assassinated during the annual victory parade in Cairo to celebrate Operation Badr.

As an MP, I met Mohamad Hassanein Heikal, editor-in-chief of *Al-Ahram*, author of *Road to Ramadan*, and considered the Henry Kissinger of Egypt. He asked how I was able to predict the war and its outcome. I explained, 'I predicted it because I understood the economics of it.'

ALLIES ON THE WORLD STAGE

By the time I was elected to Parliament, Mrs Gandhi had come to respect my assessments of West Asia. After her successful return to power in the 1980 elections, it was time to boost her standing on the world stage and fortify India's allies. I met Sheikh Ismail Abudawood, then Chairman of Jeddah Chamber of Commerce and Industry, at a conference in Delhi. He was the founder of the Abudawood Group, a diversified international conglomerate incorporating investments across West Asia, Europe and the US. Throughout his career, he had championed the growth of diversified commerce in Saudi Arabia.[29]

Over dinner, we discussed India's relations with Saudi Arabia at length and concluded that though they had been cordial for centuries, high-level visits from both sides had stopped in the last 25 years. He asked, 'Why doesn't Mrs Gandhi ever come to Saudi Arabia?' To which I replied, 'Did you invite her officially?' He admitted that he hadn't, but added that Muhammed Zia-ul-Haq, then President of Pakistan, visited often. He added that Zia-ul-Haq was establishing personal rapport with the leaders in the Middle East, a role that India had enjoyed under Pandit Nehru. I told him without mincing my words that Zia-ul-Haq did not always come on official visits, but to perform his religious obligations. He used these visits as an excuse to connect with the officials.

I also added that the then President of Pakistan claimed all his visits were by official invitation of the Saudi government: 'It is a lot easier for him to travel to Saudi Arabia and connect than it is for Mrs Gandhi. She is the leader of such a big democracy. If there is an invitation, she will definitely come.' His eyes started to shine and he sounded enthusiastic about what he could do about it.

A few weeks later, the Saudi officials contacted T.T.P. Abdullah, then Ambassador of India to Saudi Arabia. I had already spoken to

---

[29]Sheikh Ismail Ali Abudawood, Crunchbase, https://tinyurl.com/mrxvyt5s. Accessed on 18 July 2024.

him about my meeting. We decided that we needed to pursue both governments to ensure that this visit took place.

I convinced Mrs Gandhi that it was in the strategic interest of India to accept, maintain and further India's relations with Saudi Arabia. The obvious one was India's insatiable need for and dependence on imported oil, and Saudi Arabia was one of the largest producers and exporters of oil. Second, petrodollars had jumpstarted the Saudi economy and they were playing catch-up. For this, they needed a huge workforce—in construction, oil and gas, hospitals and more. We, on the other hand, had a large supply of skilled workforce that our economy could not absorb. This could be win-win for both. Third, Pakistan was using its Islamic credentials to get a foot in the door, and to secure arms, economic aid, oil and gas. What's more, Pakistan was playing India's victim to get what it wanted. We needed to dispel the lies they were spreading about India abusing its minorities, and convince the world that India, in fact, had more Muslims than Pakistan did. And their interests were safeguarded based on the rule of law.

Being custodians of Islam's most holy places, and the faith itself, gave Saudi Arabia some moral authority, so its acceptance of India's treatment of minorities was paramount. My advice to Mrs Gandhi was that India needed to decouple its foreign policy from what Pakistan was doing. Establishing our own bilateral relations could further our interests in the region independently. She was convinced.

Prior to Mrs Gandhi's visit, I invited two prominent journalists from Saudi Arabia to interview her. One was Fatina Amin Shakker, founder and editor of the first and most popular Arab women's magazine *Sayidaty*, published from London and Beirut. Shakker was a widely known personality and one of the first female voices on Saudi Radio. The other one was Farouk Luqman, a prominent journalist from *Arab News*, an English-language daily with a target readership of businessmen, executives and diplomats. Both articles were published on the day she landed for her official visit, with

Sayidaty putting her on the magazine cover.

On 21 April 1982, Mrs Gandhi began a high-profile four-day trip to Saudi Arabia, and was given a grand red-carpet welcome. As a member of her delegation, I felt proud when our national anthem, 'Jana Gana Mana', rent the air, while His Royal Highness, Crown Prince Fahad, waited at the foot of the ramp with his retinue. The tightest security was accorded to her. And she travelled in His Royal Highness King Khalid's custom-built, ultra-luxury car. It was the official recognition by the Saudis—for the first time— that India with its size, economic base and political stability was an effective bulwark against superpower geopolitics in the area.

As I travelled with Mrs Gandhi, I got the opportunity to meet King Khalid and Crown Prince Fahad. We were invited by King Khalid's wife for dinner. Crown Prince Fahad's wife was sitting next to me. In front of me was a glass of something that looked like milk. When I tasted it, she asked me if I liked it. I said, 'Yes,' but could not resist asking, 'What is it?' She smiled and explained, 'It's camel milk.' I must have pulled a face involuntarily. She said, 'You don't like it?' I told her politely that if she had not told me it was camel milk, I would perhaps have enjoyed it more. Mrs Gandhi overheard the conversation and started laughing. Then she told me in Hindi, 'Don't complain. I had to drink donkey's milk in Mongolia and had to enjoy it too.'

Even in the middle of this hectic tour, she insisted on visiting the desalination plant in Jeddah with me that I had written to her about during my earlier visits to Saudi Arabia. Apart from her official meetings, she was also invited to a horse-racing event in Riyadh. She was the first woman ever to be invited to such an event and I had the chance to accompany her. On the second day of the visit, I realized that it would be a good idea for her son Rajiv to also be a part of this delegation. It would boost his profile, and given the conservative ambience of the kingdom, it would boost her profile too. So, I suggested it to her and she agreed. The following day, Rajiv joined us in Riyadh.

Some remarkable things happened on that trip. Mrs Gandhi was able to assure the Saudis that minorities in India were safe, treated as equals and with respect. Furthermore, she convinced them to limit arms purchase aid to Pakistan. The Saudis agreed to persuade the Organization of the Petroleum Exporting Countries (OPEC) to consider India's status as a high-priority nation among aid receivers. They also agreed to replace the ad hoc export of crude oil to India with regular long-term supply. There was a verbal agreement that the Saudis would encourage the help of Indian expertise in joint ventures in Saudi Arabia and invest in India themselves.

Later, India was able to leverage the relations Mrs Gandhi had established back then. I was very happy that in some small way I had been instrumental in these developments.

A PAINFUL GOODBYE

In 1984, Mrs Gandhi had sent me to Islamabad, Pakistan, to attend a women's conference. As I was thanking the conference delegates, Krishna Dayal Sharma, then Ambassador of India to Pakistan, took me aside and said, 'Mrs Gandhi has been shot.' I was shocked and distressed. All kinds of thoughts started to cross my mind. Relations between India and Pakistan were strained. Anything could happen in a vacuum. I told Ambassador Sharma that I wanted to leave for India as soon as possible. On landing in Delhi, I went straight to Mrs Gandhi's Akbar Road residence. Her body had not yet arrived from All India Institute of Medical Sciences (AIIMS). Nathu, her man Friday for years, was woebegone and disconsolate. He took me to the spot where she had been slain by her own bodyguards—the mud was drenched in blood. I stood there in tears with Saroj Khaparde, Sheila Dikshit and Kalpnath Rai—people who had a special connection with her. We had stood by her through rain and sunshine, through good times and bad times, on easy pathways and uphill. And we were all crying. We all knew this marked the end of an era.

5

PARTY WORK AND PARTY TALK

Within hours of Indira Gandhi's assassination, her surviving son Rajiv Gandhi was sworn in as the sixth and the youngest Prime Minister of India. I had seen him and his brother Sanjay during my school vacations in Delhi. He was four years my junior. An easy-going airline pilot, he had joined politics after Sanjay's tragic death in 1980, despite his wife Sonia's protestations. His reason was simple, 'Mummy needs me.' In 1984, he was all of 40. And his dream was to transform India into a modern developed country in which citizens could achieve their full potential. As he said in a speech that resonated strongly with me: 'I am young and I, too, have a dream. I dream of an India—strong, independent, self-reliant and in the front rank of the nations of the world in the service of mankind.'[30]

Even as he took charge, Rajiv wanted the people's mandate. The election that followed turned out to be a landslide victory for him, with the Congress winning 404 of 514 contested seats in Parliament—the highest ever[31]. On 31 October 1984, he was sworn in again as Prime Minister. With Rajiv's encouragement, an army of young first-time MPs joined parliamentary politics, bringing in

---

[30]Channer, Philip, and Tina Hope, *Emotional Impact: Passionate Leaders and Corporate Transformation*, Palgrave Macmillan, 2001, https://tinyurl.com/yhbpm4fp. Accessed on 1 July 2024.
[31]ECI, *General Election, 1984 (Vol. I, II)*, Election Commission of India, https://tinyurl.com/2ds94hp3. Accessed on 1 July 2024.

a new fighting spirit and purposefulness. His Council of Ministers had a number of new, young faces. And it had two women—Mohsina Kidwai and Margaret Alva—both seasoned leaders with rich political as well as administrative experience. He did not keep me in the Council.

However, he summoned me soon, and mentioned that he hadn't taken me in as a minister because he wanted to give me a responsibility I would have liked to handle. I pointed out that the post of Deputy Chairperson of the Rajya Sabha was vacant since Shyamlal Yadav had become a Lok Sabha member, and expressed my willingness to take up that job. He went on to ask me why I thought I could do it.

I listed the reasons candidly: 'First, I have been on the panel of Vice Chairpersons of Rajya Sabha and have presided as and when the need arose. Second, I am educated, and because of that, everybody respects me. Third, I am multilingual; I am not only fluent in Urdu, Hindi and English, I can also understand Gujarati and Marathi to a certain extent. If nothing else works, I have a sense of humour! A touch of humour can help make tough moments a little easier.' I concluded by bringing my trademark humour to build my case: 'Lastly, Sir, because you will have to address me as "Madam".' He burst out laughing. H.K.L. Bhagat, Union Minister of Parliamentary Affairs, was informed. I filed my nomination paper, the notification was announced, and I was elected unanimously.

HUMOUR IN THE HOUSE

On 25 January 1985, I joined as Deputy Chairperson. I was the second of 10 women Deputy Chairpersons elected to the Rajya Sabha until then. The first woman Deputy Chairperson was Violet Alva. However, times were very different when Violet Alva had served her term (1962–69).

Even before the motion for my election could be proposed,

a section of the Opposition staged a walkout in protest. Their objection, they said, had nothing to do with me but with a technical point—they had not been given adequate time to present their views. Rajiv, as well as senior leaders of the Congress like Pranab Mukherjee (Pranab-da to us all) and Vishwanath Pratap Singh, countered with their own point-by-point rebuttals. The process of Felicitation to the Chair started with Rajiv using his classic tongue-in-cheek humour: 'It is a pleasure to see Najmaji sitting across here and it makes a very pleasant change from the faces that we are used to seeing there...' To this, M.S. Gurupadaswamy, one of the founders of the Janata Party, quipped, 'Dr Najma is a beautiful Member of the House. If the Ruling Party wanted beauty, we also could have given beauty from the Opposition benches.'[32]

Unlike Alva, I was a 'backbencher' for a few years. Hence, my first day as Deputy Chairperson came as a dose of reality, a wake-up call for the tough challenges and learning experiences that awaited me, as a member of the Opposition had aptly said during the Felicitation.

As the year progressed, the Rajya Sabha went through turbulent rounds of deliberations, debates and decisions on controversial and consequential Bills. Members locked horns for hours, sometimes even skipping their lunch break. The atmosphere in the House remained charged, be it over the 52nd Amendment to the Constitution introducing the Anti-Defection Law (ALD) that made floor-crossing almost impossible; the Terrorists and Disruptive Activities (Prevention) Bill (TADA), the first legislative effort to define and counter terrorist activities; the Bill to set up the first national open university—Indira Gandhi National Open University (IGNOU); the Lokpal Bill; the Narcotic Drugs and Psychotropic Substances (NDPS) Bill; the Airports Authority of India Bill, and

---

[32] *Lighter Moments in the Rajya Sabha*, Secretary-General, Rajya Sabha, August 1985, https://tinyurl.com/v35exh5r. Accessed on 1 July 2024.

so on. But even in the midst of confrontations, witty repartees and amusing remarks, cutting across party lines, served to diffuse tension and conflict.

I still remember with a smile some of the amusing moments in the House: Union Minister of Law and Justice Ashoke Kumar Sen's exasperation with his own slip-up: 'You will excuse me, Sir...! Madam...due to habit, we address you as Sir. But the General Clauses Act states: "A male includes a female." Eve was born out of the very flesh of Adam, that is what the Old Testament teaches us'[33]; the comment of Jagesh Desai, an MP from Maharashtra, on the Coffee (Amendment) Bill: 'Here are only two persons who take coffee and both are ministers. Therefore, this (Bill) may be passed without any discussion;'[34] a former major of the Indian Army, Jaswant Singh's repartee during a debate on the international situation: 'Whenever I have been a witness to discussions and debates on any foreign policy...I am reminded of love-making between elephants—it is always conducted at a very high level; it is accompanied by a great deal of noise, and we don't come to know of the results for at least two and a half years!'[35] And Communist leader Bhupesh Gupta's comment: 'I have a typewriter—the most expensive property I have.'[36]

In the course of that year, I learnt the value of humour in Parliament—something that stood me in good stead for years. Even if I had to scrap the lunch recess to enable the House to clear a long list of businesses slated for the day, or be strict about the time each individual or party was allotted to present their arguments, or rebut an MP, there was always place for some wit, grace, humour and light-hearted relief. The application of humour in politics

---

[33] Agarwal, Sudarshan (ed.), *The House Laughs: An Anthology of Wit and Humour in the Rajya Sabha,* Secretary-General, Rajya Sabha, Rajya Sabha Secretariat, New Delhi, 1989.
[34] Ibid.
[35] Ibid.
[36] Ibid.

became a focus of research later, but from my own experience, I gleaned that humour could be a powerful tool, if used correctly. In my first year in the Rajya Sabha, we brought out a booklet, *Lighter Moments in the Rajya Sabha*, in which Sudarshan Agarwal, then Secretary-General of the Rajya Sabha, wrote in his Foreword: 'Humour serves as oases, as it were, in the dry desert of verbal duels. None of these exchanges are pre-rehearsed or premeditated and that is precisely why they are so good.'[37]

THE KASHMIR FILES

At the end of my first year, I received a call from the prime minister's office. In fact, Rajiv called several of us—Arjun Singh, A.B.A. Ghani Khan Choudhury and myself—and asked us to resign. When I met him, he said, 'I have got another job for you,' giving me an outline of what he had in mind. Accordingly, I submitted my resignation letter to R. Venkataraman, then Vice-President of India, and said, 'I have to lay down office for party work, Sir. The prime minister has made me a general secretary of the Congress Party.' He was visibly upset. 'You were such a good deputy chairman. Now, I have to find someone else to fit in and be accepted. Anyway, it is your career.' 'Wish me luck, Sir,' I said.

Rajiv made me a general secretary in charge of Jammu and Kashmir (J&K). I was also the party spokesperson, the editor of *Congress Varnika*—the official journal of the party—and in charge of the National Students' Union of India (NSUI)—the student wing of the Congress Party. The responsibility of posters, write-ups, slogans, communication and daily press briefings was mine. Every evening, journalists would meet me and ask questions. I became a part of the team that oversaw the daily affairs of the party from the Congress Party office—a sprawling bungalow on 24 Akbar Road. I enjoyed very good relations with everybody in the party. As I used

---

[37]Ibid.

to live at 4 Akbar Road as Deputy Chairperson of the Rajya Sabha, just a stone's throw from the party office, Rajiv suggested that I should continue to stay on there, even after I had resigned the post.

As I started visiting Kashmir, I took to wearing a *pheran*, the traditional Kashmiri long woollen robe, and covering my head. I also acquired a jeep, which I drove myself most of the time. I met a range of leaders, especially the old Kashmir Congress guard—Mufti Mohammad Sayeed, who was then Union Minister of Tourism; Ghulam Rasool Kar, Vice-President of the party; Moulvi Iftikhar Hussain Ansari, Shia cleric and leader of the Congress Legislative Party (CLP) in Kashmir. I noticed that most of them functioned from home. Girdhari Lal Dogra, BJP stalwart Arun Jaitley's father-in-law, was another prominent political figure in Kashmir. A freedom fighter, he had joined the Congress from the National Conference (NC). I often sought advice from him.

Although there was no insurgency or terrorist attacks from Pakistan, they seemed scared to step out. As I interacted with the people and shared their experiences, I invited local leaders to Delhi to meet Rajiv. Iftekar Ansari Saab was one such leader who came to Delhi with me.

The Congress office in Srinagar was derelict, with hardly anyone using it. I invited the Youth Congress boys and girls over, and asked them to help me clean it up, so that I could use it. I decided to take out a march to revive the party. Apart from members of the Youth Congress in Kashmir, I also invited members of NSUI from Delhi. I decided to take them to Srinagar and then march down Maulana Azad Road—the main road running through the heart of the city. Mufti Saab vehemently advised me against it, 'Don't do it. You may just get killed.' 'It doesn't matter,' I retorted with a smile. 'I am going to do it.' I took out the march, walking shoulder to shoulder with the young people and waving party flags down the road that bore my Dada Abba's name.

Soon I realized that the Congress in Kashmir never visited people living in far-flung areas. I started visiting remote corners of Kashmir and talking to people, sometimes along the de facto border with Pakistan and at times, up the mountain roads leading to the desert terrain of Ladakh. On one such visit to a small village called Tangdhar, very close to the Line of Control (LoC), amidst snowy peaks and dense pine forests, I met Mian Bashir, the spiritual and political leader of the poor, nomadic Gujjar community. At his home was a huge vessel in which food was cooked through the day for the needy. I remember sitting at a window, taking photographs and writing verses as I took in the breathtaking view of the snow-capped mountains, the lush-green valleys and the small gurgling rivers.

PITFALLS OF TOO MUCH POWER

At the time, Rajiv wanted to achieve a major political breakthrough by ending the long impasse on Kashmir. Both his grandfather and mother had gone out of their way to accommodate the demands for special status for J&K, in terms of its autonomy and its ability to formulate laws for the state's permanent residents, but their expectations had not been met. Rajiv wanted to integrate the state into the Indian polity. To that end, on 7 November 1986, a new Kashmir Accord was signed by Rajiv and Dr Farooq Abdullah of the National Conference. A caretaker government headed by Dr Abdullah was put in place. Fresh elections were to be held within six months.

Makhan Lal Fotedar, a Kashmiri Pandit by birth, had been a close associate of Mrs Gandhi. Apart from Vincent George (whom I knew well) and R.K. Dhawan, Fotedar was another person in Rajiv's office. Though not a part of the official secretariat, he served as a political secretary to Rajiv around this time. I had never interacted with him, but knew that he treated politicians with disrespect. There was deep resentment and fear in the party over his habitual bad behaviour and his dangerous capacity to maintain a wall of inaccessibility around the prime minister. So shabbily had he treated Vasantdada Patil, a political stalwart and four-time Chief Minister of Maharashtra, that an outraged Dada had resigned from the Congress Party.

One day, Fotedar called me over to Rajiv's office. He first asked me to get in touch with a junior person in the party, and called him over to the room after I had arrived. Later, I understood that the presence of the junior was to serve as an 'audience' to Fotedar's own sense of power and to my humiliation, as he had decided to insult me. Once this person came in, he looked at me and asked why I had gone to Kashmir. I answered his question with another question, 'Don't you know I am the general secretary in charge of Jammu and Kashmir?' Not being one to relent, he carried on: 'No, you should not have gone. Rajiv is very angry.' I answered, 'If Rajiv is angry, he could tell me so himself. Why should he depute you to tell me anything? He did not depute you to inform me when he appointed me as General Secretary. Why should he ask you to say anything to me now?'

With brows furrowed in rage, he started to step up his invectives. Upset at this unwarranted behaviour, I stopped him short, and looked at the two photographs of Pandit Nehru and Mrs Gandhi in the room. Then I told him, 'I have deep roots here. My family has contributed immensely to India's freedom struggle. Never speak to me like this again.' With that, I walked off. His habitual power-flexing had rebounded on him, especially in front of his chosen 'audience'.

I told many parliamentarians about the incident. It seemed a large number of Congress members were upset with him, but dared not tell Rajiv. As the Kashmir elections drew closer, I became aware of why he might have picked on me—first, I did not necessarily follow the advice of his friends in Kashmir, and second, Rajiv had decided to leave out everybody in his camp associated with the Kashmiri 'lobby', including Fotedar, from the negotiations during the signing of the Kashmir Accord.

The day before the Kashmir Accord was signed, Rajiv had

told him, 'Tell Najma she has to come with me for the signing tomorrow.' Fotedar did not inform me. I was in Parliament and by chance came across Dr Abdullah. He looked surprised: 'What are you doing here? You should have been in Srinagar by now for the signing of the Accord tomorrow.' I informed George. A very decent man, George told Rajiv, 'I will accommodate her on your plane.' So, I went to Srinagar with the prime minister. Fotedar's plans could have caused great harm to my career and reputation, but were, fortunately, thwarted in time.

In Kashmir, I did the job I had been tasked to do successfully. The elections held after the signing of the Kashmir Accord were won jointly by the National Conference and the Congress. After the Council elections were over, I was called for a meeting. Apart from Rajiv, the other attendees were G.K. Moopanar, a veteran politician and a general secretary of the party, Ghulam Nabi Azad, then Union Minister of State in the Ministry of Home Affairs, and Fotedar. I told Rajiv, 'Sir, I have finished my job. The elections are done and the new government has been formed. Now, please take me out of Kashmir.' Rajiv said, 'Why?' I said, 'Fotedar Saab is going to push my car into a ditch someday.' Fotedar's face turned white; Azad gaped in stunned silence; Moopanar looked thunderstruck, while Rajiv was at a loss for words. I continued, 'He has behaved so badly with me, and cast such aspersions on my character that any woman with an iota of self-respect would find unacceptable. I have suffered so much, but continued to work because of you. You know my family background, my husband, that I have little children. We come to politics to facilitate progress, but it is impossible to work if we are not treated with respect. I don't need money, only respect and appreciation. Without that, what is the point?'

Finally, Rajiv said that he could not accept my resignation as general secretary, that I had done very good work, and that I should continue doing so. Later, he told me, 'Speak to George, and come to me directly if there is anything urgent.'

Throughout my political career, I came across people

corrupted by excessive power, people with massive egos and an inflated sense of self-importance, greedy, ambitious, dangerous, arrogant and contemptuous of others. Many derived their sense of self-importance from their prolonged proximity to people in the highest echelons of power. I saw them control and manipulate others to display their authority and rise in status. This, in turn, created feelings of powerlessness and insecurity among the rank and file. Such people constituted a destructive force in the body politic. Their hubris, however, heralded their end.

Unfortunately, I also saw many leaders who failed to see through such people around them. Gradually access to them was cut off, boundaries around them became impregnable, eventually leaving the leaders far removed from the ground reality.

∞

After Mrs Gandhi's death, Rajiv did not include Congress stalwart Pranab Mukherjee in his cabinet. I saw how Pranab-da suddenly became a pariah. Nobody went near him, nobody spoke to him. He used to sit alone in the Parliament lobby. I often called on him for a cup of coffee, or lunch, and brought him his favourite tobacco from my trips abroad. Some Congress members even told me, 'You are talking to him. Your numbers are down in Rajiv Gandhi's books.' I met Rajiv and said, 'When I joined the Rajya Sabha, Pranab-da was Leader of the House and I reported to him. I respect him. It is your decision not to take him in your cabinet. If you feel I should not talk to him, I will not. But I feel he stood by your mother, we owe him something.' Rajiv said, 'No, no. Please talk to him. I was not angry. I had some other reason for not keeping him in the cabinet.'

Around that time, Pranab-da wrote a book, *Beyond Survival: Emerging Dimensions of Indian Economy*. Rajiv often asked me with a twinkle in his eyes, 'How is "beyond survival"?' I used to say, 'Sir, he is surviving.' I continued to go to Pranab-da's home, meet his wife and children. He had adopted an underprivileged child, given him their name, and considered him his own son. Later, when Rajiv wanted him in his cabinet, I acted as the conduit of communication. When Pranab-da's daughter got married, only two people from Congress attended it—Narasimha Rao and myself. When his son got married, everybody was there, because by then he was back in power. I saw the same thing happen to Y.B. Chavan, Chandra Shekhar and Narasimha Rao.

IN THE GLOBAL NETWORK

These years of great learning prepared me for the global platform. Under Mrs Gandhi, I had already started taking part in the UN programmes for women and the environment. Through my work with the Indo-Arab Society, I was consulted for my views on the Arab Peninsula and had even accompanied Mrs Gandhi as a member of her delegation to Saudi Arabia. With the support of P.N. Haksar, her advisor, I had understood the importance of convincing the right stakeholders of the relevance of new ideas. But the experience of the rough-and-tumble of democratic politics on the ground taught me to transcend my limitations and be effective on a much wider scale. From visits to foreign countries to attending international conferences, I learnt to pitch myself as India's unofficial goodwill ambassador.

One such instance was during the visit of Mikhail S. Gorbachev, then President of the Soviet Union, and his wife Raisa Gorbacheva in 1986. Soon after Gorbachev became General Secretary of the Communist Party of the Soviet Union in 1985, *Glasnost* (openness) and *Perestroika* (restructuring) swept across the world. He relentlessly pushed for stronger Soviet-India ties and Rajiv reciprocated. Gorbachev's first visit to India was also his first official trip to any Asian country. Upon their arrival in November, Gorbachev and Raisa received one of the grandest welcomes given to any foreign dignitary in decades.

During this visit, Sonia arranged a small private reception at her residence for the First Lady of the Soviet Union. Along with a handful of women, I was invited too. Sonia was sitting next to me, with Madam Raisa in front of her. We were exchanging pleasantries and talking in generalities when Madam Raisa asked through her interpreter, 'What can we do to bring the women of our two countries closer?' Sonia asked me to answer. 'Madam, so many things can be done. We can send women delegates to each other's countries. Women can live with the local families for an authentic experience of each other's culture, food, way of life.' Then, Madam Raisa suggested that we bring out a magazine that women in both countries would read and enjoy. I said, 'Of course, we can do that.'

A few days later, Rajiv summoned me to his office and said, 'Raisa wants to bring out an Indo-Soviet women's magazine. She says you should be the editor in India. And Valentina Tereshkova, the first woman to travel into space, could be the editor in Russia.' I was not very keen, as I did not know much about Soviet Union. It was, however, a job I had to take up. I got in touch with a few women journalists and activists, and then I requested journalist Mrinal Pande, a friend from my Bombay days, to be the co-editor. The magazine, a quarterly, was published in English in India as *Hamari Goshthi* (our gathering) and in Russian as *Dialogue*. The magazine dummies were produced in Moscow. We sent our articles to Moscow and they sent theirs to us. In an information-starved USSR, it became extremely popular.

In 1985, a milestone year, Rajiv's vision of taking India into the twenty-first century with new ideas and technology received fresh impetus. During his trip to the US to meet President Ronald Reagan, he also met Sam Pitroda, the telecom inventor and entrepreneur, and convinced him to return to India and work on transforming India's telecom sector and especially address the digital divide between urban and rural telecom. I was a part of the delegation. Rajiv asked me to discuss the issues of drinking water, literacy, immunization, oil seeds and telecommunications with Sam, and then call the MPs to make them understand the five technology missions he and Sam were working on. My science background as well as good personal relations across the board helped me reach out and forge support for the government's plan to roll out a nationwide telecom network.

During this time, I developed a keen interest in the positive ideals of parliamentary democracy. I also became involved in the work of the Commonwealth Parliamentary Association (CPA), one of the oldest established organizations with over 180 branches across nine geographies of the Commonwealth.

India was a member of the CPA Conference of Speakers and Presiding Officers and hosted the 1986 conference. In 1987, I became the first woman to be elected Vice-President of the Executive Committee of the CPA. It provided me a great opportunity to interact with and learn from global parliamentarians.

CALL OF PARLIAMENT

After I resigned from the post of Deputy Chairperson of the Rajya Sabha in 1986, M.M. Jacob, a former freedom fighter and veteran Congress member from Kerala, took over the position. At the time, I was in Moscow. When I returned, Rajiv asked for my opinion on the appointment. I told him that Jacob was not the right person for the job. He was surprised and asked why not, noting that Jacob was a very nice man. I explained that while Jacob was indeed a gem of a person, he did not know Hindi, which was crucial for the position. I added that good parliamentarians should be multilingual and said that Jacob would be perfect as Minister of Parliamentary Affairs instead. Rajiv must have realized the truth soon enough. Within ten months of being Deputy Chairperson of the Rajya Sabha, M.M. Jacob was removed from the post and made Union Minister of Parliamentary Affairs. In November 1986, Pratibha Devisingh Patil earned the distinction of becoming the third woman member to be elected Deputy Chairperson of the Rajya Sabha. (Patil went on to become President of India from 2007 to 2012.)

Rajiv called me again to seek my views. I mentioned that I had worked with Patil in Maharashtra and pointed out her extensive experience as a minister with various portfolios since the 1960s. However, I expressed my reservation that she might be too gentle for the post. Rajiv countered that Violet Alva was also affable and gentle but had been firm when conducting House proceedings. I responded that Alva was a different person and that the House had been different at that time. The Rajya Sabha had not been as vibrant then, and the job was more challenging now. Rajiv exclaimed that it seemed nobody could please me. I replied that I would be pleased if the person chosen had the right skill sets for the job. I was proven correct, especially after the Bofors scandal broke out in 1987, making corruption a highly publicized political issue for the first time in India. Both Houses were in disarray, and someone without right qualifications would not have been able to manage either House. In 1988, Rajiv called to offer me the post of Deputy Chairperson of the Rajya Sabha again.

On 18 November 1988, I reached the hallowed hall of the Rajya Sabha. The House met at 11 o' clock. The national anthem 'Jana Gana Mana' was played. It was a very different experience from my first stint at the Rajya Sabha. Shankar Dayal Sharma, Vice President of India and Chairman of the House, proposed the motion: 'That Dr (Shrimati) Najma Heptulla be chosen as the Deputy Chairperson of the Rajya Sabha.' The motion was adopted and the Chairman announced: 'She is unanimously elected.'

Felicitations poured in from my fellow comrades-in-arms. Here are some extracts of the most memorable mentions from MPs across party lines, taken from the Rajya Sabha archives:[38]

---

[38] POI, Election of Deputy Chairman, Parliament of India, Official Debates of Rajya Sabha, 18 November, 1988, https://tinyurl.com/5ead9btd. Accessed on 7 July 2024.

P. Shiv Shanker, Leader of the House, Minister of External Affairs and Minister of Human Resource Development: '[...] In a way, it is homecoming for her [...] Tremendous encomiums were paid to her at the time when she had occupied the position in 1985 and equally, at the time when she laid down her office [...] She has a multi-faceted personality. She has tremendous educational qualifications. She had been doing quite a bit of social service. She had been an author. Therefore, when she occupies this position, she brings to bear her multi-faceted qualities on this office. In recent times, she was elected as Vice-Chairman of the Commonwealth Parliamentary Association in 1987. She had been rendering yeoman service as Chairman of the Indo-Arab Society and as Editor-in-Chief of *Hamari Goshthi*. She had been doing a tremendous service in the cultural field to establish better relations between the people of the Soviet Union and our own country.'

M.S. Gurupadaswamy, Leader of the Opposition and Leader of Janata Dal: 'She occupied the Chair and conducted the proceedings very ably as Deputy Chairman in the past. We have not forgotten her charm, her sweetness and her versatility in conducting the proceedings of the House when she occupied the Chair [...] I am sure she will be as impartial, as fair and she will be as charming as she is beautiful in the Chair [...] I would like her to be in the Chair for a long time unless she is promoted.'

Atal Bihari Vajpayee, Senior leader of the Bharatiya Janata Party: 'Najmaji comes from a family of high pedigree, a family of ancient and noble origins. Her family is traditional, but her demeanour is modern. It looks like she has managed to combine both tradition and modernity [...] She is a scientist. It is rare for such highly educated women to join politics [...] I feel happy that she is linked to Bhopal. The people of Maharashtra stake a claim on her, while those from Madhya Pradesh do the same. Bhopal is a city of lakes, while Mumbai has the ocean. The ocean has its expanse, but the lotus does not bloom in it. For that, you have to come to Bhopal.

I congratulate Najmaji. She will have our full support and co-operation.' (Translated from the Hindi.)

Shankar Dayal Sharma, Vice President of India and Chairman of the House: 'Dr Najma Heptulla has come back to this Chair after nearly three years and is bringing with her rich experience. I have no doubt that she will be able to preside over the deliberations of this House as ably and competently as she did in her last stint. During the period she was not occupying the Chair, she has been an active Member of this House and has been taking keen interest in its functioning. There is, therefore, a sort of continuity. Since she has been in touch with the methods and moods of this House, I am quite sure that she will be able to soften the ruffled tempers by her tact and charm.'

I thanked everyone for the sentiments they expressed and the confidence they reposed in me, and pointed out: 'We do not run this House only with the help of the Rule Book, but we run this House with the help and cooperation of all the Members.' Thus started my long journey as Deputy Chairperson of the Rajya Sabha. Of my 36 years as a member of the Rajya Sabha, 17 years were spent as its Deputy Chairperson—between 1988 and 2004—despite changes in government. As the longest-serving Deputy Chairperson of the Rajya Sabha, I had the honour of working with eight presidents, seven vice presidents, 11 prime ministers and numerous political stalwarts who shaped the nation. And in my capacity as Head of the Committee of Privileges that looks after the rights enjoyed by each House and its members, the Committee monitoring the Members of Parliament Local Area Development Scheme (MPLADS), and the Parliamentary Committee on Empowerment of Women, I too contributed my mite to the nation.

By an irony of fate, I was elected Deputy Chairperson of the Rajya Sabha the first time barely three months after the death of the person I considered a role model—Mrs Gandhi. When I rejoined the post in 1988, it was on the eve of her birthday—November 19.

6

A TRUE PARLIAMENTARIAN

I spent most of my work life in the massive circular building complex that was located not just in the heart of Delhi, but was also in the heart of the nation—Parliament. Here, the two parliamentary wings met in the splendid architectural assemblage of high-domed halls, tall Corinthian columns and lush lawns. A meditative bronze Mahatma Gandhi in lotus position faced the main gate, imploring parliamentarians to stand as gatekeepers of truth. In the shadow of the statue, my fellow compatriots staged protests and held press conferences to fight for their truth. Called the Old Parliament House now, it was the stage where the dynamics of national politics played out until 2023, when the New Parliament House was inaugurated as part of India's Central Vista Redevelopment Project.

The Upper House of Parliament defined my life and work. For 17 years, I presided over it as Deputy Chairperson. I witnessed democracy at work, met extraordinary world leaders. I received the award for Outstanding Parliamentarian and was written about in the annals of Parliament in glowing terms: 'She [...] has the unique privilege of becoming the longest-serving presiding officer of Parliament anywhere in the world. It is an important landmark in the history of our democracy.'[39] That landmark could be reached

---

[39] *Sixty Years of Rajya Sabha (1952–2012)*, published by Secretary-General, Rajya Sabha Secretariat, New Delhi, 2012, p. 30.

because the Rajya Sabha acted as a conduit in my journey from the home to the world.

FIGHTING FOR RAJYA SABHA

On the day I joined as Deputy Chairperson of the Rajya Sabha, Pranab Mukherjee, Leader of the House, and Dipen Ghosh, the leader of the largest Opposition group, the Communist Party of India (Marxist)—CPI (M)—approached me. They informed me that my seat was next to the Leader of the Opposition (LoP). Since there was no LoP at the time, Ghosh occupied that seat, and I was to share my bench exclusively with him. I was a little surprised but followed them. They explained that the tradition was to show some reluctance in going there. When I asked why, they laughed and mentioned that centuries ago, in England, presiding officers who displeased the House were beheaded, making people scared to take up that role or the seat.

The joke was historically accurate. The role of presiding officers was quite perilous in the UK Parliament: until the seventeenth century, seven such officers had been executed by beheading.[40] From the nineteenth century, the norm that presiding officers had to be above party interest was established and lives were spared. In the Indian context, the presiding officer sat with the LoP to show that they were unbiased. And I soon realized that the joke was apt as a political metaphor too. My job required a fine balance of robust professionalism with skills of persuasion that, if not maintained, could make or break our democratic polity and most definitely my career.

As I continued my journey in and out of the Rajya Sabha, people, places, issues and contexts changed around me constantly. Governments rose and fell, prime ministers came and went,

---

[40] UKP, 'History of the Speakerships', UK Parliament, https://tinyurl.com/2vssv9m8. Accessed on 29 July 2024.

political parties won and lost, leaders of parties surfaced and disappeared. My bench mates kept changing: at times they were Communists, at others from the Janata Party, or the Bharatiya Janata Party (BJP) or the Congress. I was sent to meet important world leaders of the day, visit the UN, preside over the IPU, be a part of Indian delegations and attend to international guests at home. In between parliamentary sessions and recesses, I engaged in community building and work related to my true calling—social justice.

When I rejoined as Deputy Chairperson of the Rajya Sabha in 1988, I got the opportunity to chase my dream—of giving back to the Upper House the dignity it deserved. The Constitution of India had conferred equal powers on both Houses of Parliament. Neither was superior to the other. In reality, however, the Lower House, the House of People or Lok Sabha (LS), did not bother about the Council of States, the Rajya Sabha. The impression was that the Lok Sabha expressed the will of the people, while the Rajya Sabha was undemocratic and subservient to it. My premise was, no one could underplay the importance of the Rajya Sabha.

My first intent was to bring Parliament closer to the government. Article 105 of the Constitution made provision for committees. Until then, committees were informal, consultative, lacked resources, and were hardly taken seriously. Without legislative channels to inform them, many MPs discussed media reports during 'zero hour' to embarrass the government, instead of focusing on substantive issues. Shivraj Patil, then Speaker of the Lok Sabha, was deeply committed to the idea of enhancing the role of Parliament through the standing committee system. The problem was, he too believed in the primacy of the Lok Sabha, and wanted all standing committees to be filled up only by MPs from his House.

I decided that it was time to bring the Rajya Sabha on equal footing with the Lok Sabha. I took up the matter with Vice President Shankar Dayal Sharma. My argument was about how there could possibly be standing committees without Rajya Sabha representation, when all the consultative committees of Parliament included it. My stance gave rise to countless meetings and debates, but I stood my ground. I argued that if we were denied membership in standing committees, we would form our own committees, like the United States Senate. These committees would be independent, and because the Rajya Sabha is a permanent body, unlike the Lok Sabha, they would be very powerful. Eventually, the Lok Sabha speaker relented, albeit reluctantly. And 17 Departmentally Related Standing Committees were inaugurated in 1993, with the Upper House getting its rightful share—one-third Rajya Sabha alongside two-third Lok Sabha—reflecting the membership of the two Houses.[41] Not only were the MPs judiciously represented, but there was also a split-sharing of chairmanship of the committees on the same ratio—1/3:2/3.

Then came the question of goodwill delegations. Sponsored by the Ministry of Parliamentary Affairs and conducted by the Ministry of External Affairs (MEA), through its exchange programme of parliamentarians, such delegations were always led by the speaker of the Lok Sabha and included only members of the Lok Sabha.[42] I questioned the rationale and contended that members of the Rajya Sabha had to be represented and the one-third to two-third rule had to be applied in this field as well. Again, a flurry of debates and counters ensued. I won again. I never pressed for the right of the Rajya Sabha to vote on Money Bills or Demand for Grants. That, I believed, could lead to a conundrum, because the day-to-day responsibility of running a government rested with the Lok Sabha. Indeed a veritable responsibility, and not a privilege

---

[41] *Parliamentary Committees*, Lok Sabha Secretariat, New Delhi, https://tinyurl.com/mr3pe54v. Accessed on 29 July 2024.
[42] Kumar, Meira, *Indian Parliamentary Diplomacy: Speaker's Perspective*, Lok Sabha Secretariat, New Delhi, 2014, p. 9.

In all other aspects, the Rajya Sabha could not be ranked below the Lok Sabha. India had accepted the Commonwealth system, but not the status of the Upper House set down by the Westminster system. The House of Lords of the United Kingdom was nominated by the Crown, while the Rajya Sabha was elected by the elected representatives of State Assemblies. Unlike the Lok Sabha, the Rajya Sabha did not represent just the constituency of its members. It was more democratic and participatory since we are a federal system. It was the Council of States and had a larger perspective on every state, apart from the 12 eminent citizens nominated by the President of India for their contribution to art, literature, science and social service. Nobody could counter my arguments, and the Rajya Sabha gained in standing.

I was very proud of what I had accomplished. I could contribute to this extent because I remained in the post of Deputy Chairperson for such a long time. With a powerful Rajya Sabha, the voice of the states was enhanced, mirroring the country's vast mosaic of diversity at every level.

AN INTERACTIVE PARLIAMENT

In 1987, when news of the Bofors scandal broke, and Parliament became unmanageable, Rajiv wanted me to get the regular business of the Upper House back on track. Easier said than done, but I decided to employ creative strategies to earn the confidence of the House. The first step was to make myself accessible to the MPs and gain firsthand knowledge of their needs and views. Thus started the lunch meets. Every day, I invited 15 MPs for lunch. I wanted them to know me personally just as I wanted to know them well. It became a great way to exchange views on what to discuss in the House, how to respond to questions, how to vote on a wide range of issues, and so on, all in an atmosphere of camaraderie and conviviality.

During this time, Sheila Dikshit and H.K.L. Bhagat, Congress leaders and Ministers of Parliamentary Affairs, approached me and demanded that I suspend members of the Opposition in the Rajya Sabha. My involuntary response was: 'Why?'

I was a stickler for rules of which I had a good understanding, having helped frame quite a few myself. They responded, 'They shout in the house,' to which I said, 'That is their right, to speak in Parliament. If they are prevented from doing so, they will take their grievances to the streets. Would you prefer that?' I also pointed out that it would be easier for me to manage and control the shouting in the House than on the streets. They realized that they had not been able to convince me and that I would not oblige them without good reason. They said that it was Rajiv who wanted the Opposition members to be suspended. My response to them was that I would take it up with him directly, and I did. I made the same argument to him as to the two ministers, and he agreed without any hesitation to support my decision.

I also opened up the Central Hall of Parliament to young journalists. The rule was, any journalist who had covered Parliament for 10 years could be allowed in. Young Rajdeep Sardesai and Arnab Goswami of NDTV used to meet me and lament this stringent rule. In 1992, when I became Acting Chairman for a month, I allowed the young brigade in. I was hauled up for this, but cited the Rule Book, that as Acting Chairman, all authority of the Chair was vested in me. Again, when only the Lok Sabha was chosen for live transmission on national television, I asked, 'Why not the Rajya Sabha?' Finally, the Rajya Sabha was included.

During my time, the Rajya Sabha was a very serious House, with a galaxy of credible politicians, who were also forceful orators. There was Ashoke Kumar Sen, a great legal mind and the longest-serving Law and Justice Minister of India, whose speeches were marked by restraint and hard facts without flourishes. There was the legendary communist Bhupesh Gupta. There was Lal Krishna

Advani, the BJP stalwart, who was a very sober person as well as a remarkable speaker and contributor to the House. There were others with great talent for public speaking, from Sushma Swaraj and Arun Jaitley of the BJP to architect-entrepreneur Piloo Mody of the Janata Party.

We had a fascinating mix of eminent citizens—novelist Amrita Pritam, artist M.F. Husain, activist Ela Bhatt, jurist Fali Nariman, danseuse Vyjayanthimala Bali, economist Bimal Jalan, ornithologist Salim Ali, sitar maestro Ravi Shankar, author R.K. Narayan, actor Shabana Azmi. They could all approach me without feeling awkward or shy. Salim Ali once asked me, 'Can I bring my binoculars to the House?' I knew he always carried binoculars, but asked, 'What are you going to watch?' 'The vultures?' Both of us burst out laughing. Another day, Shabana Azmi came in with a shaved head. I sent her a note, 'Looking very beautiful.' She wrote back, thanking me for the compliment and explained that she had shaved her head for a film. A shaved head on a woman had the power to shock. She added that my note had made her less conscious and more comfortable. She later said, 'When I shower, the water hits my head so hard, it really hurts.'

Once, a leader of the major Opposition party approached me with a request. He said that a very senior member of his party, who was elected for the first time to the Rajya Sabha, would make his maiden speech. The party was allotted a 40-minute time slot—going by the number of members it had in the Rajya Sabha—and they wanted to give him all their time. That, in my opinion, could be too long for a maiden speech. So, we agreed on a 20-minute time frame. The norm was that the first speech of any parliamentarian could not be interrupted. He insisted that if anyone did intervene, the party would revert to all of its 40 minutes. It was the last day of the session and the speech was scheduled for midnight. As was the norm, the prime minister was always present on the day marking the end of a session to thank the members for their participation and contribution. This closing session was called adjournment of the House sine die.

As was customary, Rajiv was seated to my right. Before the comrade's speech commenced, I announced that it was the honourable member's maiden speech and should not be interrupted. I, too, refrained from ringing the bell for at least 20 minutes. In all honesty, not only was the speech pedantic, it was inaudible too. Close to midnight, I could tell that the MPs were getting anxious to end the late-night session and leave. Within a few minutes of the speech, the prime minister gestured that I should ring the bell to end it. Initially, I tried to ignore his gestures. When his signalling became hard to ignore, I told him it was a maiden speech. This happened a few times. Then, exasperated by my lack of cooperation, Rajiv wrote me a private note, 'Why must we all suffer while the Honourable Member loses his maidenhood?' Luckily for me, by the time the note arrived, the speech had come to an end.

The Bofors scandal continued to rock the government. It stuck like Velcro, although by today's standard, the alleged pay-off was a pittance—₹64 crores (an apartment in Mumbai costs more than that today and all the accused had long been exonerated). Rajiv decided to call for elections in 1989 and he lost. Intrigues and power struggles became acute after his loss, both in the Congress and in the subsequent governments that were formed.

A great instability set in. The Ninth Lok Sabha, lasting between December 1989 and March 1991, started and ended in tumult. The coalition government of Prime Minister V.P. Singh lost the vote of confidence within 11 months, while Prime Minister Chandra Shekhar of Janata Dal (Socialist) remained in power for just six months. Parliament was raucous during this time. Some MPs had become so vocal that the media called them 'the shouting brigade'. Unfortunately, they were Opposition MPs from the Congress.

I approached these MPs and requested them to deal with their Opposition status with sobriety. Shouting was not helping anybody, neither their cause nor the country's. They just came across as bad sportsmen, unable handle a lost status. They said it was Rajiv who had asked them to behave this way. It was similar to filibustering, meaning an action designed to prolong, delay or prevent debates and votes. While this is sanctioned in the UK Parliament, in India there is no such formal sanction—it is just not permitted.

When I met Rajiv, I told him, 'Sir, today you are in the Opposition. Someday you will be in power. Would you want such precedents to be set? As the presiding officer, it is my duty to yield the floor and allow MPs to discuss their ideas. Whatever is the parliamentary system, let us respect it.'

I gave him the recent example of P. Shiv Shanker. He was Leader of the Opposition and a good orator, but he spoke for two hours instead of the designated half-hour time slot. Yet the House was attentive. Rajiv said: 'How did that happen?' I said, 'I did it. He was making very good points. I allowed him to speak. The Members respected my decision.' He thought for a while and said, 'They [Congress members] ask me to throw you out.' I said, 'Ok. Throw me out. No problem.' With his characteristic good humour, he said, 'No, no. I don't want to. I will tell them Najma has become too fat. I can't throw her out.' We both burst out laughing. His humour was all in good spirit.

DECORUM ON THE FLOOR

Harmony, goodwill and humour went a long way towards buffering members against resentment and hostility, but not quite far enough. Lack of decorum or etiquette either in speech or behaviour did credit to none and called for zero tolerance. Once an MP said about a fellow parliamentarian, 'What is he barking about?' The word 'barking' in Hindi was particularly jarring to me. I immediately interceded, reminding him that unparliamentary language broke the rules of politeness in the House, and pointed out that the other MP was simply speaking in his own language. Use of abusive rhetoric was an adverse trend in political culture that could set temperatures soaring. In the UK Parliament, even words like coward, hooligan, or traitor had been considered 'unparliamentary language' by speakers.

Point of Order constituted a particularly tricky parliamentary practice. They allowed a member to just stand up and elaborate on their concern relating to the procedure of the House. Unlike raising questions or flagging issues, it required no prior notice or permission, had to be dealt with there and then, and had the effect of suspending the proceedings before the House. On a Point of Order being raised, the member who spoke at that time had to give way and resume their seat. Since no debate was allowed on a Point of Order, these were often used frivolously or excessively to stall discussions and the legislative process. I used to handle these firmly, whenever I felt they were off topic or irrelevant, even if the MP happened to be a very senior politician.

I was also very clear that the time of the House could not be wasted. Once, a member made a Special Mention, while others demanded that the minister concerned make a statement on the issue. Special Mentions did not demand an immediate response and I pointed out that we would not deviate from the policy: 'Please don't ask for things that are not done.' When the member insisted on making his point even after that, I did not allow him to speak further. On any occasion, when MPs deviated from the rules, practices and procedures of the House, I tried to enforce those effectively. I had realized that if MPs could not put across their views in five minutes, they would not do so even if given all the time in the world.

Similarly, whenever a member interrupted while another was speaking, I defended the former's right to speak. As custodian of the dignity of the House, time and again I reminded the members about the need to maintain decorum on the floor of the House. Once, I observed: 'This House is known as the House of Elders and it is not becoming of elders to make such remarks against each other.' After this, the members tendered an unqualified apology.

In 1991, some members of the Opposition demanded a statement from the government on a reported excise scandal. When Yashwant Sinha, then Minister of Finance and Leader of the House, started responding, they interrupted him repeatedly. I ruled, 'Do not interrupt. When the Leader of the House is on his feet, the convention of the House is that nobody interrupts him. I am going to uphold that convention.'

Plain speaking was effective, but had to be guarded from degenerating to speaking rudely. Regarding the Finance Bill, 1992, senior Congress leader S. Jaipal Reddy had raised a Point of Order motion. He alleged that the Bill had been replaced in the list of business of the day by a Calling Attention motion and that the change had been made behind the back of the members. A Calling Attention meant a member could, with prior permission of the Chairman, call the attention of a minister to a matter of urgent public importance and request him to make a statement thereon. I explained, 'I must point out that your information is not very correct. To accept a Calling Attention or to reject one is entirely the prerogative of the Chairman [...] In his own wisdom, he has allowed that the Calling Attention be shifted.' Reddy understood and accepted my stand.

Maintaining orderly conduct in the House was paramount to me, although a flexible approach in handling ticklish procedural deadlocks and understanding different points of view strengthened democratic values. In 1999, two stalwarts, Pranab Mukherjee and Gurudas Dasgupta, said they felt the Upper House had been bypassed in the case of the Prasar Bharati Bill. Although passed by the Lok Sabha, it did not come to the Rajya Sabha, while an ordinance was issued. Even that was not placed in the Rajya Sabha for consideration. I pointed out that every government had certain privileges, but it was a constitutional requirement as well as a question of propriety that every Bill passed in the other House be brought to this House: 'Now, you know the sentiments of the House. One never knows who sits on which side in future. So, it is better that we keep up the healthy practices and traditions of this House.' The ordinance was withdrawn and the Bill was tabled on the floor of the Rajya Sabha.

Sometimes, it was not that easy to get on with one's job. I remember one such incident vividly. Sometimes MPs used to troop into the Well of the House, shouting and even fighting with each other. The Well—a sacrosanct space—was the nodal point in front of the chairman, occupied by the secretary-general of the House and their staff to assist the presiding officer and record the proceedings. No one was allowed to speak from this space.

After the Question Hour during this particular session, Buta Singh, who served as Minister of Home Affairs, intended to deliver a statement on the floor of the House. When objections were raised by some members, I advised him to 'lay his statement and documents on the table of the House', which means to read the statement. However, instead of simply announcing, 'I lay it on the table of the House,' he walked into the Well of the House and literally placed the statement on the table. This unexpected action led to a commotion, with some members breaching protocol and entering the Well of the House and picking up and tearing the statement to pieces.

Now, the members who had congregated were some of our colleagues from the South wearing dhotis fashioned as lungis, which they lifted above the knee, half-mast, as they launched an agitation in the Well of the House. The sight was so ungainly and absurd, I was embarrassed. Calling for a quick adjournment, I fled to my room. Seeing Buta Singh, I commented, 'I have seen a peaceful House, an acrimonious House, but I don't want to see an indecent House. What if they pulled at each other's lungis?' He and I both were in splits at the thought.

My policy was to tune in with the MPs and get the work done. I used to adjourn the House between 1.40 p.m. and 2 p.m. for lunch break. Several MPs asked for a longer lunch break on Fridays, because they wanted to perform namaz. The late BJP leader

Pramod Mahajan started demanding the same, to 'perform a puja', he said. Before the war of words could break out—especially with the Mandir-Masjid disputes still smouldering—I announced, 'I adjourn the House for an hour for lunch and it is up to the members to decide how they spend the time.' The animus was diffused. Announcing lunch adjournments from the Chair, however, became a practice from then on.

ART OF PERSUASION

My long tenure as a presiding officer developed in me the art of being patient and persuasive, of being able to listen to views of all political hues—both from the Treasury benches and the Opposition—of never being agitated myself, and yet trying my level best to calm down disquieted members. These could range from the simple to the very complex. An example of the former was in 1989, when Rajiv used the word 'limpets' to indict his opponents—a gaffe that attracted an amazing amount of vitriol. One day, as I was coming down the Central Hall of Parliament, an MP asked me, 'What is a limpet, Madam?' I explained, 'A limpet is a sea animal, a mollusc, that clings to rocks. It is no abuse, just a reference. You don't need to get angry.'

Nowhere, however, were my skills of persuasion more needed than in three very difficult situations I had to deal with.

In 1990, I faced the toughest situation of my tenure as a presiding officer. As Chairman of the Committee of Privileges, I had to pass a reprimand to an MP: K.K. Tewary, a two-time MP from Buxar in Bihar and former Union Minister under Rajiv. This was the first time a former Union minister was to be hauled up. It happened after Shankar Dayal Sharma indicted Congress members for rowdy behaviour and Tewary used the harshest words in response.

The following day, there was an uproar in the House, with senior Opposition leaders taking offence to the comments as an affront to the Chair and to the position of Vice President of India. The members complained to the Chair and demanded that the member in question be reprimanded for his unparliamentary language. Since the matter was about him, Chairman Sharma recused himself, referring it to me and to the Committee of Privileges for a ruling, since I was Chair. The Committee of Privileges dealt with complaints, issues relating to the privileges of MPs, as well as oversights in their conduct.

I was faced with a dilemma here. Tewary and I were colleagues, he being the senior one, from the same party. However, I needed to maintain my independence and objectivity, and get on with the job. Under normal circumstances, it would not have been such a tough call, but this was different. I had to pass a judgment on how a senior party member had behaved towards a former president of the Congress Party and a constitutional authority in the country. And I had to tell Tewary, an MP, how to behave within Parliament and outside.

The following day, when the ruling had to be given in the House, I said, 'I, as Chairman of the Committee of Privileges, believed that I was competent to rule on the violation of privileges of the Members of the House, but humbly and with humility, I would admit that as Deputy Chairperson, I do not think I am competent enough to decide on the violation of the privileges of the Chairman, who is also the Vice President of the country.' Therefore, I proposed to convert the entire Rajya Sabha into a Committee of Privileges and called on the members to collectively decide how the House should proceed on the violation of the Chairman's privileges. For the first time, every member was asked to decide what admonition was to be administered. Tewary attempted to evade the order through the Supreme Court, but failed.

Finally, Rajiv, I believe, intervened and stopped the matter from snowballing into an issue larger than it was.

Tewary agreed to be served a reprimand. A special Bar was

WIND BENEATH MY WINGS: Embracing a sunny day by the Bada Talab lake with the incredible women who shaped my journey. With (second from left) Ammi (Fatima Syed Yousuf Ali) and Chhoti Khalajan (Aysha Ansari).

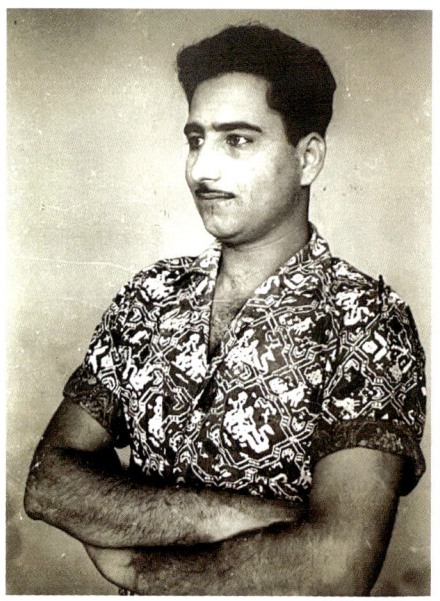

Top: **ARMED AND READY**—Dressed in traditional academic regalia at the MSc convocation ceremony at Vikram University, Ujjain, in 1960.
Bottom: **IRREPLACEABLE**—My elder brother Syed Akhtar Ali, whom I lost in a drowning accident. He was only 27 years old at the time.

THANKFUL, GRATEFUL, BLESSED: With Prime Minister Jawaharlal Nehru, whose profound affection and support have always been a cherished part of my life.

Top: **TRIP DOWN MEMORY LANE**—My maternal grandfather, Mohamad Quasim, is on my right. To my left are Prime Minister Jawaharlal Nehru, my paternal grandmother Fatima Abru, and my father Syed Yousuf Ali, in 1964.

Bottom: **FRIENDSHIP BEYOND POLITICS**—My husband Akbar Heptulla with Chandra Shekhar at the latter's farmhouse in Bondsi, late 1960s.

Top: **INHERITANCE OF LOVE**—Akbar and I with Safia Motima and Asma Motima (grandmothers-in-law) in Bombay, 1966.
Bottom: **BLISS OF MOTHERHOOD**—As a young mother at the Heptulla Park home with my eldest, Rubina, in 1967.

FRIEND, PHILOSOPHER, GUIDE: With the Iron Lady of India Indira Gandhi, without whose guidance my political ambitions would have stayed just that, ambitions. (L-R) Akbar, Indira Gandhi, sister Ozma, and Rubina, circa 1968.

Top: **INDOMITABLE**—With the founding father of Bangladesh, Sheikh Mujibur Rahman (second from right), in Bombay, 1972.
Bottom: **A GLIMPSE OF GREATNESS**—With Aruna Asaf Ali, the Grand Old Lady of the Independence Movement, in Delhi, circa 1976.

Top: **SIBLING LOVE**—(L-R) My daughters Sheba and Rubina.
Bottom: **FAMILY AND FRIENDS**—(L-R) With Lok Sabha Speaker Balram Jakhar, Sheba, Asma and Akbar, circa 1981–82.

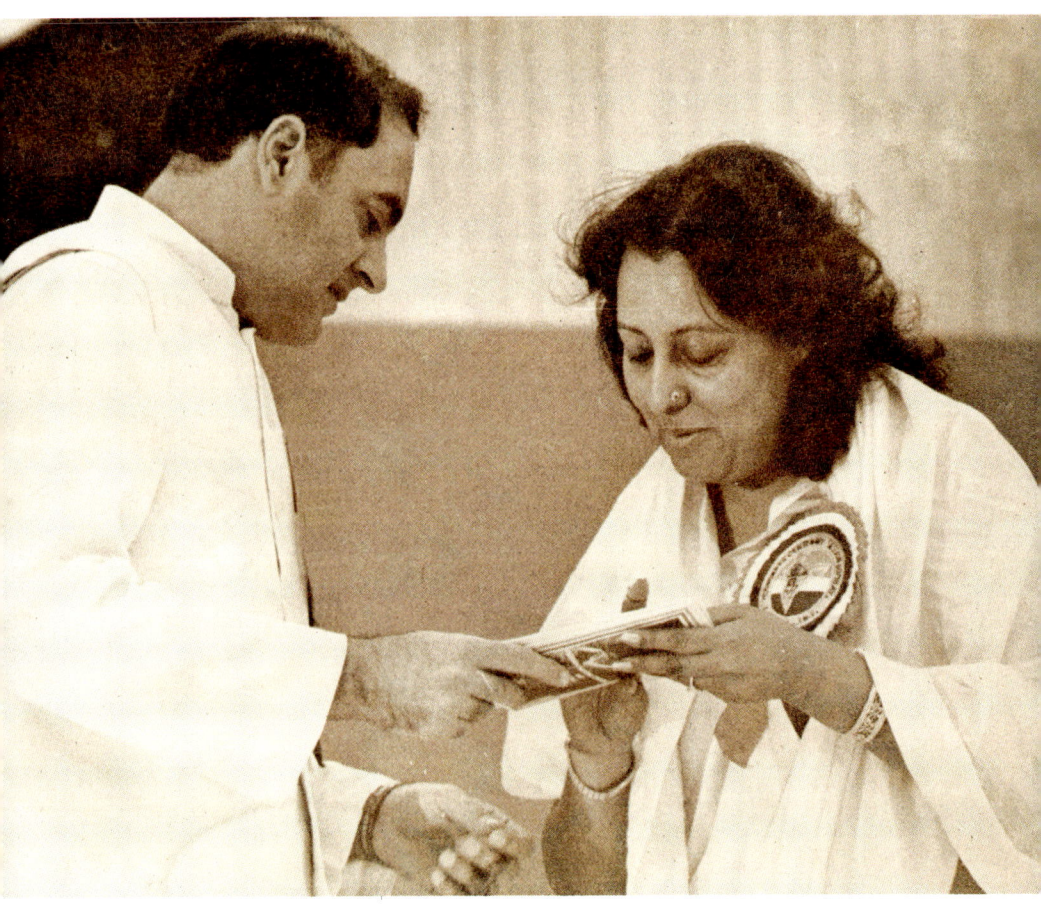

COMRADES-IN-ARMS: Presenting a booklet on the Congress Centenary to Prime Minister and Congress President Rajiv Gandhi in Bombay, 1985.

Top: **BEGINNING OF A LITERARY JOURNEY**—President R. Venkataraman launches my debut book, *India's Progress in Science and Technology: Continuity and Change*, in 1986. Bottom: **MOSCOW MEMORIES**—At Red Square with Akbar, near the Kremlin, circa 1987.

Top: **DIVINE ENCOUNTERS**—With Saint Teresa at Sahar Airport, Bombay (now Chhatrapati Shivaji Maharaj International Airport).
Bottom: With His Holiness Pope John Paul II in Vatican City.

Top: **COMPATRIOTS**—With Prime Ministers P.V. Narasimha Rao, Chandra Shekhar and President K.R. Narayanan at the Old Parliament House Annexe.
Bottom: **SMILING TOWARDS A BRIGHTER FUTURE**—(L-R) Sharing a light moment with Sam Nujoma, President of Namibia, and P.A. Sangma, Speaker of the Lok Sabha and Chief Minister of Meghalaya.

Top: **PEERS BEYOND BORDERS**— Signing the visitors' book in the presence of Avraham Burg, Speaker of the Knesset (standing on the right), in Jerusalem, 2000.
Bottom: With Betty Boothroyd, Speaker of the House of Commons, United Kingdom.

Top: **AT THE GLOBAL HIGH TABLE**—Inaugural Address at the Conference of Speakers and Presiding Officers of the National Parliaments at the Millennium Summit of the UN General Assembly in 2000.

Bottom: A group photograph at the conference.

Top: **CHANGING THE WORLD ONE CONVERSATION AT A TIME**—With the United Nations Secretary-General Boutros Boutros-Ghali.
Bottom: In a discussion with Kofi Annan, Secretary-General, United Nations, at the Parliament House, New Delhi.

Top: **IN ROYAL COMPANY**—At a meeting with His Majesty the King of Jordan Abdullah II, in Amman, Jordan, 2000.
Bottom: I was awarded the Grand Cordon of the Alawi Wissam, one of Morocco's highest honours, in recognition of my commitment to strengthening Indo-Moroccan ties.
Flanked by Akbar (to my right) and King Mohammed VI of Morocco during the award ceremony in 2001.

Top: **ADVOCATING EQUALITY**—With Fidel Castro, President of Cuba, at the IPU Conference in Havana, 2001.
Bottom: With Li Peng, Chairman of the Standing Committee of the National People's Conference (standing on the far right).

Top: **GLOBAL TIES**—With the fifth President of Indonesia Megawati Sukarnoputri.
Bottom: **STAR-STUDDED**—With actors Richard Gere and Nafisa Ali.

Top: **HOME IS WHERE THE HEART IS**—At our 4 Akbar Road home, circa 2000. (Top, L-R) Akbar, Asma and I. (Seated, L-R) My mother, Rubina with her children Nadia and Sameer.

Bottom: **FAMILY FIRST**—The whole family gathered for the first time after Akbar's passing in September 2007. We miss you dearly, Akbar. (second from left) Sheba, Asma, Rubina and my nephew Altamash.

Top: **A FAITHFUL EXCHANGE**—With His Holiness Grand Imam Gad al-Haq of Al-Azhar University, Cairo.
Bottom: **HOSTING ROYALTY**—With the King of Saudi Arabia Salman bin Abdulaziz al-Saud during his visit to New Delhi, 2014.

WITH THE POTUS: Greeting the US First Lady Michelle Obama and President Barack Obama at the Rashtrapati Bhavan in 2010.

FACE OF NEW INDIA: Presenting Prime Minister Narendra Modi a memento at his residence.

Top: **PLEDGE TO SERVE**—Taking oath as the 18th Governor of Manipur at Raj Bhavan, Imphal, Manipur.
Bottom: **PEARLS OF WISDOM**—With His Holiness the 14th Dalai Lama at Raj Bhavan in Manipur during his visit in 2019.

Top: **JINGLE BELLS**—Celebrating Christmas at Raj Bhavan, Manipur, with friends and family, Asma, Alka, and Balaji (first from the right) in December 2018.
Bottom: **REGAL**—At Raj Bhavan in Manipur. After a career navigating a man's world, it felt fitting to spend my final years of service in Manipur, a region with strong feminist traditions, known as the 'Land of Golden Girls.'

built in front of the Chair. He was formally instructed on how he needed to take the reprimand. For instance, he had to stand with hands straight down and eyes downcast, as the reprimand was read, and so on. The objective was not to humiliate him but to give him a chance at humility. As I read out the collective decision of the House, there was pin-drop silence. Tewary took it stoically and solemnly, showing the respect the representative body commanded and demanded. In the collective judgment, I mentioned that a severe penalty was not being imposed in the hope that he would reflect on his words, feel remorse and repent. That ended the ordeal, at least for me.

The second instance involved a case that shook India: an audacious stock market securities scam in 1992, in which stockbroker Harshad Mehta fraudulently laundered thousands of crores (over ₹24,000 crore, adjusted for inflation today) in the stock market over a three-year period, by exploiting the loopholes of the Indian banking system. When released on bail after three months in custody, he claimed publicly, along with his lawyer Ram Jethmalani, that he had paid ₹1 crore to the then prime minister P.V. Narasimha Rao as donation to the Congress. Rao denied this, and later, a CBI probe found no concrete evidence of this bribery claim[43].

We were discussing the report of the Joint Parliamentary Committee (JPC) on the scam, when Jethmalani, an MP, stood up to speak. It was a very tense moment. The mood among the Rajya Sabha members was already rancorous and it degenerated into acrimony, when he admitted that he was Mehta's lawyer. Some bellowed that he should not be allowed to speak, while others clamoured for him to speak. And everybody wanted my ruling. I thought for a minute. My job was to run the House as a referee, not to be a class monitor or pass judgments beyond my constitutional authority.

---

[43]Prasad, Pallavi, 'Where is the rupees 24,000 Cr Lost in Harshad Mehta Securities Scam?', *The Quint*, 28 September 2020, https://tinyurl.com/5fck7e8x. Accessed on 29 July 2024.

There was, however, no time to consult books or records for precedence. I had to give a ruling in my wisdom then and there. I said, 'Mr Jethmalani, you are an eminent lawyer and a very respected member of this august body.' He said, 'I am not eminent.' I continued, 'Alright, you are not eminent, but you are by your own admission the representing counsel for Mehta, the prime accused in the stock scam that is currently being scrutinized by the members of this House. I feel that propriety demands you should not voluntarily speak on this subject.' He sat down and did not speak.

The next day, however, he aired his views in a half-page opinion piece in *The Times of India*. He also wrote a letter to K.R. Narayanan, then Rajya Sabha Chairman and Vice President of India (1992–97), asking for the withdrawal of my ruling. He called me. I went to him and said, 'Sir, until now there has never been any instance of any ruling by a Vice Chairman or a Deputy Chairman being withdrawn by the Chairman. When you are not in the precincts of Parliament, all your authority is vested in me, because then I am in the Chair. That is what the Constitution says. You cannot withdraw my ruling officially, or constitutionally. Personally, I have no objection. You can withdraw whatever you like.' I went on to add, 'Just for my curiosity, exactly what part of the ruling are you planning to withdraw? Will you withdraw that Mr Jethmalani is an eminent lawyer and a member of this House? Will you withdraw that Mr Harshad Mehta is the main accused in the banking scam? Or will you withdraw that Jethmalani should maintain propriety of the House and not speak voluntarily? What does he want you to withdraw?'

Vice President Narayanan was quiet for a moment, reflecting on what I had just said. He responded, 'Probably nothing, since you have pointed out nothing can or should be withdrawn.' If persuasion means establishing a friendly, trustworthy presence and influencing the way someone thinks, I managed to persuade my compatriots in a way that did not offend anyone, yet maintained the constitutional position and propriety.

Another instance in 1994 involved the Congress stalwart Pranab Mukherjee, who was then Minister of Commerce. He had returned from Marrakesh, Morocco, after signing a World Trade Organization (WTO) agreement on GATT (General Agreement on Tariffs and Trade) and wanted to explain it to the members, and answer any questions they may have had. There were various means by which an MP could raise an issue: a Special Mention, a short duration discussion, or a motion. Any discussion that was not a motion did not need voting. A formal motion, however, necessitated a vote, either for or against.

Jaipal Reddy, a very articulate parliamentarian, was also the most aggressive MP at the time. He started arguing that the discussion on the agreement had to be held under a formal motion. That implied that the House had the power to reject the agreement. There was an altercation on this point between the ruling members and the Opposition, opposing and supporting the motion respectively. At the time, the Opposition had the majority in the Rajya Sabha and if the motion was defeated, it would be one of the biggest embarrassments for the government both nationally and internationally. Members approached the Chair and asked for a formal ruling: under which rule should the discussion take place?

I pointed out that according to our Constitution, any agreement or treaty signed by the government does not require ratification by Parliament. I emphasized that if the authority to ratify a treaty is not constitutionally granted, then there is no right to reject it. I explained that the Constitution does not allow me to permit a discussion of this particular matter under a formal motion, which requires voting, but it can be discussed under any other provision without voting. Pranab-da, who was one of the senior-most Members of the House, sent me a note: 'This ruling is a historic precedent, because many times such discussions would come up.' I was later asked to include this particular ruling in the seminal book *Practice and Procedure of Parliament* (1968), written by M.N. Kaul and S.L. Shakdher.

Once I noticed that Gate 11 through which I would enter Parliament had become an eyesore, with piles of garbage and weeds lying around. I decided to do something about it and wrote letters to all the MPs: 'Day after tomorrow, at 10 o'clock, I request you to come to Gate 11 for a tree planting ceremony. Every leader will plant a tree with a plaque bearing their name and party affiliation.' On the said day, I was surprised by the crowd of diverse parliamentarians, including towering leaders from Sikander Bakht of the BJP to Gurudas Dasgupta of the CPI. It was rewarding that an invitation from me could bring together leaders from such different ideologies. With horticultural upkeep, a restored fountain and repaired tiles, Gate 11 had the most attractive garden. Later on, Jaswant Singh brought a big statue of Maharana Pratap and beautified it further.

PREMONITION OF DOOM

It was 21 May 1991. The elections had just started. Political parties were racing forward with last-minute campaigns. Candidates were hitting the trail to gain support in the final hours before votes were cast. There was a mix of fear, excitement and tension in the air. On the one hand, Prime Minister Vishwanath Pratap Singh had announced the implementation of the Mandal Commission Report, to include socially and economically disadvantaged communities in government jobs and educational institutions. On the other hand, communal tensions had hit fever pitch over the question of the Ram Mandir in Ayodhya, with BJP leader L.K. Advani's chariot journey across large parts of India. With widespread violence, protests and riots rattling the foundations of our republic, a political realignment was in the offing.

I was at home in Bombay. Journalist Aditi Phadnis arrived at Heptulla Park to interview me. I had known her for a very long time and had invited her for lunch. As she left, she mentioned that she was covering Rajiv's campaign. He was on a long trail across

India, shorn of security and aloofness, interacting with people, greeting hysteric crowds. 'He is a changed man,' she said. I was supposed to go to Allahabad and Varanasi for campaign meetings and started to get ready for the airport. My husband said that those were some of the hottest places in the country and suggested I take a bath, as I might not get another chance to do so any time soon. I entered the bathroom and then something happened to me. I was filled with a strange sense of foreboding, a feeling that something bad was going to happen. I came out and said, 'I am not going.'

My husband asked why, pointing out that my meetings were all scheduled and people would be waiting for me. I responded that I just didn't want to go. He was astonished, as I had never done this before. I reassured him that I would go to Delhi the next day and take up whatever work was given to me. He simply replied, 'Okay, if you feel that way.' I telephoned some of our Youth Congress workers and informed them that my plans had changed. The entire day I was very restless. The evening was stifling hot. We watched some television programme on the environment. Then my children came back from the movies and we all got ready to retire for the night.

We had just switched off the lights, when suddenly the bell rang and there was banging on the door. I opened the door and found a large number of Youth Congress boys standing outside. They said, 'Rajiv ji is no more.' They had just seen on television that he was assassinated in Tamil Nadu while campaigning. The news shook the ground beneath my feet, sending up waves of shock and grief. I sat down on the floor. Was this why I had the uncanny feeling the whole day? Was this why I did not go to Allahabad and Varanasi and instead booked a ticket to Delhi? I was numb with sorrow as I boarded the flight to Delhi next morning.

When I reached 10 Janpath in Delhi, his body had yet not arrived, but reports were coming in that the 46-year-old former prime minister, and front-runner of the 1991 elections, had been stopped so rudely in his tracks by suicide bombers of the Liberation

Tigers of Tamil Eelam (LTTE), fighting for an independent homeland for Hindu Tamils in Northeastern Sri Lanka. I was overwhelmed by a numbing sense of déja vu. In 1984, my daughter Sheba and I were on our way to the Murree hill station of Pakistan when news came in that Indira Gandhi had been shot dead. We cancelled our journey and came back straight to Delhi. When we reached Mrs Gandhi's Akbar Road House, her body was yet to arrive from the hospital. Nearly seven years later, I was faced with a similar scenario, in the wake of yet another assassination in the same family, as we waited to receive her son's remains.

Power politics existed everywhere, even in the temple of democracy, the Parliament. I was truly happy in the Rajya Sabha. I made friends with MPs and became quite popular. I found that I could calm down heated discussions, disagreements, and even anger through mutual respect, goodwill, humour, friendship and professionalism, cutting across party affiliations. My popularity and effectiveness, however, brought unexpected challenges. I had to work closely with the Vice President of India, as he was the ex-officio chairman of the Rajya Sabha. While I had the support of many MPs, I also had a tough time under others. For instance, under Vice President Narayanan, the fact that I did not have a room to sit in and needed one, became an issue.

The chairman had two rooms in the Rajya Sabha—a big room and a smaller ante room. This room was in a mess, and was used by the Rajya Sabha staff to eat their food once the chairman had left, or to sleep in the afternoon. Since I did not have any space to even park my books and bags, I began using this as my room. Vice President Narayanan took exception to that and asked me: 'Why did you do that?' I pointed out that I worked in the House through the day and often into the night. I had no place to read, write, or grab a bite, and had to walk a long distance to use the toilet. 'Under what authority did you do it?' he asked. I said, 'When the

Chairman is on leave and I am Acting Chairman, all authority of the Chair is vested in me. I take all the decisions. On that authority, I am sitting here.' Then I added, 'If you don't want to give me the room, I will sit in the corridor because I have to sit somewhere. But imagine what people will say.' He thought about it for a moment and acquiesced. Working with the next two vice presidents—Krishan Kant (1997–2002) and Bhairon Singh Shekhawat (2002–07)—was difficult as well.

Each morning, the leader of the House, the chairman, and I used to meet to discuss the daily business to be taken up before the House. They used to take everyone's opinion but ignored what I had to say or the issues I wanted to discuss. Even the Business Advisory Committee never asked me what difficulties I was facing in the House. Their tone was generally rude, and they treated me as though I were unimportant or just not there—like many men do the 'talk to my hand' to shut up women when they try to say something or give their opinion.

That I was known for running the House well or that prime ministers found me effective did not go down well with them. Nor did it work in my favour that I was involved with international parliaments and politics.

BEYOND PARTY LINES

For me, the political could be personal too, because of my family background. I knew many people well before I joined politics. As Deputy Chairperson, I was committed to building very good relations with parliamentarians, regardless of their or my political affiliations. No easy task. There were more than 30 political parties in Parliament. I had to build my credibility with all parties of the House. This entailed my working beyond political biases with the Congress, the Communist parties, the Janta Dal, the BJP, the Samajwadi Party, or any single-member party or even independent members. P.V. Narasimha Rao, a former prime minister, had once told me, 'You are the presiding officer. Your duty first and foremost is to be above and beyond politics. You are not Najma Heptulla, the Congress member, but Najma Heptulla, Deputy Chairperson of the Rajya Sabha.'

Compassion and concern for the well-being of others were values I had grown up with and lived by. I had, however, chosen a career in politics, a supposedly dog-eat-dog world. What was difficult about my job was to stay above party lines and deliver real results. I had often faced criticism from my peers for forgetting political differences and internal power struggles. But I managed to run the House harmoniously for 17 long years without anyone ever contesting me.

Immediately after Rajiv's assassination, I found myself providing small yet crucial support to those around me. At 10 Janpath, as we awaited Rajiv's body, I noticed a visibly distressed Narasimha Rao fumbling for his medicines. Despite the chaos and shared grief, I felt compelled to fetch him a glass of water. Later, Dr Naresh Trehan, his cardiologist, told me, 'You saved his life. He needed to take his pills.'

On another occasion, while working late one night in the Rajya Sabha, I saw Bhupesh Gupta, senior communist leader and a member of the Rajya Sabha, looking exceedingly fatigued in the lobby. Concerned for his well-being, I hurried to the canteen and brought him a glass of milk, which helped him recover his energy. These gestures, though modest amidst the usually overwhelming circumstances under which we functioned, mattered just as much.

ASSOCIATIONS AND FRIENDSHIPS

I had often heard that political friendships were actually friendships driven by opportunism and self-interest. However, I forged friendships not only with individual members of the Rajya

Sabha but also with their families. I had very cordial ties with the wives of parliamentarians without caring about whose husband belonged to which party.

Advaniji and his family, for instance, always stood by me through thick and thin. Kamlaji, his wife, was a very loving person, as was his daughter Pratibha. They always invited me to celebrate Holi and Diwali with them, which I did happily. When my husband was in hospital with a heart ailment, and I did not know who to turn to, they extended a helping hand. When Akbar passed away, the entire Advani family came over to console me and share in my grief. Kamlaji told me, 'Never eat alone at home.' She called me every day to ensure that I was not alone at meal times. And if I was, she made sure I shared my meals with them.

Rajmata Vijaya Raje Scindia of Gwalior was an extremely dignified and graceful person. She would sit quietly in the House with her *pallu* (loose end of saree) always thrown over her head. Over the years, I forged a very good relationship with many royals of Gwalior. The Rajmata's son, the late Madhavrao Scindia, was a very good friend. So was her daughter, Vasundhara Raje, who offered me a seat from Rajasthan, where she was Chief Minister, when I joined the BJP and needed to be renominated to the Rajya Sabha. The Rajmata's sister-in-law, Maya Singh, a Rajya Sabha member and former cabinet minister in the Government of Madhya Pradesh, and her children became close family friends. She often mentioned that the Rajmata used to tell her how much she admired me as a woman presiding over the Rajya Sabha, especially during the turbulent session, as a fine example of women's empowerment.

Similarly, can I ever forget that I had known Ved Prakash Goyal and his wife, Chandrakanta Goyal, the parents of BJP minister Piyush Goyal, during my work on slum development in Bombay?

Mulayam Singh Yadav, founder of the Samajwadi Party, former Defence Minister of India and Chief Minister of Uttar Pradesh, was my colleague. His son and former Chief Minister of Uttar

Pradesh, Akhilesh Yadav, and his wife Dimple were very close to me. I knew Rabri Devi, not because she was Chief Minister of Bihar, but because of her husband Lalu Prasad Yadav, who I came to know very well. Lalu Yadav was a unique individual in Indian politics. As a public persona, he appeared earthy and parochial, but my understanding of him was completely different—I considered him to be one of the brightest minds in Indian politics.

Over the years, I would witness many of his personal stories. One day, he walked into my chamber and put in a request in his characteristic accent, *'Kya hum aap ke phone se Bihar ke mukhya mantri se baat kar sakte hain?'* (Can I speak to the chief minister of Bihar from your phone?) I laughed out loud, 'Why don't you just say you would like to speak to your wife, Rabriji?' He started laughing. Once I was invited to be chief guest in a programme hosted by TV personality Shekhar Suman. Lalu Yadav was also invited to the same programme. Legendary stand-up comedian, the late Raju Srivastav, impersonated Lalu Yadav in front of him, with wit, humour and satire. While the TV audience rolled with laughter, so did Lalu Yadav. He turned towards me and said sportingly, *'Bahut achchhi nakal karta hai hamari'* (He really imitates me well). It takes a lot of courage and a great sense of humour to take a joke on yourself at a public platform.

RUNNING A DEMOCRATIC PARLIAMENT

What was it like to run a democratic Parliament in a democratic way? A perfect example would be the coming together of 79 MPs from across states and party lines for relief work after a deadly tropical cyclone devastated coastal Odisha in October 1999, severely impacting 18 million people. I was instrumental in setting up a separate Parliamentary Committee in the Rajya Sabha for monitoring the Members of Parliament Local Area Development Scheme (MPLADS), started by Prime Minister Narasimha Rao in 1993. The scheme enabled MPs to recommend developmental work in their constituencies, and to create community assets based on locally felt needs. I requested all MPs to donate money from their constituencies for relief work in Odisha. This was the first time rehabilitation work was undertaken with the MPLADS funds in the wake of severe natural calamities in different parts of the country. MPs across states and political hues came forward with great enthusiasm. I asked Navin Patnaik, then Chief Minister of Odisha, what he wanted to spend the money on, and he said, 'Schools.' I appealed to all MPs to contribute ₹10 lakh from their MPLADS funds to reconstruct cyclone-damaged school buildings in different districts of Odisha. The MPs showed true leadership and almost ₹7.5 crore was pooled. However, it was not so much the amount raised that was important, but the shared pain and collective resolve of parliamentarians to help, that was worthy of appreciation.

I sought the help of experts in architectural aerodynamics to create alternative built-up spaces that took a wind-driven design approach, impacting the character of wind flow, microclimate, turbulence, wind speed and wind pressure on buildings. HUDCO (Housing and Urban Development Corporation) was entrusted with the task of reconstructing over 75 high school buildings that could withstand cyclones in the future and double up as cyclone shelters as well. Apart from providing modern safety features in the buildings, provisions for sustainable measures like rainwater harvesting, sanitation pits and other simple design elements based on sustainable consumption patterns were also introduced. Very strong ceilings were built so that food could be dropped on these at times of need.

I requested Dr A.P.J. Abdul Kalam, then President of India, to inaugurate the buildings once the developmental work was completed. He was immensely happy with the use of 'appropriate technology' that could be easily adapted to local conditions and needs. In his address at the dedication ceremony at Nirakarapur on 15 May 2003, he also congratulated all Rajya Sabha MPs for their cooperation, collaboration and concern. This became a model worth emulating.

In the last two decades, there have been many such instances of Rajya Sabha MPs resolving to help out in the aftermath of national calamities. In January 2001, after the massive Bhuj earthquake in Gujarat, which left 25,000 dead and a million homeless, MPs came forward again to help. Similarly, in December 2004, they pooled in their collective resources to help the victims of the Asian tsunami, the worst calamity in this part of the world that devastated more than 230,000 people.

WORKING WITH NARENDRA MODI

At the beginning of the new millennium, when Gujarat was devastated by the Bhuj earthquake in 2001, I had come to know Narendra Modi, then Chief Minister of Gujarat. The success of the MPLADS funds in creating honest, transparent and effective rehabilitation projects in Odisha had infused the MPs with new enthusiasm and hope. By this time, each MPLADS fund was allocated ₹2 crore annually. Once again I wrote to everyone, and again the MPs came forward and donated generously. Pramod Mahajan, then Union Minister of Communications and Information Technology, gave his entire ₹2 crore fund for Gujarat. Our relief funds totalled ₹31 crore. In May 2001, a sub-committee was constituted for an on-the-spot study of the earthquake-affected areas.

In the summer heat, we walked on foot conducting physical surveys and soil investigations, and charting vulnerability maps, local characteristics, socio-economic conditions, human resources, raw material resources, climate, and availability of infrastructure across Kutch and Rajkot. On the way, we met thousands of people and received numerous memoranda from different sections of society. Everywhere we went, we were received with so much of love and affection. People invited us, ashrams and temples offered us lunch. When we started, we had five cars with us. By the time we reached Ahmedabad, so many people had joined us that we had 500 cars. Even before we reached Ahmedabad, we had prepared the whole report.

When I met Modi in Ahmedabad, he said, *'Aap hame de do, hum korenge kharach development pe'* (Give us the money, we will spend it on development work). I said, 'Sir, I know you are a very honest man and will do the job. But I am the custodian of the project and MPs from across the country have given me the responsibility. I think, let us do it ourselves.' Modi appreciated my sentiments and said, 'That's good.' We followed the MPLADS Guidelines, the people's representations as well as communications received from the Government of Gujarat. We focused on the construction of primary school rooms along with community halls and work sheds fitted with kitchens.

The project was implemented through government agencies, namely HUDCO and National Building Construction Corporation (NBCC) in Kutch, Rajkot, Patan and Ahmedabad. I submitted the report to Parliament, to individual MPs. Chief Minister Modi appreciated our effort. Ever since, my communication with him remained consistent. I would call him 'Narendra Bhai' and he addressed me as 'Najma Behn'.

I had numerous Gujarati friends in Mumbai. One of them was Vijay Sanghvi, a writer and correspondent with *Gujarat Samachar*. His wife Mita and their two children Sneha and Kulin were very close to my family. At his behest, I once attended a programme of *Gujarat Samachar* in Surat as Chief Guest. Prime Minister Modi was presiding over the function. I was already Deputy Chairperson of the Rajya Sabha and asked for a private meeting and appointment with him over a problem, a personal issue related with a trust fund my cousin's husband ran. I asked him to help and he solved their problem. Off and on I would ring him up, speak to him in broken Gujarati. It was a very friendly relationship.

In 2002, when the Godhra riots took place, Modi was being

criticized by journalists for maintaining a studied silence through the first week of violence. In 2001, the BJP had lost the gram panchayat elections as well as three assembly by-elections in Gujarat. In October 2001, the old BJP war horse, Chief Minister Keshubhai Patel, was summarily replaced by Narendra Modi. Godhra happened just four months after he took over. He needed time to understand the issue and handle the situation.

I narrated to journalists how Modi had helped the Bohra Muslim community during the communal riots. The Bohras constituted a peaceful business community among Muslims. I had very good relations with them because my husband belonged to that community. The chief of the community had rung me up and told me that there was a large community of Bohras in Gujarat and they never participated in any rioting activity. He asked for help. I rang up Modi and told him about the Bohras: 'Please protect them.' He said, 'Don't worry. I will.' And he did. In the 2002 election, the Bohra community supported the BJP and, in particular, Narendra Modi.

7
POLITICS IN TRANSITION

The Inter-Parliamentary Union (IPU) is a world organization of parliaments of 180 countries that works in close cooperation with the UN for peace, cooperation, democracy and sustainable development.

I started my IPU journey in 1988 as Deputy Leader of a delegation to Guatemala when Rajya Sabha started to be represented just as Lok Sabha was, after my insistence. Despite my hard work, I had accepted that it was impossible for me to move up from the Environment Committee of the IPU to its Executive Committee or further. The rigidity of hierarchy between the Lok Sabha and the Rajya Sabha in our parliamentary system mandated that only the Lok Sabha Speaker could enter the global competition for IPU posts. I was, therefore, astounded when Lok Sabha Speaker Shivraj Patil suggested my name when a vacancy for a member of the IPU Executive Committee in Asia Pacific came up in 1995. 'There is a vacancy in the IPU. If anybody can win that seat, I feel it is Madam Heptulla,' he announced.

The world opened up in all directions. It was with great joy that I engaged in a campaign. I prepared my CV in different languages—English, French, Arabic, Russian, Chinese, Spanish—showcasing my background, my education, all the work I had done in Parliament and in the United Nations Development Programme (UNDP). No photocopies or cyclostyles in duplicates, but printed on art paper, with vibrant photographs and my personal letter—all presented with great care. I sent those to all the member countries through our ambassadors, many of whom were my friends.

I asked Patil if I could travel to some places and meet people. The government was very cooperative in the matter, and Parliament extended its full support. Young officers of the Ministry of External Affairs (MEA) were assigned to me to help and campaign. I travelled to some countries to campaign, reached out to my friends in various IPU committees, wrote team letters to women's groups where I had been very active, renewed contact with people I had met at various conferences. And within a few years, I climbed step by step the rungs of the IPU ladder.

THE PRESIDENTIAL RACE

The 102nd Inter-Parliamentary Conference was held in Berlin from 10 to 16 October 1999, at the invitation of the German Parliament in the Reichstag Building. Inaugural addresses were delivered by Johannes Rau, then President of Germany; Wolfgang Thierse, then President of the Bundestag, the lower chamber of the German Parliament, and also of the Conference; and Vladimir Petrovsky, Soviet scholar, Ambassador as well as then Director-General of the UN Office in Geneva; and there was a message from Kofi Annan, then UN Secretary-General. I also delivered a brief address in my capacity as Acting President of the Council of the IPU. At the time, I was also Chairperson of the IPU Executive Committee.

Conferences were the time to elect the next IPU presidents. During my speech, something in the reaction of the audience made me feel that I was the chosen one. In fact, the Women's Committee unanimously decided that they wanted me. This committee was very powerful within the IPU, and their opinions were crucial whenever candidates for the IPU presidency were chosen. In 1993, I had chaired the Meeting of Women Parliamentarians of the IPU and became a member of the Women's Coordinating Committee. I acted as Vice President of the

IPU conference held at New Delhi in 1997 on the collaboration of men and women in politics. I also engaged actively in the IPU Gender Partnership Group set up that year.

Since 1995, I was a member of the Executive Committee of the IPU. Although women's issues had entered the UN's narrative, I noticed that the IPU did not include women's issues in its main agenda. Within the IPU, I worked hard so that women's rightful leadership roles were strengthened while their views and insights could feature in the IPU agenda.

Initially, Chung-Soo Park, a friend of mine from South Korea, had also filed his nomination for the post. When the time came, however, Park withdrew his name. Meanwhile, Illahi Bukhsh Soomro, Speaker of the National Assembly of Pakistan, came up to me to say that the delegation from his country would support me.

On October 14, however, Soomro approached me with another request. General Pervez Musharraf had orchestrated a coup d'état in Pakistan, suspended the Constitution, and declared himself President. Soomro said, 'What will happen to us? There's no Parliament in Pakistan anymore.' I asked him not to worry and assured him that I would request the German government to host their delegation until they were ready to return to Pakistan. I did this and the authorities allowed them to stay on for as long as they needed to.

I also received support from members of other countries. The Egyptians were working for me, my Arab friends stood by me, the Latin Americans were on my side, all of Francophone and Anglophone Africa was with me, a large number of members from European and Nordic countries rooted for me, the Russian delegates championed for me, and North Americans were supporting me—thanks to the spirited campaign on my behalf by my friend and Canadian Senator, Sheila Finestone.

On October 16, the Council of the IPU had before it my candidature for the post of President. I addressed the meeting a second time in my capacity as a candidate for the office. The

Council heard representatives of the six geopolitical groups at the IPU, including 104 women parliamentarians from the delegations of countries. All endorsed my candidature and extensive experience at the IPU, as well as the fact that I would become the first woman President in IPU's history since its creation in 1889.

The proceedings to elect me unanimously to the office of President for a three-year term then started. I accepted the honour with a humble yet heartfelt submission: 'I am deeply conscious of the fact that this is the first time in its 110 years of existence that the IPU is electing a woman President. This is a clear reflection of the importance women have come to occupy in parliamentary life. It is also a recognition of the fact that to build a democratic society based on justice and freedom for all, equality of women and partnership between men and women are a fundamental necessity.'

Around this time, my Mexican friend, Beatriz Paredes, invited me, and I flew all the way to Mexico and then to São Paulo, Brazil. She wanted to celebrate two historic firsts—my election as the first woman President of the IPU, and her taking over as the first woman President of the Latin American Parliament.

RECEPTION BACK HOME

As soon as I became President of the IPU, congratulations started pouring in. It was a historic first and a great honour, marking the pinnacle of my journey from the Indian parliament to the world parliamentary stage. The IPU presidency had included in the past not just leading world leaders, but also former prime ministers, speakers of parliament, philanthropists, advocates, Nobel laureates and luminaries active in peace movements. As more and more parliaments from around the world joined the IPU, the choice of presidents reflected its global reach. It was all the more precious because the confidence bestowed on me echoed India's new trajectory of growth and global leadership. Both the country and its daughter were thrust into international spotlight.

I telephoned Prime Minister Atal Bihari Vajpayee from Berlin and he received my call instantly. When he heard the news, he was delighted, first because the honour had come to India, and second, it had come to an Indian Muslim woman. He said, 'You come back and we will celebrate.' I could also connect to the vice-presidential office instantly. However, when I rang up Sonia Gandhi, Congress Party President and my leader, one of her staff first said, 'Madam is busy.' When I pointed out that I was calling from Berlin, an international call, he just said, 'Please hold the line.' I waited for one full hour. Sonia never came on the line to speak to me. I was truly disappointed. After that call, I did not tell her anything. Before forwarding my name for the post of IPU President, I had taken her permission, and at the time, she had given her blessings.

If every country, culture and family has its special moments—events so important, and somehow so personal, that they transcend the normal flow of daily life—this was one such moment for me—a moment in time of such importance that it drilled a sense of rejection in my psyche forever. It was, however, a rejection that proved prescient. It prophesied a time of transition, a downward spiral and crisis in the Congress that left its old-time and experienced members, who had given their all to the party, beleaguered and demoralized. A new coterie of inexperienced sycophants started running the affairs of the party.

Around the same time, after I became the IPU President, the Vajpayee government upgraded the ranking of my office from minister of state to cabinet minister. Atalji allocated ₹1 crore in the Budget for the IPU president to travel to countries not paid for by the IPU Council. It was Vasundhara Raje who invited me and other MPs to celebrate my election as IPU President at the Parliament Annex, where we generally host all our Parliament receptions. The following year, when I invited Sonia Gandhi to attend the Millennium Conference of Presiding Officers in New York, she opted out at the last minute.

In 2001, Vajpayeeji wanted me to lead a goodwill delegation

to Iraq to meet President Saddam Hussein, to negotiate on India's behalf and secure the dues Iraq owed after the Gulf War. I requested Sonia to send someone else in my place. She told me that I should take on the responsibility. I also suggested that she recommend Natwar Singh, who was looking after the foreign affairs matter in the party, but she turned down the suggestion. Later, it became an issue with the Congress MPs close to her because nobody else from the Congress was included in that delegation. They did not know that I had taken her permission. Later, I was informed by a Congress colleague that Sonia did tell the MPs to not make it an issue as she already knew about the trip.

Besides me, a number of veteran leaders felt marginalized. In 1999, Sharad Pawar, P.A. Sangma, and Tariq Anwar moved out from the party on the issue of Sonia's foreign origin and created the Nationalist Congress Party (NCP). Frontline leaders Rajesh Pilot and Jitendra Prasada, too, stood up against the Gandhi family.

I continued in the party, but Sonia began suggesting that I would eventually leave and join Pawar. It was strange of her to think so. Sharad had specifically asked me not to leave, advising me that since I was holding office of the presiding officer, I should remain above party issues. Every time, I reassured her: 'Madam, even when Mrs Gandhi was out of power, I did not leave her.' I was one of the few who stayed with Mrs Gandhi when the Congress split and many joined Sharad Pawar's Congress (S). Long before becoming an MP, I used to come to Delhi to meet Mrs Gandhi and do whatever I could to help her—from arranging meetings with Muslim leaders such as the Shahi Imam, to dinners with ambassadors of Gulf countries. 'You are witness to all that, Madam,' I pointed out repeatedly. 'You know what role I played. Why should I leave now?' Sonia trusted very few people. And I felt she did not trust me.

Ironically, while suggesting I would join Pawar which I did not, Sonia went ahead and formed an alliance with him. So, while it would have been wrong of me to be Pawar's friend and ally, it was not so for her. Seemed hypocritical.

SONIA GANDHI'S CONGRESS

We were dealing with more than just deep mistrust. We were cut off from Sonia Gandhi and could not communicate with her. This was a sharp and serious departure from the earlier Congress culture. Indira Gandhi used to keep an open house. She was accessible to the rank-and-file members. She assiduously greeted every visitor who came from across the country to meet her every morning. I could reach out to her anytime and would inform her about things on the ground in my own way. I never critiqued her harshly but simply pointed out things I had experienced, seen or heard on the ground. For instance, when scarcity of milk products and baby food became a reality in the months following the Emergency, I wrote to her describing how busy I had become standing in queues for hours to procure milk for my children. She understood.

In 1998, when Sonia donned the party mantle, far too many layers of people sprung up between the rank and file, and the leader. That was the problem with 10 Janpath. Direct communication was cut off because of junior functionaries. They were not party workers, just clerks and other staff working there. And they blocked all access to the leader, affecting organizational health and ethics, compromising both harmony and productivity of the party members. As Congress followers, we no longer had an active role in providing feedback to our leader—so critical for a party to perform well. There was little interaction based on the quality of our exchanges, little understanding of who were part of our leader's in-groups or out-groups or even how to support our leader's vision. The decline started then. At the time, Rahul and Priyanka were not in politics but busy with their own lives. Our leader's behaviour was counter to the best practices and principles of collaboration that had evolved in the Congress over many decades.

I witnessed one such event with Sitaram Kesri, who was unanimously elected as President of the Congress Parliamentary

Party (CPP) in 1997. One day, when I was waiting for Sonia in the lobby at 10 Janpath, he came in and was also asked to wait. As moments passed, he started losing his temper, and said, 'I am Treasurer of the party and not any ordinary member. She is Deputy Chairperson of the Rajya Sabha. We have not come here to exchange pleasantries, but have serious issues to discuss. And we are made to wait like this?' He felt humiliated and departed. I was reminded of the time Vasantdada Patil quit the party as Makhan Lal Fotedar had humiliated him in a similar manner. Our only recourse was the good-natured Vincent George, long-time private secretary to Sonia, who understood that the relationship between leaders and followers depended on mutual respect, trust and support, and could potentially make or break political parties. Unfortunately, at times even reaching out to him became a problem.

THE WHEEL OF FORTUNE

I had seen enough politics and politicians to realize that the political wheel of fortune turned very fast—one could never tell who would rise or fall and when. I had also witnessed how politics changed relationships, friendships and even familial ties. I used to keep in touch with people and make time for them, even when they were out of power. I felt that they needed others during this time, when they were lonely and sidelined. They also had more time in hand and I learnt a lot about politics from their experiences and insights.

One such politician was P.V. Narasimha Rao. I still recall how ashen-faced Rao looked when we all waited for Rajiv Gandhi's body at 10 Janpath on that fateful day in May 1991. Rao was not in the good books of Rajiv Gandhi and was thinking of retirement. The assassination, however, catapulted him to power as the first Congress prime minister from outside the Nehru-Gandhi family after Indira Gandhi had consolidated her position within the party.

Yet, Rao had more adversaries within his party than outside it.

Even before he became Prime Minister, he was sidelined. I used to visit him and discuss politics over tea or coffee. A scholar, he spoke many languages, had a wealth of experience and tremendous understanding of international politics. A widower, he lived alone. His sons were in Hyderabad. Then one day, he became the ninth Prime Minister of the country (1991–96). Yet, his fall started even as he scaled the pinnacles of power.

Rao was not on good terms with Sonia Gandhi. She wanted him to report to her, and he refused. And he paid a price for this. The Congress Party failed to acknowledge the economic reforms he introduced that eventually led to the country's economic transformation. They did not stand by him when he was assailed with corruption charges—although these were never proven. And the moment he lost the 1996 elections, he was forced to step down as Congress President. He spent his last days without friends, in financial distress and in poor health. The final humiliation came after his death—the Congress did not allow his last rites to be performed in Delhi.

I did not work with Manmohan Singh when he was Prime Minister, but I always felt that like Narasimha Rao, he was not given his due by the Congress. A very quiet and decent man, he used to sit next to me as Leader of Opposition between 1998 and 2004.

Atalji was a political stalwart, with whom I had worked closely. His career had moved from the margins of party politics to the spectacular success of prime ministership of India, until he disappeared again into a hermit-like life. He was a man with a large heart. I admired him and had a very cordial relation with him for long. I used to go to his house next to Chelmsford Club in Delhi to meet him, his adopted daughter Gunnu and her husband Ranjan. Gunnu's mother, Rajkumari Kaul, knew my grandmother in Bhopal. I was perfectly aware that my colleagues were making up stories about my meeting with Atalji and his family, and complaining about me to Sonia Gandhi. I did not care, but I had to pay a steep price.

END OF THE ROAD WITH CONGRESS

New issues cropped up every now and then. When journalist Rajdeep Sardesai conducted an interview with me, and I said because of the people surrounding Sonia, I was not able to meet her, it upset her tremendously. I faced a lot of harassment from people close to her. They demanded that I leave my work in Parliament and join them whenever they organized dharnas or garlanded statues of past Congress leaders on their birth or death anniversaries. I objected: 'How can I adjourn the House on such grounds?' So, I visited their samadhis or statues with the speaker after our work hours at the House. They used to object to that as well.

When Sonia decided to take over the leadership of the party from Kesri, there was significant apprehension within the party. Concerns were raised about her readiness and suitability for the position due to her lack of experience, her Italian heritage, and her limited fluency in Hindi. Ghulam Nabi Azad and I worked tirelessly to convince the party leadership and cadre that she was indeed ready and capable of being an effective leader.

During the elections that followed her takeover, I assisted her with all her speeches. While she travelled and addressed large gatherings in various states, I conducted thorough research, liaised with local party functionaries, and identified relevant issues for her to address. Her speech writers would then use this information to draft her speeches, which were primarily in English. I ensured these were translated into Hindi and transliterated back into English for her convenience. All my support proved insufficient to convince her of my loyalty.

I felt isolated when I was excluded from critical party decisions that directly impacted me, such as selecting the district president, representatives for corporation seats, or MLA candidates for my state and district, which I had represented since 1980 and where I had developed local leadership. It felt as though nothing I did could convince her of my good intentions, leaving me feeling hopeless. I also believed that Sonia's mistrust stemmed from my close working relationship with Narasimha Rao, but my role as Deputy Chairperson of the Rajya Sabha necessitated collaborations with everyone, including Rao, who was then leader of the Congress Party and Prime Minister of India.

The Congress Party became stagnant, with leadership development stifled by Sonia's insecurities about potential challengers to her authority. Every leader was expected to operate under the umbrella of a single family controlling everything. The fact that Sonia Gandhi became the longest-serving president of the Congress Party is not a matter of pride in a democracy but rather a cause for lament. The grand old party that fought for India's independence and was led by visionaries who chose the path of democratic leadership ultimately failed to uphold the same ideals.

So disenchanted was I with the Congress leadership that I started to drift away. Ataliji was always very friendly and sympathetic. One day, when I was feeling particularly sad about something, he said '*Aa jao*. Come and join our party.' Sushma Swaraj and Arun Jaitley were very close friends in the BJP. We had never sacrificed the interests of our respective parties yet bore each other no animosity at the personal level. Unlike competition and retribution that became a dominant sub-culture in the Congress, I realized that in spirit I belonged to a Congress where camaraderie and togetherness flourished, and we could enjoy friendships within and across political lines. There did not seem much point in being with a party where the leader did not trust me. Yet, I remained undecided about quitting the party.

In February 2004, I arranged for a Devnagari transcription of Maulana Azad's *Tarjumanul Quran*, a translation of the Quran in Urdu, and requested Ataliji to release the book. He organized the release at his residence and on the sidelines of the event, told reporters, 'Najma is very welcome to the BJP, but first she has to make her mind up.' That is when I approached him and said, 'Sir, I want to join your party.' He was very welcoming. This was right after the Vajpayee government's defeat in May 2004. I resigned from the Congress. No one could say I was leaving the party to gain power and position.

The decision to leave my previous party was incredibly challenging. At the time, people remained loyal to their party because of their firm conviction about the greater good they could achieve through it, their belief in their leader, and camaraderie with like-minded individuals. It was a moral and emotional attachment. Leaving a party with which my grandfather had such a close association was not a decision I made hastily. However, I no longer saw a future for myself there.

In contrast, the BJP was not only welcoming on a personal level but I also fostered a positive rapport with key figures such as Atal Bihari Vajpayee, L.K. Advani, Sushma Swaraj and Arun Jaitley. Unlike the Congress, the BJP was more open, transparent, and democratic in its functioning. It emphasized the party over any single individual. Young leaders were not only allowed but also actively encouraged to come up. Vajpayee and Advani worked as equals, and the party was not stifled by sycophancy either. It was a breath of fresh air.

While Hindutva is a prominent aspect of the BJP's message, it is not the only one that defines the party. The party's contributions extend beyond this single narrative. Elections are not won solely on messaging; factors like development, job creation, and infrastructure investment are crucial. For instance, Atalji's investments in road and highway infrastructure connected the four metro cities, while his outreach to Pakistan aimed to reduce defence expenditures and refocus on welfare projects and fiscal responsibilities. These were all integral to the party's successes and agenda.

At the time, I felt that the BJP had a promising future and a clearer vision. I saw it as a viable challenge to the Congress and wanted to demonstrate to minorities and Muslim leadership that there was an alternative. Over years of Congress rule, the economic status of Muslims in India had steadily declined, even though they remained a reliable vote bank. I wanted to show that Muslims, like anyone else, had choices and should exercise them for their benefit rather than be a taken-for-granted vote bank.

I recall a Congress peer commenting that I would be isolated in the BJP because it was perceived as a Hindu party with no Muslims. I responded that my joining the party meant it was no longer just a Hindu party, as it now included at least one Muslim. I argued that if Muslims did not join the BJP, the party would never have any. The BJP had, in fact, had long-standing and loyal Muslim leaders like Sikander Bakht, Syed Shahnawaz Hussain, and Mukhtar Abbas Naqvi, who had served in prominent positions.

Today, the party's popularity is a testament to the work and effort put in by its leaders. Even though the party faced a setback in the year I joined, I was confident that it was only temporary and that the future looked bright.

Sonia never called me and I never contacted her. On 10 June 2004, I resigned as Deputy Chairperson of the Rajya Sabha. I resigned from the Congress. As the grandniece of Maulana Azad, it was a party I had grown up with. I was chosen by Mrs Gandhi and trusted by Rajiv. Things took a different turn after Rajiv.

In July 2004, Atalji sent Venkaiah Naidu, then BJP President, to my home with membership papers to sign. And I finally transitioned from the Congress Party to the BJP.

My life as a parliamentarian did not end. I became a member of the Rajya Sabha from the BJP, sitting now on the Opposition benches. Thus started my new innings, which continued for the next ten years—first as an MP from Rajasthan and then from Madhya Pradesh. I did not ask for anything, but new responsibilities came my way. I was given charge of the Union Territory of Dadra, Nagar Haveli, Daman and Diu in Western India. I used to travel and work on strengthening the party position there. I eventually became one of the 13 BJP Vice Presidents. Due to my long years of experience as a parliamentarian and as Deputy

Chairperson of the Rajya Sabha, I was asked to guide and mentor new members joining Parliament.

TERRORISM, UP CLOSE

On 13 December 2001, I was sitting in Room No. 35, my chamber in the Rajya Sabha. The House was adjourned. The live telecast of Parliament proceedings on Doordarshan had given way to an India vs. England cricket test match. Jayant Mishra, Officer on Special Duty (OSD), was with me. We were glancing through some documents. Suddenly, we heard a loud bang. A wicket fallen? Were people bursting firecrackers? But we were in Parliament. Who could burst crackers here? Mani, the Rajya Sabha marshal, rushed in, closed the door that opened to the outer lobby and Gate 11, and said, 'Terrorists have come.' Krishan Kant, then Vice President of India, sent someone to escort us to his room. Before we could step out, a bullet came hurtling in through a window, just a few feet away from my door. In the Vice President's chamber, security personnel were checking the CCTV footage. I saw my security man, Jadhav, who had been with me for nearly a decade, lying in a pool of blood near Gate 12. I started crying and got up, saying that I needed to go upstairs to see what was happening. The security personnel literally pushed me down.

As we huddled inside, bullets kept flying. At about 4 p.m., we came out. By then, the buildings had already been sanitized. When I came out of Gate 11, I saw a large number of hand grenades—some busted, some still live. Negi, another security officer I had known for years, was also dead. Jadhav had been the first to inform us on his walkie-talkie that terrorists had come. 'Close the doors,' he had repeatedly been heard shouting. Negi was closing our outer doors when a bullet went through his stomach. Two of the people I knew very well were gone. They were vulnerable and were completely caught by surprise. At the time, security personnel at Parliament did not carry any weapons, considered a security hazard especially after Mrs Gandhi's assassination. I was looking for my other security person from Delhi Police. I only knew him by face since he sat in a different car that followed behind. I did not remember his name because security personnel changed every fortnight, and sometimes it was difficult to keep up with the names. Where was he? He too was hurt. In the evening, I went to see him in the hospital. He had a bullet wound in his thigh.

Later, we saw on CCTV that the terrorists had come to Gate 11, the gate for the Rajya Sabha, instead of Gate 1, the main gate of Parliament. This was possibly by mistake. At the time, the Chairman was about to leave because the Rajya Sabha had adjourned. As the car carrying the terrorists obstructed his car, his security people started scolding them. At this point, they got out, started running helter-skelter and opened fire. When some of them went to Gate 1, a lady officer from Delhi Police stopped them. Those days, there were no boom barriers, one just had to show an MP pass. The terrorists had one, but she did not believe them. The commotion turned into a battle. One of them received a gunshot and then exploded because his whole body had been covered with bombs. They had put their arsenal on him. I saw blood splattered, and even bones, on the high ceilings of Gate 1.

It was found that one of them had run up to the prime minister's office and was trying to scale a wall nearby. I discovered blood stains there too. When I came out at Vijay Chowk, reporters were all over the place. I stopped my car, opened the door and was talking to them. We were live on TV, when suddenly a hand grenade exploded behind us, with the cameras still rolling. We were all shell-shocked, literally. Fortunately, it was the police detonating live bombs, but we were all on the edge. What would have happened had the terrorists managed to access Parliament? They had 30 kg of RDX in their car. India could have been plunged in complete chaos and anarchy, because MPs of both the ruling party and the Opposition were there. It was a frightening thought.

I faced a similar incident once in Turkey in 1993. Mr Mishra, my OSD, and his wife Neeru were also with me. As we were browsing stalls in the historic market district of Istanbul, a blast ripped through it. There was utter mayhem with billowing smoke and ash, splintered wood and rivers of blood. Somehow I remained calm. The shopkeeper was trembling, lighting and relighting his cigarette again and again. I told him, 'Thank Allah for saving you. Now give me the thing I bought so I can go. The security people are pressing me to leave.' That evening, when I met Süleyman Demirel, then President of Turkey, he asked me, 'How were you so calm?' I told him what I believed in, 'Nobody can save you if God doesn't want to save you.' Turkey had been fighting Kurdish insurgency since the 1980s.

In September 2001, an IPU conference was held in Burkina Faso, a francophone West African country accessible only via Paris. Speaker Ibrahim Traore had garnered African support for my IPU presidency and requested the conference. On its last day, around noon, a Kuwaiti delegate informed me of a terrorist attack in New York. I rushed to my office, turned on the TV, and saw a plane crash into the World Trade Centre. The sky turned dark as the twin towers burst into flames and collapsed. Stunned, we watched in horrified fascination and then immediately drafted and unanimously passed a resolution condemning the attack. The 9/11 attack marked the beginning of a new global war on terror.

INDIA UNDER ATTACK ONCE MORE

It was the month of November in 2008. It was a cold winter evening. I was in Delhi, at the coffee shop of The Ashok at Chanakyapuri, with a few friends. It was late evening, when I got a frantic call from my daughter Sheba. She said that her American friends, Maxine and Luis and their two sons, who were visiting

India were trapped at the Taj Mahal Hotel in Mumbai, due to a terrorist attack. She asked if I could do something to help them get out. I was shocked. Since I was out that evening, we had not heard anything. I was not sure what to do, so I called Sharad Pawar, a close friend and mentor.

Back then, he was Minister of Agriculture in Prime Minister Manmohan Singh's government, but he was still the undisputed leader of Maharashtra. I asked if he could help. He said that he needed some time to get more information and confer with the security forces before coming back to me. He called back shortly thereafter, while I was still at The Ashok and asked to get more information from them, especially the exact coordinates of where they were. I called my daughter back for the information. Her husband was in touch with Luis. My daughter called me back with the details. She said that they were in the old part of the Taj, on the first floor, which was under terrorist attack. All of them were hiding under the bed, almost coffined in, trying to be as quiet as possible and living on Toblerone chocolates and mini-bar snacks. I called back Sharad Pawar with the information.

The attack took place on November 26. It was a series of 12 coordinated shooting and bombing attacks across Mumbai's financial district and downtown, over four days. I was in constant touch with my daughter and her husband and Pawar, who in turn was in touch with the security forces. On November 28, the situation finally started to be brought under control. Security forces managed to locate them. When they called out softly, initially there was no response.

Later, I learnt that our American friends did not hear their call. When Pawar called back to say they could not get them out, I felt very disappointed. So, the security forces decided that they needed a code word only the family knew, that they could use. It was decided that they would use my daughter's name as the code word. So, I relayed it to them through my daughter. When the security forces went in the second time to rescue them, they used that code word and our friends came out of hiding.

It was a very difficult rescue. There were 12–15 commandos surrounding them, forming a human shield. They walked very slowly and the security forces asked them to wait every three feet in silence. They ensured that the area was secure and then moved forward. As they passed different rooms, they saw that the doors had been all kicked in; there were bullet marks everywhere. They were only one floor above the ground floor and were just heading down a floor, yet it felt almost like an hour to come down a few steps, since they were not sure who would suddenly jump out at them. They were brought out through the kitchen; the floor was sticky with blood. Pawar had arranged for a special car for them, and had made arrangement at an alternate hotel behind the Taj. The US embassy personnel were waiting for them with medication for their sons. They rested for a bit and were asked by the security forces to leave immediately. The car did not stop, until they reached the airport in barely 20 minutes, a trip that normally takes an hour. The airport was also closed and surrounded by security forces. They flew to the US via Brussels.

I later learnt the full extent of their ordeal. They had planned a trip across India, with Mumbai as the last stop. They were staying at the old Taj, overlooking the Arabian Sea and the Gateway of India. That evening, they explored the hotel, had dinner, and went to the pool. A band was playing 'Bye Bye Miss American Pie'. Their second son was unusually uncooperative, so they decided to return to their room.

As they climbed the stairs, they heard what sounded like firecrackers, and assumed it was a wedding party. Upon reaching their room, chaos erupted with explosions, gunshots, and smoke. They quickly decided to hide in the innermost of their two connecting rooms, messing up the outer room to look like they had fled.

All four hid under the bed, the children in the middle. The bed was right up to their faces. Luckily, the children fell asleep and slept through the entire two-day siege. They heard doors being kicked in, gunshots, and silence. At one point, they heard a woman screaming and a man pleading, followed by gunfire and then silence. Miraculously, theirs was the only room the terrorists didn't enter. It was their faith, prayers, and God's grace that saved them that day.

Later, they discovered online images of the dining tables and guests' clothing they had seen. Maxine read about a father and daughter, in Mumbai for yoga, who died holding hands under a table. The girl was her son's age.

My son-in-law asked Luis if they would ever come back to India again, and he said they would. They would not let terrorists ever win. He was right.

I found out later that another very close friend, Shabbir Bhaisaab, a prominent member of the Bohra community, was hurt in the simultaneously executed terrorist attack at The Oberoi, but managed to survive. After many years, I learnt that my niece was also staying at The Taj that day but managed to escape because of the heroism and help of the unsung heroes—the Taj staff and other hotel guests.

After the incident I went to Mumbai to personally thank Pawar. He said, 'I am just glad that I could help your friends.' Without his continuous and unrelenting support, we would have lost some very dear people. So once again, thank you, Sharadji.

8

A NEW INNINGS

On 27 May 2014, I joined Prime Minister Narendra Modi at Rashtrapati Bhavan to take oath of office as Minister of Minority Affairs. I was one of three women—along with Sushma Swaraj as Minister of External Affairs and Minister of Overseas Indian Affairs, and Nirmala Sitharaman as Minister of Commerce and Industry—who took oath in his cabinet, along with him. And I remained in the post for just two years, until July 2017.

As per the 2011 Census of India, the percentage of minorities in the country was about 19.3 per cent of the total population. The Ministry of Minority Affairs was fairly new, carved out of the Ministry of Social Justice & Empowerment only in 2006, to ensure a more focused approach towards issues relating to the notified minority communities, namely the Muslims, Christians, Sikhs, Buddhists, Parsis (Zoroastrians) and Jains.

Although Muslims constituted about 14.2 per cent of the population, I noticed that they were in the grip of a vicious cycle of poor education, unemployment, social isolation, poverty and poor life satisfaction. What could be the way out of this crisis? The only real-life, positive stories that shone amidst the gloom-ridden community were that of Muslim coaching institutes, namely the Association of Muslim Doctors, the Talent Zone Academy, Rahmani 30, the Shaheen Group and the Al-Ameen Mission. They were guiding students successfully in the fields of medicine and engineering by helping them develop the skills and knowledge they needed to succeed in competitive exams. I realized that guidance and training were the felt needs of the community and launched a number of skill development schemes for the youths, including girls. The aim was to empower them for sustainable livelihoods in the organized sector and ensure a successful future. For girls, I started training programmes in traditional arts and crafts, so that they would not face destitution in the face of livelihood disruptions.

While coaching centres served a certain purpose, a large section of minority children, especially in the Muslim community, either dropped out of school or did not enroll in the formal school system. I felt that it was essential to have programmes that would empower such children to join the national mainstream, compete at par and grow. Hence, I launched Nai Manzil (new horizons) in 2015–16 to provide them with both formal education (Class VIII or X) and skill training. Dr Arvind Mayaram, Secretary to Ministry of Minority Affairs, was of great help. Coming from the Ministry of Finance, he brought with him long-standing associations with institutions like the World Bank. He worked tirelessly with its team, so that we could launch Nai Manzil as a central scheme in record time, with 50 per cent funding from the World Bank. Starting with an initial outlay of ₹600 crore, it became a resounding success—benefitting over 100,000 youth from 20 states today. The World Bank recommended this initiative to other countries with similar requirements.

I also interacted with madrassas—centres of religious education. I suggested that they should also teach Hindi and English, not just Urdu. I pointed out that Prophet Muhammad had once said, 'Seek knowledge even if it be in China, for the seeking of knowledge is a duty upon every Muslim,' which clearly means that Islam accords very high importance to other schools of knowledge. I asked why they wouldn't follow this teaching and provide the youth with skills that could help them earn a better living. They agreed. I then connected with two central universities—Jamia Millia Islamia and Aligarh Muslim University—

to start bridge courses for madrassa-trained students, including girls, to prepare them for the civil services and other competitive exams. At my request, senior bureaucrats started taking classes in these universities.

In contrast to Muslims, the number of Parsis stood at just 57,264. Despite their diminishing numbers, Parsis, however, did not suffer from socio-economic and educational backwardness. It was an extremely talented community, with a glorious history. It had contributed immensely to the building of modern India, especially in the fields of industry, entrepreneurship, education, science, sports, arts, music, culture and philanthropy. Yet, this distinctive and distinguished community faced an existential crisis—their numbers were declining by around 12 per cent every Census decade[44], while India's population was going up by 17 per cent[45]. I felt an infusion of fresh blood was desperately needed and launched a range of campaigns and exhibitions to promote childbirth in the community, track their history and contribution and raise awareness about the community's dwindling numbers.

I planned an exciting event to showcase and promote Parsi culture through a first-of-its-kind international exhibition, 'The Everlasting Flame'. The proposal was put forth by the UNESCO-supported Parsi organization, Parzor Foundation, which was pursuing it with the Ministry of Culture for quite some time, but without success. We realized that we could bring it under our scheme Hamari Dharohar (our heritage). Held from 19 March to 29 May 2016, three unique exhibitions were organized in Delhi tracing 3,000 years of Zoroastrian history through artefacts—from the imperial Iranian-Zoroastrian legacy to the modern

---

[44]PIB Delhi, 'Declining Parsi Population in the Country', Press Information Bureau, Ministry of Minority Affairs, 21 March 2022, https://tinyurl.com/ysnc9jba. Accessed on 17 July 2024.

[45]PIB, 'Country's Population Reaches 1210 Million As Per Census 2011, etc.' Press Information Bureau, Government of India, Ministry of Home Affairs, 31 March 2011, https://tinyurl.com/2kyzh6w7. Accessed on 17 July 2024.

times, through textiles, jewellery, sculptures, coins and various manuscripts, many of which were loaned by 15 museums across the world, including Syria and Iran. These museums had never loaned manuscripts to India in the past. Therefore, it took a lot of convincing for them to agree to do so. The exhibitions were a grand success, and they allowed the Ministry of Minority Affairs to be internationally visible.[46]

I also organized a Parsi conference, which the members of the Parsi diaspora attended enthusiastically. Inaugurated by President Pranab Mukherjee, it was also attended by Ratan Tata. During the conference, we launched the Jiyo Parsi scheme to arrest, reverse and stabilize the declining trend of the Parsi population by adopting scientific protocol and structured interventions. The scheme had three components: under the medical component, financial assistance was provided to Parsi couples for childbirth treatments following standard medical protocols; under the healthcare component, financial support was provided to Parsi couples for childcare and assistance of the elderly; under the advocacy component, outreach efforts were taken up to generate awareness in the Parsi community on their declining numbers. I found out from the ministry that since the inception of the Jiyo Parsi scheme, 403 babies had been born (as on 31.12.2022).[47]

My interest in heritage conservation led me to bring under the Hamari Dharohar scheme the modernization of a unique institution—the Dairatul Ma'arifil at Osmania University. Established in 1888, the Dairatul Ma'arifil's role was to procure, transcribe, translate, collate, edit and publish priceless medieval Arabic manuscripts on medicine, mathematics and literature from around the world. The institution had fallen on hard times, with very poor infrastructure, meagre resources and dire neglect. Along with Dr Mayaram, I visited it and eventually sanctioned an

---

[46] *Annual Report, 2015-16*, Ministry of Minority Affairs, Government of India, https://tinyurl.com/2wjf8xb8. Accessed on 17 July 2024.
[47] Ibid.

ambitious project of ₹34.66 crore to modernize the infrastructure, and digitize, translate and reprint rare Arabic manuscripts. At the launch of the project, I said, 'We should showcase our rich heritage. It gives me immense pleasure to fund an institution for which Maulana Abul Kalam Azad had utmost respect.'[48]

In 2015, the Ministry of Minority Affairs also started overhauling the year-old National Waqf Development Corporation Limited (NAWADCO), formed to identify and oversee the development of Waqf properties all over India as institutional and commercial projects. Although NAWADCO's mandate was clear, the roadmap to achieving it was unclear. Deloitte, the consulting firm, was hired to prepare a comprehensive structural-functional report on making the organization more purposeful and result-oriented. I was keen to implement the recommendations as quickly as possible. Unfortunately, this project faced hurdles, with vested interests putting a spanner in the works. Some even illegally held on to Waqf properties. Today, with land prices going through the roof, these properties have become invaluable.

I could not complete this task during my tenure—just a two-year window to bring in far too many much-needed reforms.

A PEACEFUL MANIPUR

In 2016, within two years of my taking oath as a minister, as I turned 75, I was asked to resign and offered governorship of Manipur—literally a 'Bejewelled Place' in Sanskrit—in Northeast India, bordering Myanmar, Bangladesh and China. With its deep wooded valleys, sparkling waterfalls and crystal-clear lakes nestled in the mountains, I was struck by its beauty since my very first visit. Manipuris largely belong to three major tribes—the Meiteis, who are Vaishnavites or worshippers of Lord Vishnu; the Kukis and the Nagas, who embraced Christianity. Historically, they have had

---

[48]Ibid.

conflicts over land claims. Infamous for its ethnic violence now, Manipur has been renowned for a wide range of things, including its rich culture, especially the classical Manipuri dance form with its graceful Raas Leela dance depicting parts of Lord Krishna's life.

To appreciate Manipur, one needs to understand its incredibly rich geography and biodiversity. Besides the rugged hills, narrow valleys, flat plains or young rivers, the state also has the Loktak Lake, the world's only floating national park. Manipur also comes under two of the world's 36 biodiversity hotspots—the Himalayan as well as the Indo-Burma zones, characterized by rare and endangered flora and fauna. For instance, the sangai (*Rucervus eldii eldii*), or brow-antlered deer, is a species of deer found only in Manipur.

A region with strong feminist traditions, Manipur is called 'Land of Golden Girls': from boxer Mary Kom, weightlifter Mirabai Chanu, judoka Shushila Likmabam, and hockey player Sushila Chanu to archer Laishram Devi, 19 of 35 Olympians, Commonwealth and Asian Games medallists and national sporting stars in Manipur are women.[49]

It is quite fitting that I—a woman in a man's world throughout my work life—should wind up my golden years for the nation in this beautiful state. When Prime Minister Modi asked me to take over as Governor of Manipur, I was a little apprehensive. It was very far from Delhi and there were no direct flights. All flights were via Guwahati in Assam or Kolkata in West Bengal, making it a full day's journey from Delhi and even longer from Mumbai, my home.

I took oath in the month of August 2016, in Imphal, the capital of Manipur. The Raj Bhavan, a colonial building, was still under repair. So I moved into the guest house normally reserved for visiting dignitaries, adjacent to the main building. The early months were depressing and lonely since I did not know anybody.

---

[49] Hanjabam, Sukhdeba Sharma and Sanasam Yaiphaba Singh, 'Olympians and National sports awardees of Manipur', *The Sangai Express*, 10 October 2022, https://tinyurl.com/4hs94sy9. Accessed on 17 July 2024.

I did not know the local language and the position itself seemed very ceremonial, especially after my hectic Delhi life in active politics. I was assigned Z security cover, which meant whenever I went out, I had to move in a bulletproof vehicle, secured with dark panes, while a convoy of 15 cars, with commandos surrounding my car, accompanied me all the time. This isolated me from the local people—something I was not used to. Within a few months, I moved into the main building of the Raj Bhavan once it was renovated and started to make myself more at home. I even got my two dogs, Champa and Diesel, from Delhi and adopted a cat, Eva, brought to me by a Manipuri friend.

The state, however, was hardly serene when I became Governor. Though far from its current bloodshed and destruction, strikes and blockades were a constant feature of everyday life. This was largely due to conflicts between the ethnic groups, with each fighting for their own demands, over complex issues of their identity, history and land rights in the valleys and the forests. To add to it, the porous border with Myanmar facilitated the illicit flow of high-value contraband items into India, then as now, especially drugs, arms and ammunition. The border posts of Moreh and Churachandpur, the fulcrum of violence in Manipur in recent times—had been major hubs of India-Myanmar drug trafficking for long.

I found a Manipur where life had come to a standstill. Anxiety ran high about a possible intrusion upon the integrity of the state by the Indo-Naga Peace process under the interlocutor R.N. Ravi, IPS officer and Governor of Nagaland. Protests erupted, businesses shut down, and fear stalked the streets. After 8 p.m., no one came out of their homes. The basic necessities of life—vegetables, grains, pulses, bread—were not available, because markets were not allowed to operate and goods could not enter the state. I used to carry all these from Delhi whenever I travelled for work. Fuel was very expensive. And one had to wait in queue for hours to get a limited amount.

I decided that I needed to do something about the situation.

Years of experience—first as a parliamentary back-bencher, then as a presiding officer, thereafter as an international figure, and finally as a cabinet minister—had taught me one thing: things never fell into place on their own accord; somebody needed to act and take the bull by its horn. For me, as always, diplomacy, communication and engagement were key to understanding and addressing any problem. I had learnt from Dada Abba that diplomacy triumphs over aggression, violence and high-handedness. This was, and will always be, my way. I decided to call the Naga, Kuki and Meitei leaders separately and told them that their blockades and protests were putting businesses and communities in major jeopardy. My question to them was, 'Who is losing? Who does this benefit?' I pointed out to them that the prime losers were their own communities and implored them to sit across the table and talk to each other to find common ground. I also offered them the use of the Raj Bhavan as a neutral and safe place for them to come and confer to thrash out their problems. I said that it was not a government office but my residence. And I would not interfere. Somehow, with my persuasion and persistence, things gradually settled down.

A few months later, the Assembly elections took place in 2017. No party had the majority. A BJP-led coalition, under the leadership of N. Biren Singh was sworn in, with him as Chief Minister. I implored him to have at least one woman representative in his cabinet. Nemcha Kipgen, the only woman in Singh's 12-member cabinet, became Minister of Social Welfare and Cooperation. The government started working.

The first sign of normalcy was the opening of the markets on a regular basis, availability of everyday essential goods, and the normal flow of traffic in the city and on the highways. There were also signs of revival of the real estate and construction industries. When my car first passed through Imphal, I would ask myself, 'Why are all the buildings half-built, almost like somebody started a city and forgot to complete it?' I soon realized that this was due to non-availability of construction material, constant closures, and fear among the local population. After normalcy started to creep back, and people started to believe in it, I saw the completion of several buildings, and the opening of new and high-end stores. It was very reassuring and satisfying.

I decided that I needed to travel around the capital and the state to engage with the people on a one-on-one basis. I had already opened up the Raj Bhavan to the public. Anyone could come and meet me between 11 a.m. and 4 p.m., five days a week, and I always tried to help them. When I started to travel, it created a flutter among my security staff. I tried to assuage their fears that I would not interfere with the security protocols and that it was not my intention to put them in harm's way. It was just that, as Governor of the state, it was important for me to engage with the people and understand their problems. I was not there to be a silent spectator; I made up my mind to participate.

One day, in June 2017, I decided to go to the Nupi Keithel or the Ima Market—the world's largest women's market, where over 12,000 women work in a huge building. The women sell everything—from clothes, groceries and vegetables to other articles.

Mary Kom, the internationally renowned boxer, who I first met in Manipur and who later became a friend, had gifted me a *phanek*—the traditional wrap-around skirt worn by Manipuri women, with a blouse and a scarf. I wore it and went to the Ima Market. Word spread that the Governor was at the market. Immediately, shops started to shut and women came running towards me, much to the chagrin of my security staff. Women—young, old and the elderly—surrounded me. I went to every stall with them and bought something small as a token. They insisted that I change my current phanek. I was embarrassed, I had no intention of undressing in public. Within minutes, however, a new phanek was stitched to size. The women enclosed me in a circle, removed the old phanek and wrapped the new one around my waist. Then it was time for selfies, thousands of those, with the women smiling and laughing into the cameras with me. My first public outreach was a grand success. Wearing a phanek publicly became a habit. I wore different phaneks—of the Kuki, Naga or Meitei traditions—depending on the community I was meeting. It used to make the people happy.

Similarly, I started attending different sporting events. When I first attended the famous Governor's Cup boat race (which earlier governors rarely attended), my security staff panicked again. I reassured them that no one was going to kill me and asked them not worry. I went and enjoyed the race as well as the interactions. I used to go for all the football and polo matches. And I used to walk around freely in the stadium. Wherever I went, women used to come and hug me. They listened to me when I encouraged them to participate in the Thursday street market. While I was helping the bigger group of entrepreneurs, I tried to help and encourage as many individuals as I could.

During this time, someone introduced me to Bimbim, a woman who sold traditional Manipuri beaded jewellery as a way to supplement her income as a vegetable seller, at the Ima Market. Traditionally in Manipur, beaded jewellery is worn by women as a tribe identifier. Bimbim's jewellery looked very traditional, but I came to understand that they were more than just a tribe marker. The *mala*s (beaded necklaces) she made were very sophisticated and could be sold in any major fashion accessory store in the world. To encourage her, I decided to switch to her handmade malas. I encouraged all my women guests from Delhi or from elsewhere in the world to support her. The truth is, her jewellery was so beautiful that nobody needed much goading to buy those. Bimbim's business started to thrive. She hired more people, and soon went from being a vegetable seller to a small independent jewellery entrepreneur. Similarly, I tried to encourage others, especially the hand-knitted shoe designers and the artisans of other crafts. It was my way of building confidence among the people.

Major General K.P. Singh, YSM, IG-AR (S), chief of the Assam Rifles, headquartered in Manipur, once invited me to address the troops stationed there. One of the oldest central paramilitary forces in the country, administered by the Ministry of Home Affairs but under the operational control of the Indian Army, its primary duty was border security, especially along the Indo-Myanmar border. While addressing the troops at the Assam Rifles training camp, I said that we owed them a great deal for their service to the nation. They lived far from their homes and families to protect the nation's borders, allowing each of us to sleep without fear and remain safe, thanks to their vigilant presence. I added that we were also very thankful to their families, who sacrificed so much, lived alone, and brought up their children alone: 'Their sacrifices, too, must be recognized.' The men were very happy and thanked me for my thoughts and the time I spent with them. I felt grateful, too, for the time I could spend with them.

During my tenure, President Ram Nath Kovind visited Manipur with his wife Savita Kovind and they stayed at the Raj Bhavan. The president was very keen to understand the situation and ground realities in Manipur and wanted a firsthand account. Programmes and festivities showcasing the uniqueness of Manipuri culture and way of life were arranged for his visit.

Vice President Venkaiah Naidu visited too and addressed a women's meeting. Then I decided to invite scientists. I was associated with the Indian Science Congress Association (ISCA), India's biggest organization for scientists, since I was a student. Every year they held a Science Congress. I convinced them to hold the 105th Indian Science Congress, 2018, at Imphal—the first one in the Northeast. They agreed. I then went to Delhi and requested Prime Minister Modi to inaugurate it. He came to Imphal and delivered a very inspiring speech on the importance of science in society.

The Sangai Festival, an annual cultural festival showcasing the handicrafts, arts, dance and music of Manipur, across venues and districts, used to be held every November for about 10 days. The festival that had been discontinued in the troubled state was restarted during my tenure. In 2018, I invited Nirmala Sitharaman, then Minister of Defence, as Chief Guest. When I went for the inauguration of the festival, I was wearing a phanek. Nirmala was so happy, she said, 'Madam, you inaugurate.' I said, 'No, we both will.' As we went in, she saw how women reacted when they saw me in their local dress.

I realized that the biggest hindrance to the Northeast integrating with the Indian mainland was the lack of direct connectivity. The only way to get to Manipur directly was via air and that route was quite limited in scope. For that reason, tourism could not really be developed on a large scale, despite the beauty of the Northeast. Due to limited opportunities, many Manipuris had left the state to find employment in other parts of the country, even in far-off states as Karnataka, Maharashtra or Tamil Nadu. For them, visiting Manipur was harder than, say getting to Australia or the US. I decided that something had to be done about it. It was absolutely imperative that Manipur be connected to the rest of the country, and not just via Guwahati or Kolkata.

I talked to Jayant Sinha, the son of my good friend and former Minister of Finance, Yashwant Sinha. Jayant was Minister of State for Finance and Minister of State for Civil Aviation at the Centre. I explained the problem the Northeast faced. As Governor of Manipur, my priority was to get the capital city of Manipur (Imphal) connected to the rest of the country, especially to Delhi. Jayant understood and asked the Air India officials to meet me. I made sure I followed up with him and the officials he had got me connected to. Finally, Air India started a direct flight between Delhi and Imphal, every alternate day, just a three-and-half hour flight. Jayant came down to Imphal to inaugurate this flight and I remember him quipping in his speech that my persistent and unrelenting pursuance of this direct connectivity had motivated him to speed up the process. I think what he really meant was that I would finally stop bothering him at all hours of the day, all the days of the week till he relented.

Additionally, I also communicated with the authorities of all the private airlines and explained that Manipur had an international airport with all the facilities to support additional traffic and to taxi planes overnight. I argued that Imphal had the capability to support an increase in passenger traffic, both of locals going back and forth and increased tourists, nationally and internationally. This could prove to be very profitable for them. IndiGo, too, started a direct flight between Delhi and Imphal. Between Air India and IndiGo, Imphal was connected to Delhi at least five to six days a week. Since then, more direct flights from other airlines connecting Imphal to Delhi were started.

My granddaughter Nadia visited Manipur with my eldest daughter Rubina, a doctor in the United States. She had read about Manipur and wanted to do something meaningful to make her visit memorable. She implored her classmates in the US to be generous and collected a small but substantial amount of money. To encourage her, both her mother and I added to her collection. I told her about the small floating school on Loktak Lake. Loktak was known for its circular floating swamps, made of vegetation similar to tall grass—so thick, dense, and deep that entire communities settled down on those and floated along the lake. The school desperately needed funding and resources to support the 20–30 children who studied there. After consulting with Nadia, we decided to donate what the students needed. So enthused was Nadia that she bought exercise books and stationery items for the children and distributed these herself.

I always had profound faith in the ultimate triumph of religious pluralism. In Manipur, I could put that faith into action. As part of our outreach, we celebrated every festival—Holi, Eid, Diwali and Christmas. During Holi, along with the traditional dancers, I participated in their traditional dance. During Diwali, we lit up the whole place with earthen diyas and arranged for fireworks.

During Christmas, we put up a Christmas tree, decorated the Raj Bhavan, and invited carol singers from the local Baptist church. My youngest daughter Asma usually visited me in Manipur during Christmas. The Raj Bhavan always received a lot of sweets and cakes during any festival. As a norm, I always sent those to the children of the people who worked for the estate. On this occasion, Asma suggested that we drop off the cookies, candies and cakes to the local orphanage behind the Raj Bhavan. Ningombam Nilamani, the good-natured manager of Raj Bhavan, arranged for more items. Along with him and my OSD Samiuraham (Sami, as we called him), Asma took those things to the orphanage. The children were thrilled with the unexpected surprise. Their happiness was a delight to watch.

Asma kept prodding and nudging me to do something on a grander scale the following year. She wanted orphan children to have a magical experience, something to remember. At her behest, the following Christmas we invited over 200 children—tiny tots to teenagers—from across the state, irrespective of their religion. We brought in games, slides, activities, gifts and food to set up a venue where children could be children, and so could adults. There was Santa Claus and a band to spread good cheer. We wanted them to feel loved and wanted. Kipgen helped with the funding and support through her ministry, and so did all my staff and their wives. All the cabinet ministers were there to welcome the children. It was a big success. We decided to do something similar during Diwali in 2020. Unfortunately, fate had other plans and Covid struck.

Holi was one of the most elegant festivals of Manipur. With the state's strong Vaishnavite tradition, people celebrated Holi with dance, music, food and *gulal* (colourful powders supposed to be made of dried petals). Some local women appealed to me that they wanted to play Holi in the Raj Bhavan. I was happy to open up the premises for them. About 100 women came in light orange clothes, applied gulal on each other's forehead and performed the traditional dance of Manipur, accompanied by the *pung cholom* (literally, roar of the drums) and performance of the Vaishnava Sankirtana. I also joined them. Then we offered them food and light refreshments.

I loved to invite people from all over the country and the world to Manipur, to show and share the rich and unique culture of the state. Whenever we had guests, we invited the traditional Manipuri dancers and drummers to perform for us. My daughter Rubina, a paediatric endocrinologist and paediatric diabetes specialist, gave lectures on her area of specialization at the local teaching hospital in Imphal. My daughters also encouraged me to invite people for breakfast and lunch from all walks of life as a way to connect with the local Manipuri society. As part of the outreach, I invited journalists, civil society members, professors, doctors, lawyers and others almost every day until 2020. The food was always Manipuri cuisine—stew, stir-fried vegetables, fish curry and meat, piquant salads and herbs, fritters—served hot on banana leaves.

When I first visited Manipur, I did not realize how much the people, the rich culture and ecology would impress me. I thought I had seen the world, but there was so much more to see. It was a time of constant learning. One tradition that I recounted to all my friends was that of the Manipuri *nupi chenba*—eloping with the prospective bride before marriage. Local legend had it that the Manipuri princess Rukmini was being forced into a marriage against her wishes. She had lost all hope and prayed silently to Lord Krishna. A messenger turned up to inform her that Lord Krishna had accepted her request. The following day, as she headed to the marriage venue, the Lord swept her off her feet into His chariot and made her His wife. To honour that tradition, young couples chose to elope before the wedding night, spent time together, and had a formal wedding thereafter if they so wished.

When the proposal to establish a Manipur University of Culture was presented, I was thrilled and fully supportive. I actively contributed to its development through the Governor's office, eager to promote Manipur's unique culture to a global audience.

Time flies, calendar pages turn, yet memories remain intact. Years ago, British novelist L.P. Hartley wrote in his novel *The Go-Between*: 'The past is a foreign country: they do things differently there.'[50] I wasn't in Manipur very long ago, but with the current violence, it does feel like another century. A slice of history passed on in Manipur from generation to generation is the Chahi Taret Khuntakpa, or the Seven Years Devastation. It refers to the horrific experience of the Burmese invasion of Manipur that lasted from 1819 to 1826. The twist in the tale is the line that inevitably follows: 'Impossible was the task to subdue the Manipuri.'

During my tenure as Governor of Manipur, the state had become so peaceful that my friends and family, colleagues and peers not only from India but from all over the world felt safe to visit and travel within Manipur. They did not have Z security, in fact they had no security, but were safe. Today, when I hear about the unrest in Manipur, I feel dismayed and sad. My one recommendation would be to first quell the violence and then encourage dialogue and build the trust among the different communities. This is not easy but necessary, for violence cannot be the way forward. I fervently hope that the beautiful people of the bejewelled land find their peace soon. And, perhaps, remember my time with them with a smile and a nod.

---

[50]Hartley, J.P., in Quotes, *Goodreads*, https://tinyurl.com/32cmpx9z. Accessed on 17 July 2024.

SECTION III

Echoes in Time

9

A WOMEN'S WOMAN

Growing up in Bhopal in the 1940s, one could not help but be struck by paeans that proclaimed the magic of powerful women. Ballads about celebrated royal heroines, of romance, bravery, tragedy, nostalgia swirled in the air. Bhopal was enchanting as a land of legends, myths and folklore. It was the land of the ancient King Bhoj, after whom the place was named. It was also the land of the tribal Queen Kamlapati, who chose death by drowning, along with her palace maids, to escape Pathan invaders[51]. As children, we used to be thrilled whenever an elderly mendicant visited our home, singing and dancing to the beat of a small *damru*—a ubiquitous handheld drum made of wood, goat skin and cotton cords. He always received some uncooked food that my mother would set aside for him.

We did not know better and nobody corrected us either, but we called him 'Gond', which was actually the name of his tribe, but as children we thought that was his name. He was so proud of his ancestry, of the great lakes of Bhopal and of Queen Kamlapati, that he broke into a little recital whenever he saw us. He had, however, only one song in his repertoire:

Taal tau Bhopal Taal,
Baki haiin tallaiyan,

---

[51]TOI, 'Rani Kamlapati: Things you must know about the Gond queen', *The Times of India*, 15 November 2021, https://tinyurl.com/4xus7959. Accessed on 18 July 2024.

Rani tau Kamplapati,
Baki hain gadhaiyan...

(Bhopal Lake is the grandest,
All the rest are mere puddles.
Just as Queen Kamlapati is the greatest,
And all the others are no more than donkeys.)

While I marvelled at the wonderful story of the long-departed queen, the grim reality of village women around us did not escape my attention. I had noticed that the makers of beedis, the widely smoked leaf-rolled cigarette of uncured tobacco, always got their women to prepare those. The men brought the raw material—*tendu* (Indian ebony) leaves, tobacco and cotton string—and the women rolled and tied those through the day. My mother's wet-nurse, who worked at our home, once invited us for a marriage ceremony. I came to know that her son had four wives. I was angry and asked him, 'Why should you have four wives? Aren't you happy with one?' I was still in school then.

The neighbours explained that when he first got married, he taught his wife how to wrap beedis. After doing all the household chores, she made those. He sold the beedis, brought in more raw material for her, and appropriated the profit. This went on day after day. Then he got married again and the new wife also started doing the same. He amassed more money. And he kept marrying again and again. All four wives worked for his beedi enterprise. It was like a factory system, while he sat around, ate, smoked and became fat. Even at that age, I thought this was incredibly unfair. The wives worked like machines, while he enjoyed the fruits of their labour. That incident stayed with me.

STRIDES AND STUMBLES

I always believed that women's issues are everyone's issues. And all issues are women's issues. For years, I had prioritized women in my work, especially for equal pay, better workplace policies, and a healthier family-work balance. Why should men routinely receive twice as much as women, when women worked as hard and working women worked harder after coming back home? From the beginning, I strongly felt that women should have economic freedom. Only that, I believed, could free them from the exploitation, harassment and discrimination so many of them faced. Whether I was working in the Bombay slums, in Parliament, with NGOs or at the international level, my focus was always on women's economic independence.

Sometimes I succeeded, for instance in my pilot projects with women-run banks and post offices in Bombay—initiatives aimed at confidence-building among women. My personal relations with my father's friend, Shankar Dayal Sharma, was very helpful. He was Union Minister of Communications (1974–77) under Indira Gandhi and I requested him to allow a few post offices to be headed by women. I was convinced that this would have a positive impact on women, build their confidence, and set them off towards leadership roles. He agreed and we opened a couple of post offices headed by women. Pratibha Patil was then a cabinet minister in the Government of Maharashtra. I invited her to inaugurate one such post office in Chembur, headed by a woman.

The success of this pilot programme led to others and today there are close to 260 all-women post offices scattered across the country[52]. With the success of women-run post offices, I decided that this initiative could be further extended. Union Minister of Finance Pranab Mukherjee was a good friend and a mentor to me. I took my idea for women-run banks to him. Quite excited about it, he launched a State Bank of India (SBI) branch headed by a woman, at Malabar Hills in Bombay. Over the past few decades, as women did remarkably well in the finance and banking sector

---

[52]Gowthaman, Nirandhi, 'India has 260 all-women post offices: Union minister Ravi Shankar Prasad', HERSTORY, 31 August 2020, https://tinyurl.com/7nb9c4fu. Accessed on 18 July 2024.

in India, and occupied top posts in some of the leading banks, as the share of women officers grew at a fast clip—from a single-digit presence in the '80s to over 25 per cent now—it felt really good[53]. They validated the conviction of my youth.

My successes motivated me to do more. I thought it would be a good idea to link up the earlier initiative to small saving schemes. Post offices used to have the Alpa Bachat small-saving programme. I wanted more women to be involved in it. I proposed that there should be a single window in every post office, operated by women officers to help women customers. Years later, the Post Master General of India sought an appointment with me and informed me that the Alpa Bachat scheme, which I had initiated, had done tremendously well over the past 25 years. He expressed a desire for me to attend a function celebrating its success. I was really touched that they remembered my contribution and called me to share in their success. More than that, it filled me with pride that an idea I had implemented so many years ago had resonated with women across the country.

During this time, I was working to promote an organization called the Indian Housewives' Foundation, and became its president around 1985. The point was to spread the awareness that despite the key role women played in society and the economy, they were always underestimated. While the work done by men was widely acknowledged, and most men were considered economically productive, women engaged in full-time household work were categorized as 'economically unproductive' by Government of India. In fact, women attending to household chores like cooking, cleaning utensils, looking after children, fetching water, etc., were classified as 'non-workers', similar to students, pensioners and beggars.[54]

---

[53]Chavan, P., 'Women's Access to Banking in India: Policy Context, Trends, and Predictors', *Review of Agrarian Studies*, Vol. 10, No. 1, January–June, 2020.
[54]Manual on Labour Statistics (I) 2012, Government of India, Ministry of Statistics and Programme Implementation, Central Statistics Office, https://tinyurl.com/mt49hvns. Accessed on 18 July 2024.

Housewives, in reality, comprised the world's largest workforce, albeit unpaid. Women comprised the largest group of consumers, responsible for the lion's share of shopping—for groceries, clothes, household appliances, and other necessities for everyone at home—and thus contributed to economic growth. Through seminars and national-level meetings, we campaigned for identifying and redressing stay-at-home women's problems. Being a member of the Maharashtra State Government Committee for the Status of Women helped me work towards this.

All these gave me the confidence and the clout to pursue bigger, more ambitious ideas later—for instance, forming the Women's Committee of the Rajya Sabha, including women's agenda in the Inter-Parliamentary Union, capacity building for girl students as Minister of Minority Affairs in the Narendra Modi cabinet, and bringing in multiple women-centric projects in Manipur as its Governor.

There were occasions when I did not succeed. Back in the 1970s, the attitude towards sex workers was not very sympathetic. Indian society was still conservative and hardly exposed to global values. And global values were in a flux, with birth control pills introduced in the '60s and women's sexual freedom and choice still largely associated with the 'hippie movement' of peace, drugs and free love—all frowned upon. There was a constant clamour from the conservatives to clamp down on sex workers through high-handed legislation against brothels. Abuse by the authorities, customers, middlemen as well as brothel owners was rampant.

My interactions with sex workers changed my perception. I realized that most women were forced into the profession by poverty, treachery or need. An unsympathetic approach would only push the trade underground and lead to further abuse of the sex workers. I was in favour of a more practical approach to the problem—legalizing sex work as a profession. This would allow the women to be registered, get periodic health check-ups, and be protected from abuse. In addition, their earnings could contribute to the exchequer, which usually was diverted to the underground economy. Even though I had the support of Prime Minister Indira Gandhi in the women's committee she had formed for International Women's Year, 1975, the elderly members were appalled. Mrs Gandhi gave me a sympathetic hearing, but nothing much happened on that front. Finally, a three-judge bench of the Supreme Court of India issued a historic order in May 2022, recognizing sex work as a profession and putting safeguards in place to protect their rights and dignity[55]. I felt vindicated.

During the J&K elections in 1987, I used to visit remote villages, knee-deep in snow, with Farooq Abdullah Saab of the National Conference and Ghulam Rasool Kar Saab, President of Jammu and Kashmir Pradesh Congress Committee, hopping from one place to another on helicopters to campaign. Sometimes we would eat in the copter or at times on the sidelines of our speeches—usually hard-roasted chicken, bread and pink *kahwa* tea flavoured with cinnamon, cardamom, and saffron.

Once, while visiting a village in the Gool Gulabgarh tehsil, near Banihal, at an elevation of over 9,000 feet, a bit of land was cleared for a makeshift helipad, with one of the landing skids hanging above a deep gorge. I looked around for walnut trees. There were none. All of them had been chopped down, without any effort for replantation. Walnut trees took very long to grow. I wanted to involve the local women in a plantation drive, give them seeds and saplings of walnut, almond and pine, so they could grow the trees. I prepared a 17-point programme and submitted it to Rajiv Gandhi, suggesting a tree plantation scheme for women that would give

---

[55]Mishra, Bijayani and Sabiha Mazid, 'Why Supreme Court's acknowledgment of sex work as a profession is welcome', *The Indian Express*, 30 May 2022, https://tinyurl.com/bdu2tycc. Accessed on 18 July 2024.

them the freedom to look after the trees and also enjoy the fruits as an incentive. I also suggested distributing hens to the women, so that the eggs could be sold to hotels for the consumption of tourists. That way, women could be at home and earn some money. The scheme worked for some time, but like many government schemes, over time it fell through due to lack of commitment from the local political functionaries and state-level bureaucrats.

A QUESTION OF LEADERSHIP

Over the years, my experience convinced me that women were the vanguard of a new era of leadership. Our Constitution recognized women's empowerment and gender equity as a pre-requisite for strengthening the institutional structure of our democracy, but what about the participation of women in elected bodies, including in the highest forum of democracy, the Parliament? Before I joined the Rajya Sabha, there was already a demand for representation of women in elected bodies.

In 1979, 'The Convention on the Elimination of All Forms of Discrimination against Women (CEDAW)' was adopted by the UN General Assembly; it was ratified by India in 1993 and one of the recommendations for its implementation was to improve the representation of women in the upper echelons of lawmaking—affirmative actions were proposed including legislature to reserve 33 per cent seats for women in Lok Sabha and in all state legislative assemblies.[56]

When Rajiv's government had introduced the Panchayati Raj Bill in 1989, granting 30 per cent reservation to women at the grassroots, I was overjoyed. The Panchayati Raj Bill (officially the 64th Constitutional Amendment Bill) introduced by Rajiv was

---

[56]National Human Rights Commission, India, *Women's Rights in India: An Analytical Study of The United Nations Convention on the Elimination of All Forms of Discrimination against Women (CEDAW) and The Indian Constitution, Legislations, Schemes, Policies & Judgements 2021*, https://tinyurl.com/muk5nwnz. Accessed on 18 July 2024.

perceived by non-Congress state governments as an attempt to grab more power, by reducing the constitutional role of a state and promoting centralization. The need for a reformed Panchayati Raj Institution (PRI) dates back to 1978, though. A 1978 Bill had recommended reforms to enforce Article 40 of the Constitution, to organize village panchayats and endow them with powers of self-governance. The draft Bill made the establishment of Panchayati Raj Institutions mandatory, with membership to PRIs being by election. The Chief Election Commissioner (CEC) was to be in charge of all election matters and the Comptroller and Auditor General of India (CAG) was to audit all accounts. The CAG report was to be submitted to the governor of a state, who in turn had to lay it before the state legislature.[57] Panchayats could be empowered by the state legislature with executive and administrative functions, including the 'promotion of economic and social development and implementation of plans'.[58]

The proposed Bill of 1989 included all the above recommendations. It also had seat reservations for those belonging to Scheduled Castes (SC) and Scheduled Tribes (ST), in proportion to their population and to the total number of seats in a PRI. Similarly, 30 per cent of the reserved seats were to be reserved for women belonging to SC and ST and a further 30 per cent of the total were to be reserved for women. These were not perceived as problematic. However, the Bill envisaged that the collector or the district magistrate would be in control, rather than the elected representatives. Not only would the district magistrate be in charge of revenue, law and order—their traditional regulatory role—at the *zilla* or district level, but according to the new amendment,

---

[57]Chandrashekar, B.K., 'Panchayati Raj Bill: The Real Flaw', *Economic and Political Weekly*, Vol. 24, No. 26 (1 July 1989), pp. 1433–1435.
[58]Pandey, R.N., 'Women's Contribution To The Economy Through Their Unpaid Household Work', National Institute for Public Finance and Policy, Working Paper, 2000, pp. 1–33, https://tinyurl.com/29bte2z2. Accessed on 18 July 2024.

they would also be responsible for the planning, execution and monitoring, giving the bureaucracy unaccountable power, similar to the Westminster constitutional guarantees adopted by some African nations, which failed miserably.

A better system would have been the one adopted in Karnataka, which had been functioning long before the amendment Bill was introduced, where the elected Zilla Parishad or District Council was supreme in both plan formulation and execution, the president of the Zilla Parishad, at par with the rank of a state minister, was the executive head, with the chief secretary, an IAS officer, being a subordinate. The district magistrate would continue in their traditional regulatory role.[59]

The bigger issue the prime minister faced was that the Opposition did not believe in the spirit of the Bill, namely, decentralization and empowerment, but saw it as another vote-catching endeavour, as they had seen the misuse of Article 356 of the Constitution—allowing for the imposition of President's Rule on any state on grounds of the failure of constitutional machinery—and thereby devaluing the power of elected state officials.

Yet another example was the Jawahar Rozgar Yojana, where the funds were sent directly to the district magistrate or the chief secretary of the Zilla Parishad, and not through state governments.[60] This implied direct control of the centre in state-level schemes, bypassing state governments. These schemes were increasing as percentage share of state schemes.

I had never cried at the defeat of any Bill. As a presiding officer, I always believed in acting like a referee in a football match. I did not kick the ball for any team—neither the

---

[59]Chandrashekar, B.K., op. cit.
[60]*Framework For Implementation of Pradhan Mantri Awaas Yojana-Gramin (PMAY-G)* (2022), 'History of Rural Housing Programme in India', Ministry of Rural Development, Government of India, pp. 1–2, https://tinyurl.com/mryma5nz. Accessed on 18 July 2024.

Opposition nor the ruling party. I only wanted to see that the game was played fair and free of fouls. However, the night the Panchayati Raj Bill was defeated, I cried. The MPs had not understood the injustice that was done to women. The Bill could have empowered women at the most basic level of society—to help them get trained in leadership and decision-making roles. India could have been a pioneer in this. Rajiv was assassinated before the Bill could be passed. The next prime ministers—V.P. Singh and Chandra Shekhar—were not sure of their governments and never bothered about women.

It was only when Narasimha Rao became Prime Minister and there was stability in the government that the Bill was reintroduced and Parliament ratified the 73rd and 74th Constitutional Amendments in December 1992. Local self-governance was established in rural and urban India as a result of these modifications and came into effect from 1993. The amendments mandated that women be represented in municipal authorities by at least one-third of the total seats (33 per cent reservation). The best thing was, all parties, regardless of political ideals and constitution, supported the Bill this time around. By now, public discourse in India had a wider reach. When women finally became empowered at the grassroots level, I started supporting the process of women's empowerment at the panchayat level. I felt, giving women reservation and posts in local bodies, as the panchayat or zilla parishad chairperson, was one thing. But the Bill also gave them budgetary powers, monetary authority and mandate to disburse funds to various projects and schemes.

It was necessary to invest in women's capacity building. We organized training camps within the parliament annexe where we trained the new elected panchayat women on management and accountability of allocated funds. With endeavours like this, my learning curve kept rising steadily. In 1992, I chaired the Conference of Women Parliamentarians of the Commonwealth Parliamentary Association in Delhi; I was deeply involved in work being done for women by the UN; I attended several sessions of the UN General Assembly and its committees as a member of the Indian delegation; in 1997, I headed the Indian delegation to the UN Commission on the Status of Women and was a special invitee to the World Women's Forum at Harvard University; I was Founder President of the UN Parliamentarians' Forum for Human Development and was nominated as UNDP Distinguished Ambassador of Human Development. All these experiences helped me understand the different barriers, visible and invisible, that keep women from reaching the upper echelons of leadership. The fundamental learning was that I came to see myself, and was seen by others too, as a leader.

At the level of Parliament, although women's representation had increased since Independence, it was still very low. In the Rajya Sabha, it had gone up from 6.9 per cent in 1952 to 11 per cent during my tenure. The average age of women members was early 50s. The youngest were Jayanthi Natarajan and Kumari Sushila Tiria, both 32 years old when elected in 1986.[61] Most women were college-educated and belonged to diverse fields. There were advocates like Chandrika Jain, Jayanthi Natarajan and Margaret Alva; artistes like Vyjayanthimala Bali, Shabana Azmi, Hema Malini and Lata Mangeshkar; social workers like Ela Bhatt, Nirmala Deshpande and Brinda Karat; educationists like Maragatham Chandrasekhar and P. Selvie Das; scientists like Asima Chatterjee and Syeda Anwara Taimur; and writers like Amrita Pritam. Many of them went on to receive esteemed honours such as the Bharat Ratna, the Padma Awards, the Magsaysay Award, the Right Livelihood Award, the Jnanpith Award, the Akademi Awards, the Shanti Swaroop Bhatnagar Award, and the National Film Awards, among others.

Despite their numerical inferiority, women made stellar contributions to the proceedings of the House and the national

---

[61] *Women Members of Rajya Sabha,* Secretary-General, Rajya Sabha, 2003, https://tinyurl.com/bddjjsds. Accessed on 18 July 2024.

cause during my time. For instance, in 1992, Sarla Maheshwari of the Communist Party (Marxist) exposed the Hawala security scandal during a Question Hour, causing nationwide turmoil. In 1991, Jayanthi Natarajan demanded during a Motion of Thanks on the President's Address that every plan should have a women's component, and every ministry a women's cell—finally included in 1997, in the Ninth Five-Year Plan. The unrelenting demand of educationists like Bharati Ray and others committed policymakers to pass the 93rd Constitution Amendment Bill in 2002, ensuring universal education for children.

Women members always supported Constitution Amendment Bills enthusiastically, because these brought in progressive socio-economic and political reforms in the country. During my time, women were vocal and active in parliamentary activities also through the system of committees: Purabi Mukhopadhyay, J. Jayalalithaa, Sushila Adivarekar and Manorama Pandey joined the Committee on Public Undertakings; Syeda Anwara Taimur, Jayanthi Natarajan, Kumari Chandrika Premji Kenia and Renuka Chowdhury were in the Committee on Environment and Forests; Kumari Sayeeda Khatun, Kamla Sinha, Chandrika Abhinandan Jain, Savita Sharda and S.G. Indira contributed to the Committee on Science and Technology. Members like Shabana Azmi not only voiced their arguments in the committees but also took them to the floor of the House.

SHARING AND SOLIDARITY

In September 1995, the UN's Fourth World Conference on Women was convened in China. It was last century's biggest congregation of women from across the world, with over 50,000 participants. I wanted all the women from both Houses of Parliament to attend the conference, take an active part in the World Plan of Action and implement it for the advancement of women in their constituencies. I used my good offices to invite Gertrude Mongella of Tanzania, then Secretary-General of the Conference, to India. At a lunch I hosted, I introduced her to Lok Sabha Speaker Shivraj Patil and Prime Minister Narasimha Rao. Almost conversationally, I launched into the possibility of a big delegation being sent from the Indian Parliament.

It was a bit of an arm twisting, because no such prior discussion had taken place. The prime minister and the speaker were caught off-guard, because the secretary-general of the conference was sitting with them. I asked the prime minister, 'Sir, how will you choose the team? I am not speaking for myself.' I added, 'I am going with the IPU team. I could always attend as Deputy Chairperson of the Rajya Sabha. I am speaking for all my women comrades.' It was after all the largest women's congregation of the century, and India was the world's largest democracy, I pointed out. The prime minister was quiet. I urged him to send all the women, noting that there were about 65 of them, and that we all should go. I explained that the recent Constitutional Amendments aimed at empowering women at the grassroots level provided an opportunity to demonstrate the strength of our democracy. He agreed to my request.

When we went to Beijing, India had a large delegation led by Madhavrao Scindia, then Minister for Human Resource Development. I was the deputy leader. India was, in fact, represented by the maximum number of women. Apart from parliamentarians, there were also members of women's NGOs with us. They had the chance to meet so many women from across the world and participated actively in the conference. We booked a small hotel in Beijing, and also got an Indian chef from one of the restaurants to make Indian food. Many others used to come over and eat there, because it was difficult to get Indian food in Beijing at the time. All the women were ecstatic with the experience, and very happy with me because I had stepped out of line to ensure their participation.

Beijing had a ripple effect. In the early 1980s, Janata Party

MP Pramila Dandavate had tabled a Bill as a private member, demanding 33 per cent reservation for women in Parliament and state legislatures. After the success of the 73rd and 74th Amendments empowering women at the panchayat level, and Beijing, I decided to push the envelope further. In 1996, on March 8—International Women's Day—I moved a resolution in the Rajya Sabha. Among other things, my resolution proposed adequate reservation of seats for women in Parliament and state legislatures. I noted that India had been part of the Drafting Committee at the UN Women's Conference in Beijing in 1995 and emphasized that we should ensure adequate representation of women in Parliament. I had discussed it with P.A. Sangma, the then Speaker, and coming from Northeast India, where women were known to be powerful, hard-working, confident and at the forefront of society, he was very keen on a positive outcome. The Rajya Sabha unanimously adopted it.

The same year, on 12 September, the 81st Constitution Amendment Bill was introduced by Prime Minister H.D. Deve Gowda's United Front government. The Bill provided for one-third of the seats in the Lok Sabha and state legislative assemblies to be reserved for women. So great was our enthusiasm that the women members of the Rajya Sabha pressed the prime minister to pass the Bill that very day. The prime minister agreed. When the discussion began in the Lok Sabha, and the prime minister was also there, the situation turned out to be quite different. The prime constituents of the United Front—Samajwadi Party, Janata Dal, Rashtriya Janata Dal—started opposing the Bill stridently. Somehow, they thought the Bill would be a threat to men. That sealed the fate of the Bill. It took eight different governments and several women's agitations across the country to make this Bill a reality in 2023.

The other resolution I moved in the Rajya Sabha, on 8 March 1997, was for a joint Parliamentary Committee on Empowerment of Women. Simultaneously, a similar resolution was moved in the Lok Sabha by Pratibha Patil. In April 1997, we constituted the committee with 30 members and I became its first Chairperson. As we started work on what our agenda and road map should be, it was decided that we should examine what programmes and policies were being taken forward for women's education, training and employment by each ministry. Apart from that, we decided that the committee would scrutinize the functioning of each ministry for their women employees.

I was particularly pleased with my contribution to this committee on gender responsive budgeting (GRB), which the Beijing Platform for Action had outlined. The GRB was not about separate budgets or increasing allocations for women, but about the inclusion of women in the planning exercise, and about the quality of expenditure. I felt GRBs were crucial because, by all parameters, women fared far worse than men in almost every sphere—from education and health to work participation, wage disparities, livelihood insecurity, access to land and other resources. I wrote to Manmohan Singh, then Minister of Finance, to inquire about women's share in the budget allocation, for our committee to review development policies and programmes aimed at women's empowerment. He asked me what gender budgeting was. I replied that he should implement it –first, and then I would explain how to go about it. India introduced GRB in 2005–06. African and Latin American countries had implemented GRB much earlier.

THE NEW DELHI DECLARATION

At the IPU, I proposed that there should be a follow-up to the Beijing Conference, with India hosting it. It was accepted. As a member of the organizing committee, I said that there should be both men and women as delegates from every parliament. Frene Ginwala, then Speaker of the National Assembly of South Africa, asked, 'Why are you asking for men to come?' I said that, with due apologies, in Beijing we had witnessed the largest congregation of women and formulated a plan of action, which now needed to be implemented, and that in most countries, people responsible for implementation are predominantly men, not women. I stressed that unless we involved them and asserted that it was time for them to make some space for us, they would not understand our needs. She agreed with me.

It was decided that every parliament from every country would send four delegates, two men and two women. Any country which had only one woman in its parliament was to send her and three men. And countries that did not have even a single woman were to send four men. Women came from Egypt, Iraq, Jordan and even the Gulf countries—countries considered backward for not having enough women parliamentarians. At least one or two women came from African and Latin American countries. Women had no voting rights in Kuwait; it was the only country to send four men.

The Specialized Inter-Parliamentary Conference was held from 14 to 18 February 1997 in New Delhi, with delegates participating from 78 countries. The conference was entirely devoted to one chapter of the Beijing Conference, 'Platform for Action', and titled 'Towards Partnership Between Men and Women in Politics'. In our Parliament, too, women worked in partnership with men to make the conference a success. The conference was inaugurated by Shankar Dayal Sharma, President of India, in the Central Hall of Parliament; the discussions were held at Vigyan Bhavan and the reception at The Ashok.

After four days of lively debates, exchanges, questioning and mutual enrichment, the participants agreed that women's arrival on the political stage would not lead to the exclusion of men, as some feared, but rather to the strengthening of the democratic process. What emerged from the conference was the New Delhi Declaration, with recommendations on the best ways to train women to exercise their political rights, to run an electoral campaign, obtain clean funds and deal with the media. Since women often did not contest elections due to lack of funds, the declaration highlighted financial support from the government for this. It was a knotty issue in many countries. Democracies where political parties had the list system were asked to place women at a higher level on the list. One pledge of the declaration was that every parliament should have a women's committee to look after women's issues.

∞

We had three chief guests, representing the three main regions of the world: Europe, Asia-Pacific and Africa. Two were women heads of state—Vigdís Finnbogadóttir from Iceland and Sheikh Hasina from Bangladesh—and the only man on the list was President Robert Mugabe from Zimbabwe. My association with Sheikh Hasina went back to the days of her father, Sheikh Mujibur Rahman, founder of modern-day Bangladesh. Both Akbar and I had supported the separation of East Pakistan (now Bangladesh) from West Pakistan (now Pakistan).

In the late 1960s, a delegation of three people came to India with evidence of atrocities and inhuman treatment of East Pakistanis by West Pakistan. On its eastern borders, India struggled with the influx of one million refugees fleeing the violence. This convinced many in India that we needed to support the independence of East Pakistan, after which India went to war with Pakistan, and Bangladesh was liberated in 1971. Prior to the liberation, Sheikh Mujibur Reham was under arrest in West Pakistan. After the liberation of Bangladesh, he was released. On his way to the newly formed Bangladesh, he had stopped at Bombay. Akbar, myself and the children had gone to receive him at Santa Cruz Airport.

Sheikh Hasina knew of our support from back then. Always gracious, when she became Prime Minister of Bangladesh and visited India, she asked me to pay her a visit. So, when I invited her to the conference to be a chief guest, and share the stage with the presidents of Iceland and Zimbabwe, she was delighted. We continued to be in touch and she also invited me officially to visit Bangladesh to meet and engage with members of their parliament and other leaders. This was a milestone in furthering diplomatic interests of India with a strategically important partner and neighbour.

ASIAN WOMEN LEADERS

Throughout my lifetime, I have witnessed a significant transition in women's political power. Since 1940, there have been 133 women who served as heads of state. Over the past 40 years, one of the most notable developments has been the rise of Asian women to the highest levels of political leadership—positions once dominated by men. This despite enduring sexism, misogyny, and gender stereotyping. Asia has had women leaders earlier than many advanced Western nations. For instance, Ceylon's (now Sri Lanka) Sirimavo Bandaranaike became the world's first female prime minister in 1960; her daughter Chandrika Bandaranaike Kumaratunga became President of Sri Lanka in 1994; Indira Gandhi served as Prime Minister of India four times, while Bangladesh's Sheikh Hasina and Begum Khaleda Zia have alternated as prime ministers since the 1980s, highlighting some of the subcontinent's female political figures in leadership positions.

In the new millennium, the trend of women in leadership positions has continued to grow, with an increasing number of countries electing female heads of state. Data from Pew Research indicates that the number of countries with women leaders has risen from less than 20 in the year 2000 to 59 today. Notably, many of these women come from political families, are well-educated, and emphasize the benefits of female leadership. Yet, fact is that women still hold relatively few top political positions globally, with only about 32 women serving as presidents or prime ministers and over 50 per cent of nations having never had a woman in such roles. However, research suggests that women's leadership often has positive outcomes such as reduced violence, improved living standards, legal reforms, and increased trust in democracy. This demonstrates that women's leadership is not confined to economically advanced democracies, as developing nations too have seen significant progress in this area.

10

THE WORLD AS MY FAMILY

Looking back, I could say that I had a protected childhood, but not overprotected. My family let me go about my activities without too much monitoring or too many restrictions. A confident, happy child, I loved ideas and action. I was especially cheerful outdoors, where I could withdraw into my own wonderful secret world for hours.

When I was about seven years old, several things clicked in my head, giving me a grand idea for action. Often, the world used to enter our living room through a box—a radio. On one such occasion, I heard on that radio that something called the 'United Nations' (UN) had been set up to make our lives and the world a better place. I did not understand what it meant, but I thought it sounded like something very important. So I asked my Khalajan, 'What does United Nations mean?' Being a teacher, she explained it to me beautifully: 'All the countries have joined hands to work together for a better world through this organization—the United Nations.'

Around the same time, my father had given me a toy spade and a little tin bucket, so I could do my own gardening. What added a special touch was a globe Nana, my maternal grandfather, had bought for us. He told us, 'Here is India and right across is America.' He had also pointed out New York, which I knew was home to the UN. All these became a potent mix in my head, firing up my imagination. I decided to dig a tunnel in our garden, so

I could go straight to New York and to the UN. At some point, Nana noticed the small hole I had dug and asked what I was up to. I said, 'I am digging a tunnel.' 'A tunnel? For what?' I said solemnly, 'I am making this tunnel to go to the UN in New York, America.' I did not like the laughter that greeted my answer: 'Why are you laughing?' 'Don't worry.' I was told. 'Continue digging your tunnel.'

Call it chance or causality, happenstance or hard work, destiny or divine intervention, but my life and work not only took me to New York and to the UN, but all around the world. My experiences taught me that one needed to have a vision for the future—for oneself, one's family, the community, the country, and for the world. The point was to catch a dream and nurture it. That's what made life great.

'VASUDHAIVA KUTUMBAKAM'

Ayaṃ nijaḥ paro veti gaṇanā laghucetasām.
Udāracaritānāṃ tu vasudhaiva kuṭumbakam.[62]

(This is mine, that is his, say the small minded.
The large-hearted believe the whole world is one family.)

This verse from the *Maha Upanishad* about an interconnected planet and living beings was engraved at the entrance of the Central Hall of Parliament. It greeted me every day. Of utmost salience was the phrase *'Vasudhaiva Kutumbakam,* meaning 'The world is one family,' that always reinforced a deep sense of expansion, as though the lines had suddenly stretched up to the sky, transporting me with them. I wasn't, however, always conscious that the phrase had transitioned from an intensely philosophical meditation to an enlivening political alternative in course of 3,500 years or more.

---

[62]In Kavishala, https://tinyurl.com/4da36z8b. Accessed on 18 July 2024.

It was inserted in the Preamble to our Constitution as 'world fraternity' by Dr Bhimrao Ramji Ambedkar. For Pandit Jawaharlal Nehru, it meant an amicable foreign policy culminating in the Non-Aligned Movement. Indira Gandhi invoked it in 1983 to say: 'Our world is small but it has room for all of us to live together in peace and beauty.'[63] For Rajiv Gandhi, it formed the credo of the 'earth citizen',[64] while Atal Bihari Vajpayee expanded it to mean our core human rights values. For Manmohan Singh, it marked India's approach to climate change and global warming. Under Narendra Modi, it became a diplomatic lexicon, a proud Indian mantra.

For me, however, *Vasudhaiva Kutumbakam* had a personal nuance. It played out in my life in a consistent and strikingly dynamic manner, opening up the world in stages.

The first stage came through my Arab ancestry. We had relatives who continued to live in Saudi Arabia. Although we had not seen most of them, I knew that two of my uncles held influential positions in the Saudi Government: Uncle Yousif Fazil was a sought-after person as Director of Passport Services, while Uncle Saleh Bakhuthma was Director of Expansion of Mosques in Mecca, the holiest and the most important city in the Muslim world.

The second stage of befriending the world began when I started undertaking foreign visits as a parliamentarian. One such visit was to Saskatchewan in the Canadian Prairies. I was part of the delegation for Commonwealth Parliamentary Association (CPA) conferences to be held at the cities of Saskatoon and Regina in September 1980. I was in a car with Balram Jakhar, then Speaker of the Lok Sabha, while 21 speakers of state assemblies followed

---

[63] *7th Summit Conference of Heads of State or Government of the Non-Aligned Movement, New Delhi, India, 7-12 March 1983*, https://tinyurl.com/mwurct75. Accessed on 6 August 2024.

[64] Palanithurai, G. (comp.), *Memorable Quotes from Rajiv Gandhi and on Rajiv Gandhi*, Concept Publishing Company, 2009, https://tinyurl.com/mwmre8rz. Accessed on 6 August 2024.

us in a bus. We travelled across vast stretches of wheat fields and occasional bushes, shrubs and homesteads, where a typical farming family lived surrounded by land, livestock and tractors. We stopped at one such homestead, and learnt that the size of the farm was 5,000 acres. 'How many people work here?' Jakhar asked. A farmer himself, he nearly choked on his coffee when the owner said, 'Two. My son and myself.' The marvel of mechanized farming!

More marvels were in store for us. The Indian Foreign Service (IFS) officer travelling with us went through the telephone directory to locate all the Shahs and Patels in the region. Even in the remotest places, he found at least 10–15 Indian families, mostly Gujarati, running grocery stores, motels and eateries. He called them up to say, 'Indian parliamentarians are in your town and would like to meet you.' Immediately, they invited us for lunch or dinner. He came back laughing, 'I have arranged for Indian food for you. Pure vegetarian. Don't worry, Sir.' Getting food of our choice was difficult. Jakhar was a pure vegetarian as were half the delegates. The rest of us were stumped because this part of Canada did not eat chicken, mutton or fish—just beef.

A TRIP TO PAKISTAN

My interactions with heads of states started long back, under Mrs Gandhi. One day in 1984, she called me and said that she wanted me to go to Pakistan for an international conference of women. I said, 'Madam, I am not really interested. My grandfather was not in favour of Partition. Although Pakistan is now a reality, still, I am not very keen.' She insisted: 'The relation between India and Pakistan is very strained. That's why I want you to go there.' When I went to Islamabad, Abdul Sattar, then Minister of Foreign Affairs of Pakistan, received me at the airport. At some point, he told me that he had arranged a meeting with General Zia-ul-Haq, President of Pakistan. I had not asked for one, but I could hardly refuse.

I had carried a few gifts with me and chose a box of carved

sandalwood from those for him. When I met the president, he was very cordial and offered me tea. Then he said, 'Why is India so much against us?' I said, 'India is not against you, Mr President. The thing is, the hijacker of the 1981 Indian Airlines flight, who demanded repatriation of imprisoned Sikh leaders, are staying in your country. They are spreading the propaganda that they are guests of your government and that you are against us.' He was taken aback and said, 'No, no, we are not against India. We want friendship.' I told him that it was sad and surprising that Indians visiting Pakistan needed to report to the police. 'That should not happen between two friendly countries.' I took up yet another sensitive issue: 'Our journalists want to visit Pakistan, but Mr President, you do not clear their visa applications. It is not something that India does to Pakistani journalists. In our country, there is so much of freedom, anybody can come. India is like an open book.' I could see that he was surprised again by my plain speaking.

Before leaving, I gave him the sandalwood box and said, 'Mr President, while presenting you this box, I would like to remind you that when Emperor Akbar was born, his father Humayun was in the wilderness, somewhere in this part of your country. He had nothing to give away, because he was not on the throne. So he took out a *mushk-e-nafa*—a pod of deer musk—and distributed it among his people, saying, "As long and as far as this fragrance goes, my son's fame too should go and remain." I am a guest to your country. I have nothing but this to give you—a sandalwood box from India. I hope, as long as the fragrance in the sandalwood remains, you will remember that a member of Parliament had come from India with a message of our goodwill.'

He was visibly moved by my comment. He did not know quite what to say. So he gave me a coffee table book, *Journey through Pakistan* by Mohamed Amin, Duncan Willetts and Graham Hancock. I told him, 'Mr President, now that you have given me this book, I think I can be free to move around in Pakistan, and not have to report to the police when I come to your country next?' He was smiling when I left him. When I joined Krishna Sharma, then Ambassador of India to Pakistan, in the car, he said, 'Mrs Heptulla, you had a great visit. I don't think anybody has ever spoken to the president in such a manner. I am going to send a message to Mrs Gandhi that your visit was very, very successful.'

He may have sent that message but Mrs Gandhi never received it. She was assassinated while I was still on that trip.

THE EMISSARY OF PRIME MINISTERS

Mrs Gandhi understood the depth of my knowledge of West Asia and that I invested time and energy to understand the dynamics of the Arab world. Ever since, the successive prime ministers I worked with—Rajiv Gandhi, V.P. Singh, Chandra Shekhar, P.V. Narasimha Rao and Atal Bihari Vajpayee—took into account my knowledge, analysis and contacts in most of their West Asia-related decisions. I was sent to meet global leaders, especially in West Asia—from King Hussein of Jordan to King Abdullah of Saudi Arabia—with messages from our prime ministers. These were not just goodwill visits.

In 1990, when the Gulf crisis was raging, Prime Minister Chandra Shekhar sent me to meet King Hussein of Jordan. My Congress colleagues told me, 'Why are you taking Chandra Shekhar's chestnut out of the fire?' I retorted, 'It is not Chandra Shekhar's chestnut, it is India's chestnut. If I can help serve the nation in any capacity, I will.' Around this time, Rajiv had undertaken a peace mission. When he returned to India, he made sarcastic comments to reporters about Chandra Shekhar's frequent trips to his farmhouse at Bhondsi in Haryana. I had a feeling that Chandra Shekhar would not last very long. Soon enough, two Haryana constables were found snooping around Rajiv's residence and Chandra Shekhar's government was brought down on charges of spying. I was upset. The charges were neither probed properly nor proven. I respected Chandra Shekhar. He was a superb orator and his commitment to India was unshakeable, but he did not get his due.

Around the time V.P. Singh became Prime Minister of India (1989–90), Pakistan was using a good deal of propaganda against India on the issue of Kashmir. They were going to all Islamic countries and holding forth on how we were exploiting the Kashmiri people. We were in a very vulnerable situation. One day, we were attending a conference at Vigyan Bhavan in Delhi. At some point, Shankar Dayal Sharma, then Vice President of India, was in the elevator with the prime minister. He was my immediate boss and also knew of my background. He told the prime minister casually, 'Najma knows the Arab people very well. Why don't you use her services?' V.P. Singh called me to his office and said that he wanted me to go to the Arab countries as his emissary.

I could not go without the permission of my party leader. Hence, I met Rajiv and sought his consent. I also told him that in August 1990 a meeting of the Organization of the Islamic Conference (OIC) was being held at Cairo. The OIC was a very influential platform of Islamic countries and its meeting was the best time to apprise the Arab world about the real situation— the propaganda, the misconceptions, the real villains behind the scene, the history and the background—which most of them did not know (as was confirmed later when I met them). Rajiv agreed, since it was in the larger interest of the country. I was ready to take up the assignment entrusted to me.

The task was not easy. I had to meet a number of heads of state and convince them about the reality of the propaganda being disseminated. I met King Hussein of Jordan, King Hassan of Morocco, Sheikh Sabah, Emir of Kuwait, and Hosni Mubarak, President of Egypt. In Saudi Arabia, I met Prince Sultan bin Abdulaziz Al Saud. I also got in touch with Abdullah Bin Omar Nasseef, the Secretary-General of the Muslim World League (or Rabitah Alam Islami), in Mecca. They all seemed to be under a false impression. Apparently, during the partition of India, it had been decided that enclaves with Muslims in India would go to Pakistan. I was astonished. Clearly, they did not know how India had been partitioned.

I said that they were mistaken if they thought there were significant Muslim and Hindu enclaves throughout India. I explained that in one village, there might be 20 Muslim homes and five Hindu homes, while in another village, there might be 20 Hindu homes and five Muslim homes, and so it was not possible for there to be traces of Pakistan all over India. I mentioned that Pakistan had given them this impression, but it was not true. I then elaborated on the circumstances surrounding Independence, detailing the events and what Muhammad Ali Jinnah was doing at the time. I clarified that these were extensive discussions. I pointed out that legally and constitutionally, Kashmir was part of India, noting that in 1947 Maharaja Hari Singh of Jammu and Kashmir had signed the Instrument of Accession, thereby allowing J&K to join India.

I reported that my visit had been successful and that it was clear that the Arab nations had come to understand the extent of the false information they had been given. I expressed my happiness, which was shared by the officials of the Ministry of External Affairs who had travelled with me. They prepared reports and sent them to every country I had visited. However, upon my return, I encountered the same questions I had faced after my visit to King Hussein of Jordan. Romesh Bhandari and Natwar Singh, the two advisors to Rajiv on foreign affairs, asked me why I had gone to those countries. I explained that it was because it was a serious issue, and my visit had been successful. I had met with the heads of state, presented the prime minister's letter, and managed to convince them of our strategic bilateral interests and shared values. Bhandari countered that this was not the point, and questioned why I had pulled V.P. Singh's chestnut out of the fire. I was shocked and replied that, first, I had obtained permission from Rajiv, who agreed that the country's interests should take precedence over party politics. Second, I emphasized that Kashmir was not V.P. Singh's chestnut alone; it was everyone's. I insisted that undertaking such missions for the country was more important to me than my own life or party affiliation.

※

In 1990, Saddam Hussein invaded Kuwait, marking the beginning of the Gulf War. By the time Chandra Shekhar became Prime Minister, the Gulf crisis had become a nightmare. Thousands of Indian expatriates were trapped in 'No Man's Land' on the Jordanian border, living in deplorable conditions in makeshift camps. There was rising anger in India with the government's inability to alleviate their plight. Under the V.P. Singh government, I.K. Gujral, then Minister of External Affairs, had gone to Baghdad to meet Saddam Hussein, but he returned with only a few Indian citizens, mainly people he knew.[65]

Bringing back the expatriates became top priority for the Chandra Shekhar government. He asked me to go to Jordan to meet King Hussein. When I went to Jordan (Amman), I was pleasantly surprised to discover that the then Crown Prince, Prince Hassan, was married to Princess Sarvath, who came from the distinguished Suhrawardy family of India. Her mother was from Calcutta and her father from Bhopal. Her paternal uncle was none other than Mohammad Hidayatullah, former Chief Justice of India, who had also served as Vice President and Acting President of India. I communicated to the King of Jordan the prime minister's request for better conditions for Indian expatriates and their speedy repatriation. Following our visit to Jordan, 170,000 expatriates were airlifted from Amman to Bombay between August and October 1990 via 488 Air India flights.

---

[65] Sreenivasan, T.P., 'Before Vande Bharat, India airlifted 1.7 lakh expats when Iraq annexed Kuwait in 1990', *Onmanorama*, 16 May 2020, https://tinyurl.com/2vbyb5bn. Accessed on 1 July 2024.

Even after Saddam Hussein withdrew from Kuwait, the tension continued. This was, however, around oil, which could now only be bought from Iraq, through a quota system sanctioned by the president of Iraq. In 2001, while I was sitting in my office in the Rajya Sabha, Jaswant Singh, Minister of External Affairs in the Vajpayee government, came to see me. He informed me that the prime minister had asked me to lead a delegation to Iraq for discussions on oil. I responded that as Minister of External Affairs, he should go instead, as I was not particularly fond of Saddam Hussein. Jaswant Singh clarified that it was a request from Atalji. Not wanting to upset Atalji, I sought Sonia's permission, explaining that although I was not enthusiastic about the request, Atalji was insisting on the trip. I asked Sonia if she would approve of my participation or if she would like to appoint someone like Natwar Singh to accompany me. Sonia gave her consent to me but decided not to send anyone else with the delegation.

Atalji had chosen nearly 100 people—from parliamentarians to business owners, academics to civil society members, politicians to the mullahs—for a three-day visit to Baghdad. Digvijay Singh, then Minister of State for External Affairs, was also part of the delegation. There were, however, no journalists. I asked Rajdeep Sardesai if he would like to come along. He said, 'Yes.' On September 4, a special Indian Airlines flight took us to Baghdad after the Ministry of External Affairs received the green signal from UN to undertake this travel, since there were sanctions on Iraq. We were received well. As leader of the delegation, I carried the prime minister's letter for the president of Iraq. This was also a successful trip.

When Prime Minister Rao and his Finance Minister Manmohan Singh were ushering in a comprehensive policy of economic reforms, they felt the need to send me on a diplomatic mission to forge new associations and alliances. Prime Minister Rao called me and said, 'Why don't you visit the West Asian countries and ask them to invest in India?' I went to the Gulf countries to apprise them about the great transformation taking place in the Indian economy—the open-door policy reforms. I travelled to Saudi Arabia and met Sheikh Ismail Abudawood, Chairman of the Saudi Chamber of Commerce, and proprietor of the Abudawood Group, whom I had met earlier during Mrs Gandhi's time. The meeting went off very well. He promised to ask the members of the chamber to invest in India, through joint ventures and foreign direct investment (FDI). He had organized a big lunch and took me to it.

When we entered, I was shocked to see that I was the only woman amidst at least 100 men. I had never felt more uncomfortable in a crowd as on that day. But the lunch was well organized. I was introduced to business magnets with offices all over the world. On 24 July 1991, Manmohan Singh presented the outline for economic reforms in his Budget. New trade policies promoting exports and removal of import controls gradually made the economy vibrant. Non-resident Indians started sending money to the motherland in droves, with Gulf countries ranking at the top. Saudi Arabia gradually emerged as one of India's major partners in bilateral investment, FDI and joint ventures.

LEARNING FROM THE UNITED NATIONS

The UN was the peg around which the fourth stage of my engagement with the world started. In 1983, the chance to go to the UN for three months came up. India used to send a delegation to the UN every year. That year, I was assigned work in the special political committee of the UN. I participated at different levels, especially in the drafting committee—a work I loved. This experience at the UN led to a lesson I never forgot—a parliamentarian should be involved in advocacy and diplomacy internationally to further India's interests more effectively rather than leave it solely to officials of the External Affairs Ministry. I realized that when parliamentarians are involved, it helps the government further its policy agenda in a more participative way. I became very involved with the UN and its agencies—UNESCO, UNDP, WHO, and also UNIFEM (United Nations Development Fund for Women). I was organizing and helping in conferences at the international level through the UN and the IPU, while at home, I was working with NGOs in various sectors: population control, human development, HIV-AIDS, environment and, of course, women's empowerment.

Around 1989–90, I met Mahbub ul Haq, the renowned Pakistani economist who had created the widely-respected Human Development Index (HDI) to measure development by well-being, rather than by financial income alone. At the time, he was serving as a special advisor to the UNDP in New York. One day, he invited me to his office. He was preparing the Human Development Report and asked me if I would like to get involved. He was particularly keen to get people's participation in his project. I said, 'India has a three-tier system of democracy—village panchayat, state assembly and Parliament. If we could involve the members at each tier, then the human development concept could spread among the people.'

I started working with the full cooperation of the UNDP. Yet, it was difficult. For instance, Manmohan Singh, then Finance Minister, used to mock me: 'What is this Human Development?' Brenda McSweeney, UN Resident Coordinator and UN Development Programme Resident Representative of the UNDP in India, faced similar resistance. Eventually, I had a breakthrough when Yashwant Sinha became Finance Minister. He cooperated and we were able to get people involved.

Naveen Patnaik was the first to give me a platform to launch the Human Development Report in Bhubaneswar. We then rolled it out across the country. The government started collecting data—how many schools were there, what was the educational status of the people, how was development taking place, and so on. A number of NGOs got involved and slowly the MPs came around. I became a Distinguished Human Development Ambassador for UNDP. In 1993, I set up the Parliamentarians' Forum for Human Development. It was very heartening when India's HDI started improving.

FROM UNITED NATIONS TO INTER-PARLIAMENTARY UNION

It was a short step from the UN to the IPU. Despite my involvement with the UN and all its international conferences, I had a little concern. I noticed a disconnect between the UN's focus on developing countries and the commitments of its members. Heads of states made commitments and adopted resolutions at the UN, but when it came to transfer of technology and resources to help the developing world, nobody came forward. Everything could remain at the level of tall promises, I rationalized, because the UN was an organization of governments.

When the heads of states came back to their parliaments, either they ratified the UN resolution or in some parliaments—like ours—the governments did not even need to do that. They could just inform their parliaments about the UN resolution and the commitment they had made. In contrast, the IPU was a parliament of the people, in which the ruling government as well as the Opposition were represented. Hence, the IPU as an organization could be involved in every negotiation on the ground.

Due to this conviction, my involvement with the IPU became intense, active and prolonged. We drafted a resolution in support of the United Nations Conference on Environment and Development (UNCED), the Earth Summit, in Rio de Janeiro, Brazil, in June 1992. One of the most daring programmes of action at Rio was Agenda 21, which called for new strategies to achieve sustainable development in the twenty-first century.

I firmly believed that the UN and the IPU should work hand in hand for any initiative of governments to be implemented on the ground. Hence, we organized a supportive conference at Yaounde, Cameroon, for the IPU member countries to commit themselves to Agenda 21. For any budgetary allocation towards protection of the environment, or any legislation to be passed in Parliament, they needed to be aware of the issues at hand, and be prepared in their own constituencies to deal with them. We also organized a follow-up conference at Brasilia in November to review the outcome: how far the IPU members had managed to implement Agenda 21. Eventually, with my efforts, the UN realized the importance of partnering with the IPU. The IPU received recognition, first as a UN Observer, and then obtained a place in the UN General Assembly to sit and participate. While achieving this, my personal horizon widened exponentially, broadening my view of the world and my role in it.

REFLECTIONS ON FRIENDSHIPS

As my horizons widened, I came to cherish and treasure many shades of friendship. They were not the great friendships of childhood, that came with the constant promise of availability and companionship. Instead, they were great friendships, of unspoken bonds and undocumented interactions. They were also intriguing, allowing friends to disappear from each other's lives for some time or forever—with fondness and no regrets. At a time when technology had not yet made relationships just a phone call or WhatsApp away, slices of memory sufficed.

A remarkable friendship developed in course of my work in the 1990s. I came to know Li Peng, fourth Premier of the People's Republic of China (1988–98), quite well through my work at the IPU. Although the Chinese economy had flourished during his long premiership, he was personally infamous for his role in the violent suppression of the Tiananmen Square demonstrations of 1989. When I came to know him, he was one of the most powerful figures in both the Communist Party and the government, for his position as Chairman of the National Legislature of China (NPC) as also in the Political Bureau.

At the beginning of the third millennium, the UN had decided to hold the Millennium Conference from 6 to 8 September 2000, at its headquarters in New York, to present a new development strategy for the twenty-first century. Starting in 1998, it had launched an information campaign preceding the conference. It was, at that time, the largest gathering of heads of state and governments. Complementing the UN's Millennium Conference, the IPU had also decided to organize a Millennium Conference at the same time in the UN, to be represented by heads of parliaments. In preparation for the IPU Millennium Conference of 2000, a drafting committee was constituted with 31 members.

We had a meeting at Geneva, Switzerland, at the IPU headquarters. Lord Meghnad Desai, celebrated economist and Labour Party leader in the UK, was also a member of this committee. We drafted our agenda and declaration to be adopted at the IPU's Millennium Conference. All member countries of the IPU accepted the declaration, and the drafting committee was dissolved.

Before IPU's Millennium Conference, and after the dissolution of the drafting committee, we had another conference at Amman in Jordan (the 103rd conference of the IPU on 30 April 2000). Here I came across Lu Shaye, Ambassador of China to France. He presented the best wishes of Li Peng and said that Li Peng had requested changes to the closed draft of the IPU Millennium Conference. I explained to him that it was not possible anymore to reopen the draft or to make any changes. The draft was approved, completed, signed and sealed.

Shaye then came to Geneva again with the same request. We humbly requested him not to ask for such a thing because it was not possible. Wherever I went, the Chinese delegation followed, with the same request. Each time, he started with the compliments of Li Peng, adding that 'India and China are very good friends,' before asking me about the status of Li Peng's suggestions. Finally, I got so tired of explaining that I told him, 'Ambassador Shaye, I know you have no courage to go and speak to Li Peng, because if you do, I am sure he will put you in Tiananmen Square. So, I will come to Beijing and explain to Li Peng. Alright?' He looked delighted and within two hours he came back to say, 'Madam, it is all fixed. Everything is organized.'

I went to China with a few of my teammates, and we were received by Shivshankar Menon, then Ambassador of India to China. Shaye and others, however, were already waiting with an enormous black limousine, with Indian and Chinese flags flying on both sides. To my shock, I saw four motorbike riders ahead of us, forming a convoy. Shaye informed me that I had a meeting with Li Peng at 6 p.m. that day. He then mentioned that there would be a banquet in my honour after the meeting, and I agreed. Shaye enquired about our meeting schedule for the next day. I questioned the necessity of the meeting, explaining that I planned to visit the Pearl Market to buy pearls and the Silk Market to buy silk. I wondered aloud why we would need to meet. He suggested it was for further discussions, but I reassured him that no further discussions would be necessary as I intended to close the deal with Li Peng that very day. Subsequently, he took us to the 7-Star China World Hotel.

Our small delegation was received by Li Peng and his wife Madam Zhu Lin. I explained to him that if I opened the resolution again for discussion, not only his two or three suggestions but hundreds of other suggestions would come in, and we would have to accommodate those. There were so many people we had to satisfy and they could all demand for the inclusion of fresh suggestions. And some of those could be a resolution against him. He said, 'Ok. Are you speaking at the next conference?' I said that the next conference was scheduled to be held at the UN headquarters in New York in September the same year, and I was opening it. 'Can you make my suggestions a part of your speech,' he asked. 'Done,' I said. 'But if you like, I can say these are your suggestions.' He started laughing: 'No, no, no, I don't want you to say that to anybody.'

In the years since that strange beginning, Li Peng became a very good friend. I heard him sing along to the famous Raj Kapoor song 'Mera Joota Hai Japani', watched him preside over sessions at the 2000 Millennium Summit of the UN in New York with other world leaders, have been witness to him holding wonderful programmes for the Indian delegation in China, and also arranging for us to visit Urumqi and Kashgar on the Silk Route and other historic places. I invited him to India and he came. He was given a grand reception at The Ashok. At my request, he addressed our parliamentarians. It was really a memorable relationship. It helped to further India's strategic and diplomatic interests with an important, but many a times an adversarial, neighbour.

—

The 105th IPU Conference at Havana, Cuba, in April 2001 was inaugurated by President Fidel Castro. I had met him earlier as an MP, but this time around I was President of the IPU. On stage, I moved a resolution condemning the destruction of the Bamiyan Buddha by the Taliban. I was so upset by the criminal vandalization of a world heritage that tears rolled down my face. Later, President Castro sent somebody for me. When I met him, he asked, 'Why were you crying, Mrs Heptulla?' I said, 'Mr President, that was a world heritage, the Bamiyan Buddha. I had seen it in Afghanistan many years ago. I know how magnificent it was.'

He invited us to the Palace of the Revolution the next day around 4 p.m. When we reached there, we saw at least 30–40 young people sitting around him, along with his cabinet colleagues and his brother Raúl. When we all sat down, Castro said something to them, which was translated to us: 'I want to discuss something with Dr Heptulla and I want you people to know about it.' He told them that I was crying as I moved the resolution on the Bamiyan Buddha. 'We don't know anything about Buddhism,' he pointed out. 'We don't know that part of the world.' And to my horror, he added, 'I would like her to speak to us about the various cultures and religions of India.' It was a difficult task, given India's complex history and culture spanning over 5,000 years and more.

I did not even have a piece of paper to refer to, yet I spoke until 10 p.m., answering questions all the while. A thick National Geographic atlas was brought in and I had to locate the places where the Buddha's message had spread: Kandahar and Bamiyan to the Thousand Caves of the Buddha in the mountains of Urumqi and Kashgar; Afghanistan, Indonesia, Malaysia, up to Japan, China, Tibet, Mongolia and all across Asia. President Castro also wanted to know more about Hinduism and Islam, the other two major religions of India. I also talked about Jainism, Zoroastrianism, the multiple languages and cultures, the richness and diversity of the fabric of India, which I explained was our strength, not our weakness.

Over dinner, President Castro said, 'We are so thankful to you because we do not know what is happening outside our part of the world. We are so involved with our own issues. I would not have known about the Bamiyan Buddha if it hadn't been destroyed by the Taliban.' He asked if I had been to all those places. I replied that I had visited most of them, including the Thousand Caves, Indonesia, Malaysia, Myanmar, Cambodia, and even Ulaanbaatar in Mongolia. I then explained my observation of a common pattern in India's presence outside the subcontinent, noting that India had never occupied an inch of any other land in its history. However, the spirit of India had travelled to all these places, and had influenced the ethos, minds, thoughts, and beliefs of the people there.

CELEBRATING THE TASTE OF THE WORLD

If I forayed into a world without borders, I was also up for an adventure into taste without borders. In my travels around the world, I uncovered different traditions, cultures, festivals and also unique dishes—not necessarily haute cuisine and crystalware, but the authentic foodways of a country, home-cooking at its best, but often with mysterious ingredients. I was served octopus in Tunisia, kangaroo meat in Australia, roasted wild antelope in Zimbabwe, snake meat in China, and crocodile delicacies elsewhere in Africa. Sometimes I enjoyed the food wholeheartedly. Sometimes I came up with ingenious ways of coping with unfamiliar food. And sometimes—just sometimes—I closed my eyes and swallowed the dishes that came my way. Fortunately, I was not a vegetarian, or else, I would have gone hungry frequently. My non-vegetarianism, however, had its limits.

At one of the IPU conferences, the Speaker of Mongolia, Natsagiin Bagabandi, invited me to visit his country. When the formal invitation arrived, it was for a conference-cum-workshop on democracy for the members of their parliament. Kushak Bakula, then Ambassador of India to Mongolia, and a former MP from Ladakh, came to receive me. He was also a revered monk in Mongolia. When we landed in Ulaanbaatar, the capital of Mongolia, we saw everybody at the airport, from the police to the travellers, prostrating in reverence. My friend Sheila Finestone whispered, 'Why has a monk come to receive us?' I told her, 'He is our ambassador here.' She said, 'Oh, you appoint monks as ambassadors?' I laughed out loud, 'Yes, anything that helps diplomacy. He is a parliamentarian as well as a Buddhist religious leader from Ladakh.'

After the conference, the president wanted to meet us. We were taken to a beautifully decorated tent, where everybody was sitting along two sides: one side was ours and the other side his. Behind us was a huge statue of the great Mongol empire-builder, Genghis

Khan. To my surprise, the president turned out to be the young speaker I had once met at a conference in Sweden. For days he had tried to arrange a meeting with me, but I had been very busy and only managed to meet him over coffee. He had discussed his desire to strengthen Mongolia's ties with India and host an IPU conference. Now, as president, he asked if I remembered him. I felt a bit embarrassed for making him wait previously but was touched by his humility and impressed by his decency and honour as a host.

While we were in conversation, some people started serving a milky drink in small glasses. Anders Johnsson, IPU Secretary-General, had a wicked sense of humour. He asked me loudly, 'Mrs Heptulla, do you know what it is made of?' The president said excitedly, 'It is the milk of a mare.' I had drunk the milk of a camel in Saudi Arabia. This seemed to top that experience. They explained how the drink was made. The custom was to ferment the milk for 15 days inside a sac made of goatskin or sheepskin, like a *mashak* I had seen villagers in Bhopal use to carry water. While I was hesitating to take a sip, Johnsson added, 'Mrs Heptulla, please drink up. It's very good for your complexion.' I vowed to make him pay for this later. For now, I drank and thanked God it was a really small glass. It was not so much the taste but the fact that it was something I was not used to. After all, we do drink the milk of a cow but don't really think about it. It seems very natural.

This wasn't the only experience of its kind. When Timoci Bavadra, former Prime Minister of Fiji, died in 1988, Rajiv asked me to represent India at his funeral. The day after the funeral, when I went to pay my condolences to his wife, something in a small cup was being passed around, with everyone taking a sip from the same cup. When it came to me after six people, I was told that it was a sacred ritual and I had to drink it. So I did not even ask what it was. I just closed my eyes and took a sip. It tasted like herbal tea of some kind. Those were the days before Covid. I don't think we could do this anymore, no matter how sacred a ritual is.

I tasted another kind of a drink when I was in King George

Island, in the Antarctica. We stayed in a very small hotel run by a family of three. The father would man the counter, the mother would cook, and the son would serve. And the entire day, I would see the boy drink something from a coconut shell with a straw that looked like a spoon. I asked him, 'What kind of spoon is that?' He said, 'It's a closed spoon, with holes in it.' He used it to draw in and sip a brownish liquid. He then gave me a similar spoon and some of that liquid, that tasted like our paan, except it was made from the bark of a tree, not a leaf. After trying it, I felt light in the head and became happy and energetic for the rest of the day. There were no after-effects, like a headache or nausea. He gifted me a beautiful silver spoon.

At another conference held at Burkina Faso, Ibrahim Traore, Speaker of Parliament, had hosted a special dinner for us. I wore their national dress, a very colourful and heavy ensemble which his wife had gifted me. There was rhythmic music and dancing with drums and djembes, in which I was invited to participate, much to the amusement of my IPU colleagues. As the night wore on, the music became louder—in fact so loud that we had to shout at the top of our voices to talk to each other. When the music suddenly stopped, much to our embarrassment, it seemed as if we were fighting with each other. When we sat down for dinner under a huge tree, I saw a big bowl containing something like green mulberry. We had a mulberry tree in Bhopal and I said, 'Oh, after a long time, I see mulberry.' I was about to reach out, when Sheila Finestone grabbed my hand and pinched me hard. She said, 'Najma, this is not mulberry but maggots.' 'Oh God,' I said. 'Sheila, I will thank you all my life for telling me what they are. I can't really make out in the dark and might have eaten it, quite unaware.'

Generally, I found Indian restaurants everywhere, even in the remote Saskatchewan prairies. At Ouagadougou, the capital of Burkina Faso, however, there was none. Yet, we did not miss out on Indian food, thanks to an enterprising Indian couple who came over from one of the neighbouring countries and opened a makeshift tin-shed restaurant, when they heard that a large international delegation was coming. It was clean and they served good Indian food. The couple did brisk business as many of the delegates ate there. I took Blaise Compaoré, President of Burkina Faso, and his wife there. Later, it became so popular that the couple built a proper restaurant and stayed back in Burkina Faso.

It has been a long journey for me. The little girl who tried to dig a tunnel to New York and the UN has turned grey navigating her way around the world. Starting with her mother's home-cooked *pasanda*—a culinary delight with flattened pieces of meat in browned onion gravy—she has learnt to celebrate world cultures through their cuisines. I have grown up in an extremely hospitable family, where the norm was to share food with people. That's why in 1986, when Mrs Raisa Gorbacheva wanted to know how the women of India and Russia could be brought closer, my first response was 'through food'—sharing food, learning and teaching each other's foodways.

It makes me happy that food is increasingly a part of what is being called soft power, a tool of public diplomacy, recognized by many countries. I can only conclude by saying that food is part of my identity as an Indian. It is my culture. It is food that brings me closer to my fellow Indians, whether from Maharashtra, Kerala, Kashmir or Manipur. I have much more in common with them than with my co-religionists elsewhere in the world. As my Dada Abba Maulana Azad used to say: 'It is culture that ultimately unites people, not religion or politics.'

Epilogue
AN ODE TO CHHIPKALIS AND MENDAKS

As this book, *In Pursuit of Democracy*, winds to a close, I am reminded of a certain day. I was young and doing my PhD. I travelled to Lucknow to attend a cousin's wedding. Being family, I arrived early to do my bit in the pre-wedding preparations. It was customary for the girl's family to offer ceremoniously packed gifts to the groom's family. Creatively inclined, I joined my cousins as they meticulously packed the gifts, decorating the baskets and boxes with silk ribbons and glitter paper.

When we were almost done, the father of the bride walked into the room. He seemed pleased at our efforts and proud to see the wealth he was effortlessly able to bestow on the groom's family. With great pride, he pointed out to me the value of the jewellery, the clothes, the trousseau, and the dowry he was giving his daughter at the time of her marriage. Unable to contain himself, he went a step further and said, partly in jest and partly in boastful arrogance, 'Take a good look at all these gifts. Your father will probably give you only *chhipkali*s (lizards) and *mendak*s (frogs) as your marriage gifts.'

It was not hard to understand his implications—that while he was equipping his daughter with a robust reputation of having come from wealth, the best my father could do was to send me out into the world with a PhD in zoology. At the time, I must admit, it hurt and I had tears in my eyes. I did not say anything out of respect for his age and seniority. What he said, however, stayed with me, boring a deep hole in my heart. I remember that stinging comment even today. Of course, now it only reminds me of all the strengths I have recognized within myself, those that have equipped me to make the most of my life.

My family was of humble means but they instilled in me a deep love and desire for learning, which I treasure even at this ripe old age. My education in 'chhipkalis and mendaks', as my uncle put it, developed in me a scientific bent of mind. I internalized an approach based on questioning, observation and hypothesis-testing before reaching any conclusion. If for any reason I found that an observation contradicted my conclusion, I had the ability to throw it all out and go back to the drawing board. The ability to think critically has influenced my approach to all aspects of life—in my role as a mother, a party worker, a parliamentarian, a presiding officer, or a citizen. Critical thinking is what has allowed me to survive for close to 40–45 years in a competitive 'man's world', with its dog-eat-dog mentality.

I also learnt that no matter the task at hand, it had to be done diligently, efficiently, whole-heartedly, with love and 'single-minded devotion'. As Dada Abba Maulana Azad always said, 'There are no small jobs or tasks; all jobs are equal.' Dada Abba always said, 'Whatever trade you take up, make yourself the best at it so that you are known for your trade and not your family.' A country cannot be run or a policy cannot be made by giving your 50 per cent or even 90 per cent, but by giving your infinity to it. That has been my guiding principle in life.

For the generations of tomorrow, my first and foremost advice is something I learnt as a young girl. Underlying all my achievements has been a deep commitment to education and learning. Knowledge is wealth, something nobody can take away from you. And knowledge can be power, if you know how to use it well. Knowledge also has no limitations—no beginning or end, no age or address, no language or gender. So, learn something every day.

For girls, remember, don't ever make 'being a girl' the reason for doing something or the excuse for not doing something. I truly believe women can do anything and everything, only if they want to. Growing up in Bhopal, I saw women rulers who could ride horses as well as fight with a sword. In the course of my work, I came across numerous strong, powerful women who, by dint of sheer merit and determination, led their country, worked with global organizations, or ran their own enterprises successfully. As I included in the Delhi Declaration of 1997, 'The time has come to make way for women.'

While it is widely believed that behind every successful man is a woman, I believe behind every successful woman is a man. I have long advocated that girls are more likely to pursue higher education and women are more likely to have successful careers when they have generous and supportive grandfathers, fathers, brothers, and husbands. My grandfather, father and my husband have not only treated women with respect, dignity and equality, but also taken care of children. It is only my husband's affection and trust that made it possible for me to work in a man's world, travel incessantly, and thrive in my career. Hence, for boys and young men, my only word of advice is—treat the girls and women in your life as your equal and they can be your strength. Women carry the next generation. It is very important that the lap on which a child is reared is lined with love, care, knowledge and education.

Finally, if you have the will and desire, you will achieve your dream. Nothing is impossible: I wanted to see the world and I saw the world. Always look ahead, never back. Yesterday is gone, today is yours. Do your work and plan for tomorrow.

For all future generations, a poem by writer, philosopher and politician Muhammad Iqbal, one that has guided my life, sums up wonderfully my wish for you:

Khudi ko kar buland itna ke har taqder se pehle
Khuda bande se khud pooche bata teri raza kya hai.

My interpretation of Iqbal's couplet is:

> Live so beautifully that if death is the end of life,
> God may feel sorry for having ended thy career.

Here is another poem, 'How Old Are You?' by H.S. Fritsch, that I always recount to my young friends:

> Age is a quality of mind.

> If you have left your dreams behind,
> If hope is cold,
> If you no longer look ahead,
> If your ambitions' fires are dead,
> Then you are old.

> But if from life you take the best,
> And if in life you keep the jest,
> If love you hold;
> No matter how the years go by,
> No matter how the birthdays fly,
> You are not old.

ACKNOWLEDGEMENTS

In 2021, I was faced with a daunting health crisis that left me feeling drained and defeated. In those darkest moments, my youngest daughter Asma urged me to pen my memoirs, and she would not take no for an answer. Recalling my journey and recounting it took me back to my childhood, through the triumphs and tribulations of my career, and made me revisit the mentors and milestones that shaped me. As I embarked on this reflective odyssey, a remarkable transformation unfolded in me—with each written page, my health began to rebound, and my spirit revived. I owe a debt of gratitude to Asma for nudging me towards this cathartic journey, which has not only birthed this book but also gifted me a new lease of life.

I am grateful to the countless individuals who have shaped my life over the past eight decades. While acknowledging each one of them here would be difficult for lack of space, I must express my heartfelt thanks to all those who had a profound impact on me.

First and foremost, I thank my parents Fatima and Syed Yousuf Ali and my aunt Aysha Ansari for their unwavering support, guidance, and trust. Their generosity and kindness have always enabled me to face challenges with courage and humility.

I am deeply grateful to my loving husband, Akbar Ali Heptulla, whose wise counsel, unwavering trust, and steadfast support have been a constant source of strength. His guidance has illuminated my path, and I cherish his presence in my life.

I also want to express my heartfelt gratitude to my three incredible, beautiful, ferociously strong and independent daughters—Rubina, Sheba and Asma—whose infinite patience and resilience have allowed me to pursue my commitment to my country, even when it meant sacrificing precious moments with them. I hope that this book fills them with pride, knowing that the journey has been worth it.

I extend my sincere thanks to Sharad Pawar for his gracious Foreword and to Honourable Ram Nath Kovind, former President of India, Nitin Gadkari, Nirmala Sitharaman, Ghulam Nabi Azad, Aamir Khan, Rajdeep Sardesai, and Aditi Phadnis for their kind endorsements.

I would like to give special thanks to Joanna Punjabi, who has been a lighthouse guiding this project to safe harbour. I would also like to acknowledge Hamdi Attia for a beautiful rendering of the old Parliament House; 'Pealing Memory' truly embodies the emotions of achievement and loss.

I am extremely grateful to Kapish Mehra, Managing Director of Rupa, and his wonderful team at Rupa Publications, including Yamini Chowdhury, Rohan Datta and the copy, design and quality editors, for their tireless efforts in making my life's story take shape in this book.

I am especially indebted to Damayanti Datta, Arvind Mayaram, Rolinda Farooqi, Sami Ur Rahman, and Ningombam Nilamani, helping me through the process of researching, recollecting, recording, collating and organizing my thoughts and memories from years past.

I would also like to thank the many men and women at the Rajya Sabha Secretariat, Library, Television and many other departments whose hard work and dedication ensure the protection, preservation and continuation of our nation's most important history for all future generations. I would like to acknowledge Sayed Sarfarz Husain, video librarian at Sansad Television, for his support.

I would also like to acknowledge my friends Suresh and Damayanti Hatiwalla, who have read and reread many versions of this manuscript and offered invaluable feedback and commentary. Finally I would like to thank Sajid Malik for his support over the years.

Thank you all for your contributions, which have made this book possible.

ANNEXURE

Here are some more extracts of the most memorable mentions from members across political parties when Dr Najma Heptulla was re-elected in 1988, as taken from the Rajya Sabha archives:

Samar Mukherjee, Member of Polit Bureau, Communist Party of India (Marxist), and General Secretary, Centre of Indian Trade Unions (CITU), West Bengal: '[…] I congratulate Mrs Heptulla on her being unanimously elected as Deputy Chairman […] She will have to tackle this House which sometimes become, so turbulent […] Able tackling and impartiality are the requirements of the present situation if really democracy is to be upheld.'[66]

P. Upendra, Member of Telegu Desam Party, Andhra Pradesh, and General Secretary of the National Front: 'Yesterday, we had proposed a name from the Opposition side […] But the moment we came to know that she was the choice of the ruling party, we were quick to retrace our step. That shows she could charm the Opposition […] When she was moved from here for a party assignment, I had my own doubts whether such a sophisticated person would fit in the humdrum of the political office [… So] we are very happy that she is here to conduct the proceedings of the House and if she has lost any objectivity during her small assignment in the party office, I am sure she would regain it very soon and be fair to all sections of the House. When some Members like me came new to the House, we had the privilege of being

---

[66]POI, Election Of Deputy Chairman, PARLIAMENT OF INDIA, OFFICIAL DEBATES OF RAJYA SABHA, 18 November 1988, pp. 277–295, https://tinyurl.com/2s4z452b. Accessed on 1 July 2024.

guided by her and she knew the art of moulding the ebullient and the irrepressible [...] Whenever she found somebody was going to be troublesome, she used to call him for dinner [...], feed us fully with biryani and *firni* [...] Sir, she could handle the proceedings of the House with great tact and objectivity and with a sense of fairness. Coming from an illustrious family, the family of the great Maulanaji, it is an added qualification for her [...].'[67]

Aladi Aruna, alias V. Arunachalam, Member of All India Anna Dravida Munnetra Kazhagam, Tamil Nadu: 'We are aware of the fact that in political life [...] a few establish their prudence, wisdom and knowledge. I frankly admit that Mrs Najma Heptulla is one amongst them [...] Maulana Azad wrote *India Wins Freedom*; our Najma has created a record by her deed and demeanour: she has won the Opposition. To administer an elected body, especially Rajya Sabha, is not an easy task because the Chair has to deal with equals. It requires patience, tolerance and eminence [...] The Chair has to decide what is reasonable in the midst of controversy and various interpretations [...] I honestly believe that she will be very successful in her task.'[68]

G. Swaminathan, All India Anna Dravida Munnetra Kazhagam, Tamil Nadu: 'I had an opportunity of meeting her when I was one of the Presiding Officers of Tamil Nadu in one of the conferences which was held in Ooty [...] We were really surprised to see a young lady [and] we were all very much impressed not only by her erudition, by her cleverness and her parliamentary acumen, but also by her presence [...].'[69]

Ghulam Rasool Matto, National Conference, Jammu and Kashmir: 'I extend Dr Najma Heptulla heartiest congratulations [...] When she was first elected as the Deputy Chairman, [...] she said, though she belonged to the Congress Party, but when she will be in the Chair, she will think that she is [...] the custodian of the

---

[67] Ibid.
[68] Ibid.
[69] Ibid.

entire House [...] She has known every Member by name and even closely [...] I hope that she will live up to the traditions that she had set forth here in the House during her previous term as also the genetic genealogy she has inherited from the great Maulana Abul Kalam Azad.'[70]

Bijoya Chakravarty, Bharatiya Janata Party, Assam: 'In my two-and-a-half years of Parliamentary life, I came in contact with Najmaji on many occasions. Probably, I have hardly met such a scholarly lady with dignity and grace, who has commanded the confidence of the entire House. We women feel greatly flattered when we see one of us being elected to the high office of Deputy Chairman, and that too unanimously, in a House where women are in a negligible minority.'[71]

Jagesh Desai, Congress, Maharashtra: 'I am very happy that Najmaji has become the Deputy Chairman. We have worked together in Bombay. I have seen her quality. She has a very intelligent and a very tactful attitude. She has the ability to solve every problem. I am also happy for the reason that she is my sister. On every Rakhi Day, she ties a rakhi on my hand. On many occasions, tempers run high in the House. I am sure, with her smiling face, tempers will cool down and tension will disappear.'[72]

---

[70] Ibid.
[71] Ibid.
[72] Ibid.

INDEX

9/11 attack on, World Trade Centre, USA, 140
9th Asian Games, 72
17-point programme, 168
20-Point Programme, 60
33 per cent reservation for women, 172, 176
52nd Constitutional Amendment, 83
64th Constitutional Amendment, 3, 169
73rd Constitutional Amendment, 172, 176
74th Constitutional Amendment, 172, 176
81st Constitution Amendment Bill, 176
93rd Constitution Amendment Bill, 174
102nd Inter-Parliamentary Conference, 126
103rd Conference of the IPU, 196
105th Indian Science Congress, 2018, 154
1972 Shimla Agreement, 70
1977 general elections, 48
1978 Camp David Accord, 76
1980 general elections, 49, 65–6, 77
1989 general elections, 104
1991 general elections, 115
1996 general elections, 133
2002 Gujarat election, 124
2011 Census of India, 144

Aamna Begum, father's eldest sister, 19
Abbas, Khwaja Ahmad, 37
Abdullah, Dr Farooq, 87, 89, 168
Abdullah, T.T.P., 73–4, 77
Abudawood Group, 77, 192
Abudawood, Sheikh Ismail Ali, 77, 192
Abul Kalam, xii, 10–11, 148
Abun Nasir, 10
abuse, 61, 109, 167–8
academic background, 40
academic career, 9
Acting Chairman, 102, 117
active politics, 38, 150
activism, 7, 20
Adivarekar, Sushila, 174
adjournment of the House, 104
adult education, 60
advanced democracies, 181
Advani, Lal Krishna, 102–3, 114, 119, 136
Afghan dynasty, 12
Afghanistan, 9, 198–9
Africa, 43, 127, 177, 179, 200
African countries/nations, 171 177–8
Agarwal, Sudarshan, 84–5
agrarian economy, 47
A History of the World in 100 Objects, xi
Ahmedabad, 14, 123
Ahmed, Fakhruddin Ali, President of India, 59
Ahmednagar Jail, Maharashtra, 21
Airports Authority of India Bill, 83
Akademi Awards, 173

Akbar, my husband, 33–8, 49, 59, 66–7, 73, 179
Akhtar, Jan Nisar, 18
Akhtar, Javed, 18
Akhtar, my brother, 14
Al-Ahram, 76
Al-Ameen Mission, 144
Al-Balagh, 11
Al-Hilal, 11
Aligarh, 6, 13, 18, 145
Aligarh Muslim University, 13, 18, 145
Allahabad High Court, 59
Allahabad (now Prayagraj), 21, 34, 59, 65, 115
All India Anna Dravida Munnetra Kazhagam, 62
All India Congress Committee (AICC), 45
All India Council for Technical Education (AICTE), 21
All India Institute of Medical Sciences (AIIMS), 80
All-India Muslim Women's Conference, 6
Alpa Bachat (small-saving) programme, 166
Alva, Margaret, 82–3, 94, 173
Ambedkar, Dr Bhimrao Ramji, 184
Amchi Mati Amchi Mansan, 72
America, 182, 183
American Heart Journal, The, 29
ancestry, 24, 163, 184
Annan, Kofi, then UN Secretary-General, 126
Ansari, Moulvi Iftikhar Hussain, 86
Antarctica, 74, 202
Anti-Defection Law (ALD), 83
Antulay, A.R., Chief Minister of Maharashtra, 67
Anwar, Tariq, 130
Arab countries, 44, 188
Arab diplomatic community, 65
Arabian Sea, 142
Arabic language, 7, 125, 147–8

Arabic manuscripts, 147–8
Arab League, 76
Arab News, 78
Arab Peninsula, 91
Arab purchasing power, 75
arms and ammunition, 150
arms purchase aid to Pakistan, 80
Article 40 of the Constitution of India, 170
Article 105 of the Constitution of India, 99
Article 356 of the Constitution of India, 171
arts and crafts, 6, 12, 145–6, 154
Aruna Asaf Ali, 37
Arundale, Rukmini Devi, 42
Asaf Ali, 37
Asha Bhabi, 35–6
Ashoka, Mauryan emperor, 34
Asia, 43, 75, 77, 125, 179–80, 187, 199
Asian Games, 71–2, 149
Asian tsunami, 122
Asian women leaders, 180
Asma, daughter, 64, 157
Assam, 149, 154
Assam Rifles training camp, 154
assassination, xv, 4, 51, 76, 81, 115–6, 118, 132, 139, 172, 187
assessments of West Asia, 77
Association of Muslim Doctors, 144
associations, 118, 145, 191
atheism, 11
Australia, 155, 200
autonomous government organization, 74
Awaara, 37
award for Outstanding Parliamentarian, 97
Aysha Ansari (Chhoti Khalajan), mother's sister, 7–9, 17–19, 25, 182
Azad, Ghulam Nabi, 89, 134
Azad, Maulana Abul Kalam xii, 10–11, 14, 17, 19–25, 31, 37–8, 86, 135, 137, 148, 151, 185, 203, 206–7,

Index

Azmi, Shabana, 103, 173–4

Bada Talab, 8, 11, 14
Bagabandi, Natsagiin, 200
Bakht, Sikander, 114, 137
Bakhuthma, Saleh, 184
Bakula, Kushak, 200
Bali, Vyjayanthimala, 103, 173
Bamiyan Buddha, destruction of the, 198–9
Bandaranaike, Sirimavo, 180
Banerjee, Mamata, 5
Bangladesh (East Pakistan), 22, 70, 148, 179–80
banking scam, 112
Bar Lev Line, 75–6
Bareilly, 34
Barkley, Dr, 13
Bashir, Mian, 87
Bavadra, Timoci, 201
BBC Radio, xi
Begin, Menachem, 76
Begum Khaleda Zia, 180
Begum Maimoona Sultan, 33
Begum Sultan Jahan, 17
Begums of Bhopal: A History of the Princely State of Bhopal, The, 14
Beijing, 175–8, 197
Beijing Platform for Action, 177
Berlin, 126, 129
betrayal, 64, 76
Beyond Survival: Emerging Dimensions of Indian Economy, 90
Bhagat, H.K.L., 82, 102
Bhaijaan, 27, 28, 31, 33, 68
Bhandari, Romesh, 189
Bharat Heavy Electricals Limited, Bhopal, 28
Bharatiya Janata Party (BJP), xiv, 86, 95, 99, 103, 108, 114, 117, 119, 124, 135–7, 151
Bhatnagar, Professor S.P., 27
Bhatt, Ela, 103, 173
Bhindranwale, Jarnail Singh, 50

Bhopal, xi–xii, 5–8, 11–14, 17–18, 20–21, 23, 25–6, 28, 30–35, 43–4, 74, 95, 133, 163–4, 190, 201–2, 207
Bhopali dishes, 15
Bhopal Lake, 8, 164
Bhopal society, 13
Bhuj earthquake in 2001, 122
Bihar, 40, 109, 120
bilateral investment, 192
bilateral relations, 78
biodiversity, 149
bipartisanship, 23
Birkinshaw, Matt, 40
birth of Pakistan, 22
birthday gift, 25
Bisariya, Raja Awadh Narain, 13
black-and-white programme, 72
black marketing, 56
Blitz, 37
blockades, 150–51
Board of Control for Cricket in India, 12
Bofors scandal, 94, 101, 104
Bohra Muslim community, 33, 124, 143
Bohra Shia Muslims, 31
Bombay (now Mumbai), xiii, 9, 19, 30–32, 34–8, 40–44, 49, 51, 55, 57, 59, 61, 63–6, 68, 92, 95, 104, 114, 119, 123, 141–3, 149, 165, 179, 190
Bombay film industry, 19, 37
Bombay Pradesh Congress Committee, 38
Bombay Spinning and Weaving Company, 57
Bose, Dr, family physician, 13
Bosnia, 22
Bourbons and the Begums of Bhopal: The Forgotten History, 14
Bourbon, Sheila, 13
Brazil, 128, 194
bribery, 111
brinkmanship, 48
Britain, 39
British Empire, 20, 73

British government, 11, 65
British Museum, xi
British policies, 11
Buddhism, 199
Buddhist monuments, 34
Buddhists, 144
Bukhari, Maulana Syed Abdullah, Shahi Imam of Delhi's Jama Masjid, 61
Bundestag, 126
bureaucracy, 171
Burkina Faso, 140, 202–3
Burmese invasion of Manipur, 159
burqa, 7
business ethics, 31
business of governing the nation, 23

Calcutta (now Kolkata), then the capital of India, 10–11, 14, 149, 155, 190
Calling Attention motion, 107
camaraderie, 101, 135–6
Cambodia, 199
Cambridge School, Bhopal, 8, 17
Cameron, David, 39
campaign meetings, 115
capacity building, 167, 172
Capote, Truman, xiv
career, 8, 89, 99, 207
career in politics, 118
Carter, Jimmy, 76
Castro, Fidel, President of Cuba, 198–9
CBI, 111
Central Bombay, 40
Central Hall of Parliament, xii, 22, 102, 109, 178, 183
Central India, xii, 11, 34
central universities, 145
Chahi Taret Khuntakpa (Seven Years Devastation), 159
Chairman of the Committee of Privileges, 109–10
Chairman of the Indo-Arab Society, 95
Chairperson of the IPU Executive Committee, 126
Chandra, Bipan, 45
Chandrasekhar, Maragatham, 173
Chandrashekar, B.K., 170–71
Chandra Shekhar, 91, 104, 172, 187–8, 190
Channer, Philip, 81
Chanu, Mirabai, 149
Chanu, Sushila, 149
charkha (spinning wheel), 25
Chatterjee, Asima, 173
Chavan-Naik dominance, 48
Chavan, P., 166
Chavan, S.B., 48
Chavan, Yashwantrao Balwantrao (Y.B.), 45–51, 91
Chechnya, 22
Chhachhi, Amrita, 58
Chhota Talab, 11, 26
Chibber, Maneesh, 45
Chief Election Commissioner (CEC), 170
childhood, xi, xiii, 19, 27, 182, 195
China, People's Republic of, 39, 46, 73, 145, 148, 174, 195–200
Chinese economy, 195
Chinese language, 125
Choudhury, A.B.A. Ghani Khan, 85
Chowdhury, Renuka, 174
Chowk Bazar, 13
Christianity, 148
Christmas, 14, 156–7
Christmas festival, 14, 156–7
civil services, 146
climate change, 39, 73, 184
coalition government, 48–49, 104
Coffee (Amendment) Bill, 84
Cold War, 43
collective decision of the House, 111
colonial policy, 16
colonial rule, 11, 21
colonialism, 24
Committee of Privileges, 96, 109–10

Committee on Environment and Forests, 174
Committee on Public Undertakings, 174
Committee on Science and Technology, 174
Commonwealth, 93, 95, 101, 149, 172, 184
Commonwealth Parliamentary Association (CPA), 93, 95, 172, 184
communal riots, 124
communal tensions, 114
Communist parties, 117
Communist Party of India (CPI), 62, 114
Communist Party of India (Marxist) {CPI (M)}, 98, 174
Communist Party of the Soviet Union, 91
Compagnie Française des Pétroles (CFP), 63
Compaoré, Blaise, 203
Comptroller and Auditor General of India (CAG), 170
Conference of Women Parliamentarians of the Commonwealth Parliamentary Association, 172
confidence-building, 165
Congress culture, 131
Congress (I), 48, 50, 64
Congress (Indira), 64
Congress Legislative Party (CLP) in Kashmir, 86
Congress Parliamentary Party (CPP), 131, 132
Congress Party, xiii–iv, 4, 21, 30, 37–8, 41, 44–6, 48, 50, 62, 64, 67, 81, 83, 85–6, 88–91, 93, 99, 102, 104–5, 107, 109–11, 113, 115, 117–8, 129–37, 154, 168, 170, 187
Congress (R), 45–6, 64
Congress split, 46, 130
Congress (U), 48

Congress Varnika, 85
Constituent Assembly of India, 22
Constitutional Amendments, 172, 175
constitutional guarantees, 171
Constitution Amendment Bills, 174
Constitution of India, 83, 99, 112–3, 127, 169–71, 174, 176, 184
control of the Suez Canal, 75
Convention on the Elimination of All Forms of Discrimination against Women (CEDAW), 169
conviction, 22, 136, 166, 194
cooking, 8, 57, 166, 200
cooperation, xiii, 96, 98, 104, 122, 125, 193
cooperative movement, 47, 48
corruption, 63, 94, 133
cottage industry, 42
Council of Scientific & Industrial Research (CSIR), 28, 73
Council of States, 99, 101
Council of the IPU, 126–7
coup d'état in Pakistan, 127
Covid, 157, 201
CPA Conference of Speakers and Presiding Officers, 93
creation of Bangladesh, 22, 70
cricket, 5, 12, 15, 138
crimes against humanity, xv
criminal conspiracy, 63
crochet, 8
culinary culture, 31
cultural immersion, 43
cultural inheritance, 43
culture(s), 12, 18, 21–2, 31, 44, 92, 105, 129, 131, 135, 146, 149, 154, 158, 159, 199–200, 203
custodian of the dignity of the House, 106

Dadi, Maulana Azad's elder sister, 31
Dairatul Ma'arifil, Osmania University, 147
dance, 149, 154, 156–7, 158

Dandavate, Pramila, 176
Dasgupta, Gurudas, 107, 114
Das, P. Selvie, 173
decentralization, 171
decision-making process, 71
decorum, 105–6
de facto border, 87
defence expenditures, 136
Defence of India Act, 1915, 11
Delhi Declaration of 1997, 207
Delhi Police, 139
Delhi politics, 47
Demand for Grants, 100
demand for representation of women in elected bodies, 169
demands for special status for J&K, 87
Demirel, Süleyman, then President of Turkey, 140
democracy, xii, xiii, 3, 5, 21, 45, 61, 77, 93, 97, 116, 125, 135, 169, 175, 181, 193, 200
democratic leadership, 135
democratic Parliament, 120
democratic politics, 91
democratic right, 4
democratic society, 128
democratic values, 107
Deputy Chairperson of the Rajya Sabha, xiii, 3, 82–3, 86, 93–4, 96–9, 101, 110, 117–8, 123, 132, 135, 137, 175
Deputy Leader of a delegation to Guatemala, 125
Desai, Jagesh, 84
Desai, Morarji, 44, 48, 62
desalination, 74, 79
descendants of the family, 10
Deshpande, Nirmala, 173
Deshpande, Prachi, 46
Deve Gowda, H.D., 176
developing countries, 43, 81, 194
developmental work, 121
development economics, 42
development of Bhopal, 14

development policies, 177
Dharti Ke Laal, 37
Dhawan, R.K., 50, 87
Dialogue, 92
dignity, xiii, 99, 106, 168, 207
Dikshit, Sheila, 80, 102
diplomacy, 12, 21, 151, 192, 200, 203
diplomatic mission, 191
Director of Girls' Education, Bhopal, 6
discrimination, 17, 59, 165
discussions and debates on foreign policy, 84
dissertation, 26–7
Diwali festival, 119, 156–7
Dogra, Girdhari Lal, 86
Doon School, Dehradun, 25
Doordarshan, 72, 138
dowry, 27, 41, 60, 205
dowry, abolition of, 60
drugs, 150, 167
Dutta, Prabhash K., 45

East India Company, 14
East Pakistan (now Bangladesh), 179
economic aid, 78
Economic and Political Weekly, 46, 58, 170
economic reforms, 133, 191–2
Economic Times, The, 61
economy, 47, 60, 78, 166, 168, 192, 195
Editor-in-Chief of *Hamari Goshthi*, 95
educated women, 5, 24, 95
education, xii, 10, 12, 21, 41, 43, 60, 72, 125, 144–6, 174, 177, 206–7
Egypt, 43, 75–6, 178, 188
Egypt-Israel peace agreement, 76
Eid festival, 14, 35, 156
election campaign(s), 55, 63, 65, 178
Election Commission of India, 81
electoral malpractice, 59
electoral politics, 37
Eliot, T.S., xi
embroidery, 6, 8
Emergency, declaration of the, 59–62, 131

Emergency powers, 61
Emotional Impact: Passionate Leaders and Corporate Transformation, 81
Emperor Akbar, 186
employment, 17, 155, 177
empowerment, 3, 5, 41, 119, 169, 171–2, 177, 193
end of the road with Congress, 134
engagement, 31, 39, 151, 192
England, 5, 98, 138
English language, 78, 82, 92, 125, 145
entrepreneurship, 6, 146
environmental problems, 72
environmental studies, 69
environment and resource management, 71
Environment Committee of the IPU, 125
equality, xiv, 56, 128, 207
equality of women, 128
equal wages for equal work, 58–9
eradication of the caste system, 60
esteemed Anatomical Record in Philadelphia, 29
ethnic groups, 150
ethnicities, 41
ethnic violence, 149
ET Online, 61
Europe, 75, 77, 179
European countries, 127
European powers, 75
excessive power, xiii, 90
exchange programme, 100
exhibition(s), 7, 146–7

factionalism, 48
Fahad, Crown Prince, 79
Faiz, 18
familial ties, 132
family, 5, 7, 9, 17, 23, 26, 28, 32, 34, 43–4, 89, 117, 123
family connections, 37
family conversation, 19
family gathering, 19

family planning (limiting to two children), 60
family responsibilities, 32, 67
family tragedy, 29
family-work balance, 165
famines, 73
Fanaswalla, Ismail Bhai, 32
farmers, 47–8, 56, 72
farming, 56, 69, 72, 185
farm management programmes, 72
father, 14, 15, 17–19, 28, 30, 33
Fatima Arzu Begum, my grandmother, 6–7, 10–11, 13–15, 20, 25, 31, 35, 133
Fazil, Yousif, 184
federal polity, 46
federal system, 101
feminist traditions, 149
festival greetings, 56
festival(s), 14, 28, 56, 154–7, 200
festivities, 28, 154
fight against the two-nation theory, 37
fight for Hindu-Muslim unity, and, 11
fighting for Rajya Sabha, 98
film industry, 19, 35, 37
Finance Bill, 1992, 107
Finance Commission, 50
financial assistance, 147
financial distress, 133
financial support, 147, 178
Finestone, Sheila, 127, 200, 202
Finnbogadóttir, Vigdís, 179
first day as Deputy Chairperson, 83
first trip to Delhi, 37
first woman to be elected Vice-President of the Executive Committee of the CPA, 93
first year in the Rajya Sabha, 85
fiscal responsibilities, 136
Five-Point Programme, 60
forcible sterilization, 61
foreign affairs, 130, 189
foreign direct investment (FDI), 192
foreign-owned companies, 70
foreign policy, 42, 78, 84, 184

forest-dwelling communities, 16
formal school system, 145
Fotedar, Makhan Lal, 87–9, 132
Founder President of the UN Parliamentarians' Forum for Human Development, 173
freedom fighter, xii, 86, 93
French Revolution of 1789, 13
friendship(s), 14, 30, 37, 116, 118, 132, 135, 186, 195
fundamental rights, 60

Gadgil, Dr D.R., 47
Gandhi, Indira, xiii, 13–14, 22, 24–5, 34, 44–6, 48–51, 55–6, 59–81, 87–8, 90–91, 96, 116, 130–32, 137, 139, 165, 168, 180, 184–5, 187, 192
Gandhi, Mahatma, 25, 45, 50, 97
Gandhi, Priyanka, 131
Gandhi, Rahul, 131
Gandhi, Rajiv, 3–4, 25, 79, 81, 83, 85–94, 101–2, 104–5, 109–10, 114–5, 118, 132, 137, 168–9, 172, 184, 187–90, 201
Gandhi, Sanjay, 25, 48, 60, 67–8, 70, 81
Gandhi, Sonia, 81, 91–2, 129–35, 137, 191
Gateway of India, 142
Gaza, 76
gender, 17, 41, 59, 169, 177, 180, 206
gender discrimination, 59
gender equality, xiv
gender equity, 169
gender responsive budgeting (GRB), 177
gender stereotyping, 180
General Agreement on Tariffs and Trade (GATT), 113
geopolitical groups, 128
geopolitics, 79
George, Vincent, 4, 87, 132
German Parliament, 126
Germany, 126
Ghalib, 18

ghazal, 18
Ghosh, Dipen, 98
Ghubar-e-Khatir (The Dust of Memories), 21
Ginwala, Frene, 177
Giri, Varahagiri Venkata, 45
girlhood, 15
Glasnost, 91
global leadership, 128
global parliamentary organizations, xiii
global warming, 184
Goan Catholic community, 35
Go-Between, The, 159
Godhra riots of 2002, 123–4
Golan Heights, 75, 76
gold medal, 26, 27
goodwill, xiii, 91, 100, 105, 116, 129, 186–7
goodwill delegations, 100, 129
goodwill missions, xiii
Gorbacheva, Raisa, wife of Gorbachev, Mikhail S., 91, 203
Gorbachev, Mikhail S., 91
Gorbachev's first visit to India, 91
Goswami, Arnab, 102
governance, xii, 3, 5, 170, 172
government agencies, 123
Government of India, 146–7, 166, 171
government schemes, 169
Governor of Manipur, xiv, 149, 155, 159
Governor's Cup boat race, 153
Gowthaman, Nirandhi, 165
Goyal, Chandrakanta, 119
Goyal, Piyush, 119
Goyal, Ved Prakash, 119
gram panchayat elections of 2001, 124
grandaunt, 7, 13
Grand Old Party, 46
grassroots institutions, 3
grassroots women, 5, 42
gravitating towards politics, 36
grief, 28, 67–8, 115, 118–9
Gujarat, 46, 71, 122–4

Gujarati language, 42, 47, 63, 82, 123, 185
Gujarat Samachar, 123
Gujjar community, 87
Gujral, I.K., 190
Gulf countries, 130, 178, 192
Gulf crisis, 187, 190
Gulf War, 44, 130, 190
Gulrukh, 31
Gungi Gudia (dumb doll), 45
Gupta, Bhupesh, 84, 102, 118
Gurupadaswamy, M.S., 83, 95
Guwahati, 149, 155
Gwalior, 119

Hajj pilgrimage, 9, 75
Haksar, P.N., 69–71, 73, 91
Hamari Dharohar scheme, 146–7
Hamari Goshthi, 92, 95
Hamidia College, Bhopal, 26
Hamidullah Khan, Nawab, 12
handicrafts, 6, 154
handmade artefacts, 7
Hanifa Abru (Abru Begum), Chhoti Amma, 6–7, 10, 13, 20
Hanif, Mohammad, the eldest son of Kalay Khan, 31
Hanjabam, Sukhdeba Sharma, 149
Hartley, J.P., 159
Hartley, L.P., 159
Harun al-Rashid, Caliph, 9
Haryana, 187
haunted tree, 16
Hawala security scandal, 174
Head of the Committee of Privileges, 96
Hebbar, K.K., xii
Heikal, Mohamad Hassanein, editor-in-chief of Al-Ahram, 76
Hejaz, Saudi Arabia, 9
Hema Malini, 173
Heptulla, 187
Heptulla, Akbar Ali Adamji, 31
Heptulla Park, xiii, 31, 35, 38, 40, 114

heritage conservation, 147
Hidayatullah, Mohammad, 190
higher education, 21, 207
Hindi language, 19, 37, 44, 72, 79, 82, 93, 96, 105, 134, 145
Hindi cinema/film, 19, 37
Hindu(s), 11, 13–14, 51, 116, 137, 189
Hindu-Muslim unity, 11
Hindu party, 137
Hindustani classical vocals, 18
Hindustan Times, 37
Hindutva, 136
History of Maharashtra, Ancient Period, 47
HIV-AIDS, 193
Holi festival, 14, 28, 119, 156–7
honour, xiv, 13, 96, 128–9, 158, 197, 201
Hope, Tina, 81
House Laughs: An Anthology of Wit and Humour in the Rajya Sabha, The, 84
House of Elders, 106
House of Lords of the United Kingdom, 101
household chores, 164, 166
Housing and Urban Development Corporation (HUDCO), 121, 123
human development, 193
Human Development Index (HDI), 193–4
Human Development Report, 193
human rights, 184
Humayun, Mughal Emperor, 186
humiliation, 88, 133
humility, 110–11, 201
Hum Kisise Kum Naheen, 19
humour, xiii, 82–85, 105, 116, 120, 201
Hurley, Siobhan Lambert, 12
Husain, M.F., 103
Hussain, Dr Zakir, the President of India, 45
Hussain, Syed Shahnawaz, 137
Hussein, Saddam, President of Iraq, 130, 190–91
Hyderabad, 6, 133

Iceland, 179
idea for women-run banks, 165
identity, 34, 46, 150, 203
Iftikhar Ali Khan, Nawab of Pataudi, 12
Ima Market, 152–3
imperial Iranian-Zoroastrian legacy, 146
Imphal, 149, 151, 154–6, 158
import controls, 192
incarceration, 20
In Cold Blood, xiv
independent India, xii, 10, 17, 68
India and Pakistan relations, 80, 185
India-Myanmar drug trafficking, 150
India Today, 30, 45, 63
Indian Army, 84, 154
Indian banking system, 111
Indian cinema, 19, 37
Indian Council for Historical Research (ICHR), 21
Indian Council of Cultural Relations (ICCR), 21
Indian delegations, 99
Indian delegation to the UN Commission on the Status of Women, 173
Indian Express, The, 168
Indian Institute of Technology (IIT Kharagpur), 21
Indian Kanoon, 60
Indian Muslim diaspora, 65
Indian Muslim woman, 129
Indian National Congress, xiii, 21, 30, 37, 44
Indian Ocean, 75
Indian Parliament, xii–xiv, 3–5, 8, 18, 22, 48, 60, 62, 71, 73, 75, 77, 81, 84, 89–90, 96–7, 99–102, 104, 109–10, 112–4, 116–7, 120, 123, 125–9, 134, 138–9, 165, 169, 172–6, 178, 183, 186, 193, 195, 202
Indian Parliamentary Diplomacy: Speaker's Perspective, 100
Indian politics, 120
Indian polity, 87
Indian princes, 12
Indian Science Congress Association (ISCA), 154
Indian spices and delicacies, 23
India's approach to climate change, 184
India's Central Vista Redevelopment Project, 97
India's dependence on imported oil, 74, 78
India's first expedition to Antarctica, 74
India's foreign policy, 78
India's forest wealth, 16
India's freedom struggle, 23, 25, 36, 4588
India's higher education, 21
India's independence, 11, 135
India's relations with Saudi Arabia, 77–8
India's telecom sector, 92
India's treatment of minorities, 78
India's unofficial goodwill ambassador, 91
Indira Gandhi National Open University (IGNOU), 83
Indira Gandhi's arrest, 63
Indira Gandhi's assassination, 51, 81, 139
Indira, S.G., 174
Indo-Arab Society, 42–4, 65, 91, 95
Indo-China war of 1962, 46
Indo-Myanmar border, 154
Indo-Naga Peace process, 150
Indonesia, 10, 199
Indo-Pakistani disputes, 70
Indo-Pakistan war of 1965, 46
Indo-Pakistan war of 1971, 60, 179
Indore, 34
Indo-Soviet women's magazine, 92
industrial and agricultural production, 60
industrial growth, 60

industry(ies), 19, 35, 37, 42, 57, 146, 151
inflation, 60, 111
infrastructure investment, 136
inhuman treatment of East Pakistanis, 179
insecurity, 90, 177
inspiration, 19, 24
Instrument of Accession, 189
insurgency, 86, 140
integrity, 25, 150
interactive Parliament, 101
internal party democracy, 45
international conferences, 91, 194
international exhibition, 146
International Journal of Research in Social Sciences, 12
international politics, 55, 133
international relations, 43
International Women's Day, 176
International Women's Year, 168
Inter-Parliamentary Union (IPU), xiv, 99, 125–9, 140, 167, 175, 177, 193–6, 198, 200–202
intricacies of politics, 49
IPU agenda, 127
IPU conference, 127, 140, 201
IPU Council, 129
IPU Executive Committee, 125–7
IPU Gender Partnership Group, 127
IPU Millennium Conference, 196
IPU presidency, 126, 128–9, 140
Iqbal, 18, 207, 208
Iran, 147
Irani, Khodabux Rustom, 65
Iraq, 130, 178, 190–91
Islam, 27, 78, 145, 199
Israel, 75–6
Iyengar, Indira, 13, 14

Jabalpur, 34
Jacob, M.M., 93
Jahan Begum, Nawab Sultan, 12–13
Jahan Begum, Sultan, 12–14, 17

Jain, Chandrika Abhinandan, 173–4
Jains, 144
Jaipal Reddy, S., 107, 113
Jaitley, Arun, 86, 103, 135–6
Jakhar, Balram, 184–5
Jalalabad, 12
Jalan, Bimal, 103
Jama Masjid, 13, 37, 61, 65
Jamia Millia Islamia, 21, 145
Jammu and Kashmir (J&K), 85–9, 168, 188–90, 203
Jammu and Kashmir Pradesh Congress Committee, 168
Janata Dal, 95, 176
Janata Dal (Socialist), 104
Janata Party, xiv, 48, 62–3, 83, 95, 99, 103, 175
Janata Party alliance, 62
Janta Dal, 117
Japan, 199
Jawahar Rozgar Yojana, 171
Jayalalithaa, J., 174
Jeddah Chamber of Commerce and Industry, 77
Jethmalani, Ram, 111–2
jewellery, 13, 147, 153, 205
Jhala, Digvijaysinh, Maharaja of Wankaner, 71
Jinnah, Muhammad Ali, 37, 189
Jiyo Parsi scheme, 147
J&K elections in 1987, 168
Jnanpith Award, 173
job of Assistant Professor, 28
jobs, 39, 57–8, 114, 206
Johnsson, Anders, 201
joined the Rajya Sabha, 90, 169
Joint Parliamentary Committee (JPC), 111
joint Parliamentary Committee on Empowerment of Women, 176
joint ventures, 80, 192
Jordan, 76, 178, 187–90, 196
Journey through Pakistan, 186
Junior Research Fellowship, 28

justice, 99, 128

Kalam, Dr A.P.J. Abdul, 121
Kalay Khan, 31
Kamaraj, Kumaraswami, 44
Kant, Krishan, 117, 138
Kapoor, Shammi, 36
Karanjia, Russy, 37
Karat, Brinda, 173
karchobi, 6
Kar, Ghulam Rasool, 86, 168
Karnataka, 48, 155, 171
Kashmir Accord, 87–9
Kashmir elections, 88
Kashmir Files, 85
Kashmiri 'lobby', 88
Kashmiri Pandit, 87
Kaul, M.N., 113
Kaul, Rajkumari, 133
Kenia, Kumari Chandrika Premji, 174
Kerala, 93, 203
Kesri, 131, 134
Kesri, Sitaram, 131
Khadi Bhandar, 25
Khadija Begum, 10
Khalid, Royal Highness King, 79
Khan, Aamir, Tahir bhai's son, 19
Khan, Azad Rao, 19
Khan, Genghis, 200–201
Khan, Shaharyar M., 14
Khaparde, Saroj, 80
Khatun, Kumari Sayeeda, 174
Khilauna, 18
Khusrau, Amir, 20–21
Kidwai, Mohsina, 82
King Abdulaziz City of Science and Technology, 74
King Abdullah of Saudi Arabia, 187
King Bhoj, 163
King Hassan of Morocco, 188
King Hussein of Jordan, 187–90
Kipgen, Nemcha, 151
knitting, 8
Kolukheri, 15

Konkani language, 46
Kovind, Ram Nath, 154
Krishi Darshan, 72
Krishna Menon, V.K., 38
Kukis, 148, 151, 153
Kumaratunga, Chandrika Bandaranaike, 180
Kumar, Dilip, 37
Kumar, Meira, 100
Kumar, Santosh, 33
kundan jewellery, 13
Kurdish insurgency, 140
Kutch, 122–3
Kuwait, 178, 188, 190–91

Lab to Land Policy, 69
Labour Party, UK, 196
Lady Hardinge Medical College, Delhi, 25
Lahore, 6
Laishram Devi, 149
Lalit Kala Akademi, 21
Land of Golden Girls, 149
land reforms, 47
land rights, 150
language politics, 46
languages, 7, 46, 72, 125, 133, 199
Lata Mangeshkar, 173
Latin American countries, 177, 178
Latin American Parliament, 128
Leader of Common People, 46
Leader of the House, 90, 95, 98, 107
Leader of the Opposition (LoP), 48, 95, 98, 105, 133
leadership, xiv, 39, 44, 47–9, 76, 121, 127–8, 134–6, 151, 165, 169, 172–3, 180–81
leadership roles, 127, 165
learning, xiii, 7, 12, 42, 56, 83, 91, 158, 172–3, 203, 206
learning experiences, 83
learning the value of humour, 84
Left-leaning ideology, 36
legacy, 11–12, 36, 146

legal reforms, 181
legislation against brothels, 167
lesson on surviving, 64
liberal atmosphere at home, 17
liberation of Bangladesh, 179
Liberation Tigers of Tamil Eelam (LTTE), 115–6
Libya, 65
license raj, 70
life as a parliamentarian, 137
life partner, 32–3
Lighter Moments in the Rajya Sabha, 83, 85
Likmabam, Shushila, 149
Line of Control (LoC), 70, 87
Li Peng, fourth Premier of the People's Republic of China, 195–8
literacy, 93
literature, 18, 101, 147
livelihood, 40, 145, 177
livelihood insecurity, 177
live telecast of Parliament proceedings on Doordarshan, 102, 138
living standards, 181
L.K. Advani's chariot journey, 114
local government, 41
Local self-governance, 5, 172
Lohia, Ram Manohar, 44–5
Lok Sabha (Lower House), 3, 38, 45, 48, 59, 62, 82, 99–102, 104, 107, 125, 169, 175–6, 184
Lok Sabha, election of, 1971, 59
Lok Sabha Speaker, 45, 125, 175
Lokpal Bill, 83
Loktak Lake, 149, 156
London School of Economics, 69
longest-serving presiding officer of Parliament, 97
Lord Meghnad Desai, 196
Lucknow, 19, 34, 205
Luqman, Farouk, 78
Lu Shaye, 196–7

Machchhu River, 71

Madhya Pradesh, 95, 119, 137
madrassas, 145–6
Magarief, Dr Mohammed Yousef, 65
Magsaysay Award, 173
Mahajan, Pramod, 109, 122
Maharani Laxmi Bai Girls College, 26
Maharashtra, 21, 34, 44–51, 58, 67–8, 72, 84, 88, 94–5, 141, 155, 165, 167, 203
Maharashtra: Land and Its People, 46
Maharashtra politics, 47, 49
Maharashtra State Gazetteers, 47
Maharashtra State Government Committee for the Status of Women, 167
Mahatma Gandhi's vision, 50
Maha Upanishad, 183
Mahbub ul Haq, 193
Maheshwari, Sarla, 174
Majaz Lakhnawi, 18
Malaysia, 199
Mamola Bai, Bhopal's first woman ruler, 13
Mandal Commission Report, 114
Mandal, Prasanta Kumar, 12
Mandir-Masjid disputes, 109
mandi (wholesale market), 56
Manipur, xiv, 148–9, 167, 203
Manipur Assembly elections of 2017, 151
Manipuri cuisine, 158
Manipuri culture, 154
Manipuri dance, 149
Manipuri society, 158
Manipuri women, 152
Manipur University of Culture, 158
Mansoor, Nasir Bhai's son, 19
Manual on Labour Statistics, 166
manuscripts, 147–8
Maratha hegemony, 48
Maratha leadership, 47–9
Marathas, 46–7
Marathi language, 46, 49–50, 82
market securities scam, 111

marksmanship, 12
marriage, xiii, 25, 27, 32–5, 37, 158, 164, 205
martial arts, 12
Marxism, 39
Mary Kom, 149, 152
maternity leave, 58
Mathur, Professor Ravi Prakash, 27
Maulana Azad's family, 14
Maulana Azad's political persona, 11
Maulana Khairuddin, 9, 10
Maulana Munawaruddin, 9
Mayaram, Dr Arvind, 145, 147
Mayawati, 5
Mazid, Sabiha, 168
McSweeney, Brenda, 193
Mecca, 9–10, 184, 188
mechanization, 58
mechanized farming, 185
media, 39, 60, 99, 104, 178
media reports, 99
media training, 39
Medina, 10
Meeting of Women Parliamentarians of the IPU, 126
Mehta, Har, 112
Mehta, Harshad, 111–2
Meitei(s), 148, 151, 153
Member of Parliament (MP), 22–3, 43, 45, 49, 68, 76, 81, 84, 93–4, 99–101, 104–6, 108–11, 113–4, 116, 120–23, 129–30, 137, 139, 172, 176, 194, 198, 200
Member of Rajya Sabha, 34
Members of Parliament Local Area Development Scheme (MPLADS), 96, 120–23
Menon, Shivshankar, 197
mentors, xiv, 34, 40, 51
mentorships, 40
Mexico, 128
middle classes, 69
Middle East, 77
migrants, 40

Millennium Conference of Presiding Officers, 129
Ministry of Culture, 146
Ministry of External Affairs (MEA), 75, 100, 126, 189, 191–2
Ministry of Finance, 145
Ministry of Home Affairs, 89, 146, 154
Ministry of Minority Affairs, 144–8
Ministry of Parliamentary Affairs, 100
Ministry of Rural Development, 171
Ministry of Social Justice & Empowerment, 144
minorities, xii, 78, 80, 136, 144
minority children, 145
minority communities, 144
Mir, 18
Mishra, Bijayani, 168
Mishra, Jayant, 138
misogyny, 180
mistrust, 65, 131, 135
modern democracy, 5
modern India, xi, xiii, 146
modernity, 12, 95
modernization, 47, 58, 147
Modi, Narendra, xiv, 122–4, 144, 149, 154, 167, 184
Mody, Piloo, 103
Mohammad Sayed, 10
Money Bills, 100
Mongella, Gertrude, 174
Mongolia, 79, 199–201
Moopanar, G.K., 89
Moradabadi, Jigar, 18
Morarji government, 62
Morocco, 113, 188
Motilal Vigyan Mahavidyalaya, 26
Motion of Thanks on the President's Address, 174
MPLADS funds, 121–2
MPLADS Guidelines, 123
Mrs Gandhi arrested, 63
Mrs Gandhi's assassination on 31 October 1984, 51, 80, 90
Mrs Gandhi's campaign, 65

Index 229

Mrs Gandhi visited Saudi Arabia, 74, 79
Mrs Gandhi voted back to power, 49
Mubarak, Hosni, 188
Mugabe, Robert, President of Zimbabwe, 179
Mughal court, 9
Mughal Empire, 9
Mukherjee, Aditya, 45
Mukherjee, Mridula, 45
Mukherjee, Pranab, 83, 90–91, 98, 107, 113, 147, 165
Mukhopadhyay, Purabi, 174
murder, 12, 61
museums, 147
mushairas (poetry recitals), 18
Musharraf, General Pervez, 127
music, 18, 146, 154, 157, 202
musical journey, 19
Muslim(s), xii, 6, 9–14, 22, 31, 61, 65, 74, 78, 124, 129–30, 136–7, 144–6, 184, 188–9
Muslim intellectuals, 65
Muslim leadership, 136
Muslim women, xii, 6
Muslim World League (*Rabitah Alam Islami*), 74, 188
mutual respect, 116, 132
Myanmar, 148, 150, 154, 199

Nadia, granddaughter, 156
Naga(s), 148, 150–51, 153
Nagaland, 150
Nagpur, 47
Naidu, Venkaiah, 137, 154
Naik, V.P., 47
Nai Manzil (new horizons), 145
Naini Jail, Allahabad, 21, 65
NAM's policy, 43
Naqvi, Mukhtar Abbas, 137
Narasimha Rao, 4, 91, 111, 117–8, 120, 132–3, 135, 172, 175, 187, 191
Narayanan, K.R., 112, 116
Narayan, R.K., 103
Narcotic Drugs and Psychotropic Substances (NDPS) Bill, 83
Nariman, Fali, 103
Narmada River, 11, 28
NASA, 29
Nasir, 35
Nasir Bhai, 19, 35, 36
Nasir Hussain, 19
Nasseef, Abdullah Bin Omar, 74, 188
Nasser, Gamal-Abdel, 43, 75
Natarajan, Jayanthi, 173, 174
National Building Construction Corporation (NBCC), 123
national calamities, 122
National Conference (NC), 86–7, 89, 168
National Film Awards, 173
National Forest Policy of 1988, 16
National Geographic, 17
National Human Rights Commission, 169
National Institute for Public Finance and Policy, 170
Nationalist Congress Party (NCP), 130
nationalization of banks, 70
National Legislature of China (NPC), 196
national parties, 39
national politics, 23, 47, 55, 97
national security threats, 60
National Students' Union of India (NSUI), 85–6
National Waqf Development Corporation Limited (NAWADCO), 148
Nawab Begums, 11–12, 14
NDTV, 102
negotiation(s), 58, 88, 194
Nehru-Gandhi family, 132
Nehru, Pandit Jawaharlal, 17, 22, 24–8, 38, 42–3, 45–6, 50, 65–6, 68–9, 77, 88, 184
Nehruvian vision on foreign relations, 43
Nene, Professor Dr, 27

neorealism, 37
New Delhi Declaration, 177–8
new India, 24
newly independent countries, 43
New Parliament House, 97
New York Times, The, xi, 48
NGOs, 165, 175, 193–4
nikah (marriage) ceremonies, 33
Nilamani, Ningombam, 157
Ninth Five-Year Plan, 174
Ninth Lok Sabha, 104
Nixon, Richard, 76
nominated as UNDP Distinguished Ambassador of Human Development, 173
nomination to the Rajya Sabha, 67
Non-Aligned Movement (NAM), 43, 184
non-Indira breakaway faction, 48
Non-resident Indians, 192
Nordic countries, 127
Northeast India, 62, 148, 154–5, 176
North India, 34
North West District Congress Committee, 38
nostalgia, 163
Numaish (exhibition), 7, 146
Nupi Keithel, 152
Nuruddin, Maulana Azad's nephew, 17

Obaid, Dr Rida, 74
Odisha, 120, 121, 122
Oil and Natural Gas Corporation Ltd (ONGC), 63
Old Parliament House, xiii, 97
Onmanorama, 190
open-door policy reforms, 192
Operation Badr, 76
Operation Blue Star,, 50
opportunism, 118
Opposition, the, 4, 48, 83, 95, 98, 102, 105, 107, 109, 113, 137, 139, 171–2, 194
opposition to Emergency, 61

opposition to Mrs Gandhi, 61
orderly conduct in the House, 107
Organization of the Islamic Conference (OIC), 188
Organization of the Petroleum Exporting Countries (OPEC), 80
organized sector, 145
Ottoman Empire, 9
outdoor sports, 17
Ozma, my sister, 8, 15, 28, 31

Padma Awards, 173
painting, xii
Pakistan, 22, 37, 46, 60, 70, 77–8, 80, 86–7, 116, 127, 136, 179, 185–9
Pakistan Movement, 37
Pakistan's recognition of Bangladesh, 70
Pakistan (West Pakistan), 22, 37, 46, 60, 70, 77–8, 80, 86–7, 116, 127, 136, 179, 185–9
Palace of the Revolution, 198
Palanithurai, G., 184
Panchayati Raj Bill, 169–70, 172
Panchayati Raj Institution (PRI), 3, 169–70, 172
Pande, Mrinal, 92
Pandey, Manorama, 174
Pandey, R.N., 170
Pandit Nehru's vision, 69
Paredes, Beatriz, 128
Parekh, Asha, 36
Park, Chung-Soo, 127
Parliamentarians' Forum for Human Development, 173, 194
Parliamentary Committee, 96, 111, 120, 176
Parliamentary Committee on Empowerment of Women, 96, 176
parliamentary committees, 100
parliamentary democracy, 93
parliamentary politics, 81
parliamentary practice, xiv, 106
parliamentary system, 105, 125

Index

Parsi community, 147
Parsi conference, 147
Parsi culture, 146
Parsi diaspora, 147
Parsis, 144, 146
participation of women in elected bodies, 169
partition of India, 22, 37, 185, 189
party affiliations, 116
party decisions, 134
party interest, xiii, 98
party leadership, 48, 134
party lines, 84, 94, 117–8, 120
party politics, 133, 190
Parzor Foundation, 146
passion, 16, 24, 40
Patan, 123
Pataudi, Mansur Ali Khan, 12
Patel, Keshubhai, 124
Patel, Rajni, 37
Pathak, A.S., 46
Pathan invaders, 163
Patil, Pratibha Devisingh, 93, 165, 176
Patil, Shivraj, 99, 125, 175
Patil, Vasantdada, 88, 132
Patnaik, Navin, 121, 193
patriarchal patronizing of women, 5
Patriot, 37
patriotic alliance, 37
Paul Kurian, 58
Pawar, Sharad, 46, 50, 130, 141–3
peace, 14, 43, 56, 76, 125, 128, 159, 167, 184, 187
peace movements, 128
Perestroika, 91
periodic health check-ups, 168
perseverance, 40, 72
Persian, 7, 20
personality, 35, 45, 56, 78, 95, 120
personality cult, 45
personal letters, 125
personal relations, 93, 165
personal sacrifices, 23
personal stories, 120

Petrovsky, Vladimir, 126
Pew Research, 180
Phadnis, Aditi, 114
PhD in zoology, 9, 26, 28–9, 36, 205
philanthropy, 7, 146
physical fitness, 17
pilot programme, 165
Pilot, Rajesh, 130
Pitroda, Sam, 92–3
plurality, 21
poetry, 6, 8, 18
poetry recitals, 18
Point of Order motion, 106–7
police brutality, 60
political activism, 20
political allies, 62
political biases, 117
political blunder, 63
political career, xiii, 62, 68, 89
political culture, 105
political family, 40, 180
political friendships, 118
political instability, 48
political institutions, 39
political issues, 17, 94
political leadership, 39, 180
political metaphor, 98
political parties, 41, 99, 114, 117, 132, 179
political power, 44, 47, 180
political powerbrokers, 61
political realignment, 114
political reforms, 174
political rights, 178
political stalwarts, 44, 46, 88, 96, 133
political system, xii, 4
political wheel of fortune, 132
political work, 34, 40, 42
politics, xiii, 22–3, 36–40, 44, 46–51, 55, 57, 64, 81, 84, 89, 91, 95, 97, 116–8, 120, 127, 131–3, 150, 178, 190, 203
politics in transition, 125
politics of patronage, 64
population control, 193

positive impact on women, 165
post-doctoral research, 32
post-doctorate, 29
poverty, 60, 144, 167
power-flexing, 88
powerlessness, 90
power of institutions, 21
power politics, 116
power struggles, 104, 118
Practice and Procedure of Parliament, 113
Pradhan Mantri Awaas Yojana-Gramin (PMAY-G), 171
Prakash, Professor Ravi, 27–8
Prasada, Jitendra, 130
Prasad, Pallavi, 111
Prasad, Ravi Shankar, 165
Prasad, Ravi Visvesvaraya Sharada, 62
Prasar Bharati Bill, 107
Preamble to our Constitution, 184
presidential election, 45
President of the IPU, 128, 198
President's Rule, 171
presiding officer, xiii, 4, 97–8, 105, 108–9, 118, 130, 151, 171, 206
Press Information Bureau (PIB), 146
princely state of Bhopal, xii, 30, 44
Prince Sultan bin Abdulaziz Al Saud, 188
Princess of Wales Ladies' Club, 7
Print, The, 45
Pritam, Amrita, 103, 173
privileges of MPs, 110
procedural deadlocks, 107
proceedings of the House, 95, 106, 173
progressive women, 12
promise to Pandit Nehru, 27
propaganda, 39, 48, 55, 60, 186, 188
propaganda against India, 188
Prophet Muhammad, 145
ProQuest LLC, 12
protests, 97, 114, 151
public gatherings, 61
public life, 6
public policing, 60
public scandal, 62
public service, xii, 25, 60
public speaking, 39, 103
Pune College of Agriculture, 14
Punjab, 50, 51
Purani Dilli, 37
purdah, 17

Qasim, Dr Syed Zahoor, 74
Qayamat Se Qayamat Tak, 19
Queen Kamlapati, 163, 164
Queen Zubaida, 9
Question Hour, 108, 174
Quint, The, 111
Quit India Movement, 21, 37
Quran, 135
Qureshi, Shamim, 67

Raas Leela dance, 149
Rabia, Princess, 12
Rabri Devi, 120
radical food policy, 56
Rae Bareli, 59, 62
Raga Jaijaiwanti, 19
Raga Khamaj, 19
Rahmani 30, 144
Rahman, Sheikh Mujibur, 179
Rai, Kalpnath, 80
rainwater harvesting, 121
Rajasthan, 119, 137
Raje, Vasundhara, 119, 129
Rajiv Gandhi's assassination, 115, 118, 132
Rajiv Gandhi's encouragement, 81
Rajiv Gandhi's government, 169
Rajiv Gandhi's vision, 92
Rajkot, 122–3
Raj Narain, 59–60, 62
Rajya Sabha (Upper House), xiii, 3–4, 34, 42–3, 49, 67–8, 70, 82–6, 90, 93–4, 96–103, 107–8, 110–13, 116, 118–23, 125, 132, 135, 137–8, 139, 167, 169, 173, 175–6, 191
Rajya Sabha membership, 67

Rashtrapati Bhavan, 144
Rashtriya Janata Dal, 176
Rashtriya Mill Mazdoor Sangh (RMMS) Swadeshi, 57–8
Rau, Johannes, 126
Ravi, R.N., 150
Ravi Shankar, 103
Ray, Bharati, 174
Ray, Siddhartha Shankar, 60
Reagan, Ronald, 92
Red Sea, 75
refugees, 60, 179
regional conflicts, 76
regional politics, 46–7
relentless diplomacy, 12
relief funds, 122
relief work, 120–21
religions, 22, 157, 199, 203
religious pluralism, 156
religious polarization, 22
Representation of the People Act, 1951, 59
reservation, 3–4, 94, 169, 172, 176
Reservation of seats for women, 3–5
resignation as general secretary, 89
resignation as Deputy Chairperson of the Rajya Sabha, 137
resignation from the Congress, 88, 136–7
resource management, 69, 71–2
responsibility(ies), 31–2, 67, 82, 85, 100–101, 123, 130, 136–7
Review of Agrarian Studies, 166
revolutionary nationalism, 11
riding, 5, 12
Right Livelihood Award, 173
right to be heard, 5
right to equal opportunity, 5
right to vote, 5
rights, 5, 16, 60, 96, 150, 168, 178, 184
Rio de Janeiro, Brazil, 194
riots, 114, 123–4
road and highway infrastructure, 136
road-building programmes, 58

role of Parliament, 99
role of presiding officers, 98
romance, 163
royal children, 14
royal family, 12–14, 31
royals of Gwalior, 119
Rubina, daughter, 35, 156, 158
Rule Book, 96, 98, 102
rule of law, 78
ruling party, 3, 48, 83, 139, 172
rural India, 69, 74
rural women, 58
Russia, 92, 203
Russian language, 92, 125

Sadat, Anwar, 75–6
Safiya, wife of Jan Nisar Akhtar, 18
Safvi, Rana, 37
Sagar,, 34
Sahitya Akademi, 21
Sahni, Balraj, 37
Sajida, Princess, 12
Salim Ali, Dr, 30, 36, 103
Samajwadi Party, 117, 119, 176
Samant, Dr Datta, 57
Samvidhaan Hatya Diwas, 61
Sanchi, 34
Sangai Express, The, 149
Sangai Festival, 154
Sangeet Natak Akademi, 21
Sanghvi, Vijay, 123
Sangma, P.A., 130, 176
sanitation, 12, 41, 121
Sanjay Gandhi's tragic death in 1980, 81
Sanjiva Reddy, Neelam, 45, 46
Sardesai, Rajdeep, 102, 134, 191
Saskatchewan, 184, 202
Sattar, Abdul, 185
Saudi Arabia, 5, 9–10, 43, 65, 73–4, 77–80, 91, 184, 187–8, 192, 201
Saudi Arabian National Center for Science and Technology (SANCST), 74

Saudi Radio, 78
Sayeed, Mufti Mohammad, 86
Sayidaty, 78–9
Sayyid Yusuf Ali, 14, 30
scam, 111, 112
Scheduled Castes (SC), 170
Scheduled Tribes (ST), 170
schemes for underprivileged women, 12
school vacations, 81
science and technology, 68, 71
Scindia, Madhavrao, 119, 175
Scindia, Rajmata Vijaya Raje, 119
sculptures, 11, 147
Sea of Galilee, 76
secularism, 37
Sen, Ashoke Kumar, 84, 102
Senior Research Fellowship, 29
senior women, 59
Sen, Justice Ashoke Kumar, 84
sentiments, 96, 107, 123
Sethi, P.C., 63
sexism, 180
sexual freedom, 167
sex work, 167–8
sex workers, 167
Shabbir Bhaisaab, 143
Shaheen Group, 144
Shahi Imam of Delhi's Jama Masjid, 61, 65, 130
Shah Jahan, 37
Shakdher, S.L., 113
Shakker, Fatina Amin, 78
Shanti Swaroop Bhatnagar Award, 173
Sharda, Savita, 174
Sharma, Krishna Dayal, 80, 187
Sharma, Shankar Dayal, 30, 33, 38, 59, 94, 96, 99, 109, 165, 178, 188
Shastri, Lal Bahadur, 44
Sheba, daughter, 116, 140
Sheikh Hasina, 179–80
Sheikh Mohammad bin Zahire Watri, 10
Sheikh Sabah, Emir of Kuwait, 188

Shekhawat, Bhairon Singh, 117
Shiv Shanker, P., 95, 105
shouting brigade, 104
Shree 420, 37
Shri Mahila Griha Udyog Lijjat Papad, 42
Shyamala Hills, 14
Sikhs, 144
Sinai, 75–6
Sinai Peninsula, 75
Singh, Arjun, 85
Singh, Buta, 108
Singh, Charan, 43, 49
Singh, Digvijay, 191
Singh, Dr Manmohan, 133, 141, 177, 184, 191–3
Singh, Hari, 189
Singh, Jaswant, 84, 114, 191
Singh, Major General K.P., 154
Singh, Maya, 119
Singh, Natwar, 130, 189, 191
Singh, N. Biren, 151
Singh, Neetu, 36
Singh, Sanasam Yaiphaba, 149
Singh, Simpreet, 40
Singh, Vishwanath Pratap, 83, 104, 114, 172, 187–90
Sinha, Jayant, 155
Sinha, Kamla, 174
Sinha, Yashwant, 107, 155, 193
Sino-Indian relations, 27
Sitharaman, Nirmala, 144, 155
Six-Day War, 75
Sixty-third Amendment Act, 1989, 171
Sixty Years of Rajya Sabha, 97
skill development schemes, 145
skills, 6, 98, 109, 144–5
slums, 40–42, 61, 119, 165
social development, 170
social isolation, 144
social justice, 99
socially and economically disadvantaged communities, 114
social recognition, 5

social reforms, 12
social service, 95, 101
social work, xiii, 34
society, xii, 5, 13, 41–2, 68, 122, 128, 154, 158, 166–7, 172, 176, 191
socio-economic backwardness, 146
socio-economic reforms, 174
sojourns, 10
Sonia's insecurities, 135
Soomro, Illahi Bukhsh, 127
South Africa, 177
South Korea, 127
Soviet-India ties, 91
Soviet Union (USSR), 43, 91–2, 95
Spanish language, 125
Specialized Inter-Parliamentary Conference, 178
Special Mention, 106, 113
special political committee of the UN, 192
spiritual guide, 9, 22
sports, 12, 17, 146, 149
spying, 187
Sreenivasan, T.P., 190
Sri Aurobindo, 11
Sri Lanka, 116, 180
Srinagar, 86, 89
Srivastav, Raju, 120
Stamp, Laurence Dudley, 17
standard of living of the people, 50
Standing Committees, 99–100
state governments, 170–71
state protection for women, 59
state's politics, 46
statue of Maharana Pratap, 114
stay-at-home women's problems, 167
Straits of Tiran, 75
strategic significance of the Suez Canal, 43
struggle against colonialism, 24
struggle for independence, 36, 45, 65
success of the MPLADS funds, 122
Suez Canal, 43, 75
Sufi pir (spiritual guide), 9–10

sugar cooperatives, 47–8
Sultania Girls School, Bhopal, 17, 23
Sultania Hospital, Bhopal, 13
Sultan of Turkey, 10
Sultanpuri, Majrooh, 36
Suman, Shekhar, 120
summer holidays/vacation, 17, 19
Sunak, Rishi, 39
superpower, 43, 79
Supreme Court of India, 110, 168
Surat, 123
suspicion, 63, 65
sustainable consumption patterns, 121
sustainable development, 125, 194
sustainable livelihoods, 145
Swaraj, Sushma, 103, 135–6, 144
Sweden, 201
swimming, 12
Switzerland, 196
sycophancy, xiii, 136
Syria, 76, 147

Tahir Bhai, 35
Tahir Hussain, 19
Taimur, Syeda Anwara, 173, 174
taken-for-granted vote bank, 137
Talent Zone Academy, 144
Taliban, 198, 199
Tamil Nadu, 4, 44, 74, 115, 155
Tangdhar, 87
Tanzania, 175
Tarjumanul Quran, 135
Tata, Ratan, 147
teachings of Sri Aurobindo, 11
technology, 39, 47, 68, 71–2, 92–3, 121, 194–5
Teen Murti Bhavan, New Delhi, 25
Teesri Manzil, 19
tenure as a presiding officer, 109
Tereshkova, Valentina, 92
terrorism, 138
terrorist attack in Mumbai, 141
terrorist attacks, 86

Terrorists and Disruptive Activities (Prevention) Bill (TADA), 83
terrorists attack on Indian Parliament, 139
Tewary, K.K., 109–11
textile industry, 57
textiles, 147
Thakkar, Professor M.S., 28
'The Everlasting Flame', 146
The Oberoi, Mumbai, 143
The Taj Hotel, Mumbai, 143
Thierse, Wolfgang, 126
Third World, 43
three-tier system of democracy, 193
Tiananmen Square demonstrations, 195, 197
Tibet, 199
Times of India (TOI), The, 112, 163
Tiria, Kumari Sushila, 173
Tito, Josip Broz (popularly known as Marshal Tito), 43
togetherness, 135
tongue-in-cheek humour, 83
tourism, 86, 155
Towards Partnership Between Men and Women in Politics, 178
trade route, 75
trade unions, 41
tradition of learning, 9
tradition(s), 9, 12, 33, 95, 98, 108, 149, 153, 157–8, 200
traditional dance, 156, 158
tragedy, xv, 19, 28–9, 51, 163
training camps, 39
training for democracy, 39
training programmes, 145
transfer of technology, 194
Traore, Ibrahim, 140, 202
Treasury benches, 109
tree plantation, 60, 168
Trehan, Dr Naresh, 118
trip to Pakistan, 185
tropical cyclone in coastal Odisha in October 1999, 120

trust, 64, 123, 130, 132, 135, 159, 181, 207
Turkey, 10, 140
two-nation theory, 22, 37

UK Parliament, 98, 105–06
underground economy, 168
underprivileged women, 12
unemployment, 144
UN's Fourth World Conference on Women, 174
UN General Assembly, 169, 173, 195
UN's International Women's Year celebrations, 56
UN's Millennium Conference, 196
UN Observer, 195
UN peacekeeping forces, 75
UN programmes for women and the environment, 91
UN Women's Conference, 176
UNESCO, 146, 193
UNIFEM, 193
unimpeachable integrity, 25
Union Territory of Dadra, Nagar Haveli, Daman and Diu, 137
United Front government, 176
United Kingdom (UK), 29, 98, 101, 105–6, 196
United Nations Conference on Environment and Development (UNCED), 194
United Nations Development Fund for Women, 193
United Nations Development Programme (UNDP), 125, 173, 193–4
United Nations Environment Programme (UNEP), 73
United Nations (UN), xi–xiv, 43, 56–7, 73, 75, 91, 99, 125–7, 169, 172–4, 176, 182–3, 191–8, 203
United States (US), 5, 39, 43, 60, 76–7, 92, 100, 142, 155–6
universal education for children, 174

universal human yearnings, 6
University Grants Commission (UGC), 21
University of Newcastle, 29
unparliamentary language, 105, 106, 110
unqualified apology, 106
unrest in Manipur, 159
unwritten rules, 15
upbringing, 6
uplift of Indian women, 6, 13
Urban Design Research Institute, 40
Urdu language and literature, 6–7, 11, 13–14, 17–18, 82, 135, 145
Urdu literature, 18
Urdu poetry, 18
Urs, D. Devaraj, 48
US emergency military aid to Israel, 76
Ustad Hafiz Ali Khan (Ustad Amjad Ali Khan's father), 18
Uttar Pradesh, 5, 40, 65, 119

vaccination drives, 12
Vaishnava Sankirtana, 158
Vaishnavites, 148
Vaishnavite tradition, 157
Vajpayee, Atal Bihari, xiv, 95, 129, 133, 135–7, 184, 187, 191
Vajpayee government, 129, 136, 191
Varanasi, 115
Varhadi language, 46
vasectomy camps, 61
Vasudhaiva Kutumbakam, 183, 184
Venkataraman, R., 85
Vice-Chairman of the Commonwealth Parliamentary Association, 95
Vice Chairpersons of Rajya Sabha, 82
Vigyan Bhavan, 178, 188
Vikram University, Ujjain, 26
village panchayats, 170, 193
village women, 164
violating the Representation of the People Act, 1951, 59
violation of privileges of the Members of the House, 110
violation of the Chairman's privileges, 110
violence, 21, 41, 114, 124, 149–51, 159, 179–80
violence against women, 41
violence of the colonial rule, 21
visited China, 197
visited Jordan, 190
visited Saudi Arabia, 79
vivacious personality, 35
voluntary teaching, 29
vote banks, 61, 137
vote of confidence, 104
voting bloc, 61, 65
voting rights, 178
voting system, xii
V.P. Singh government, 190

wages and bonuses, 57–60, 177
Waqf properties, 148
way of life, 8, 92, 154
wedding, 10, 14, 31, 33–4, 61, 142, 158, 205
wedding cards, 33
wedding preparations, 33, 205
Well of the House, 108
West Asia, 43, 77, 187
West Asian strategy, 75
West Bengal, 5, 60, 149
Western India, 137
Western knowledge systems, 11
Western nations, 76, 180
Westminster system, 101
West Pakistan (now Pakistan), 179
whip, 17, 45
withdrawal of Israel from Gaza and the West Bank, 76
withdrawal of Israeli forces from Sinai, 76
Woman and Home, 17
woman President of the IPU, 128
woman President of the Latin American Parliament, 128

woman ruler of Bhopal, 12
women delegates, 92
women in leadership positions, xiv, 180
women journalists, 92
women leaders, 55, 180
Women Members of Rajya Sabha, 173
Women's reservation bill, 170, 172, 176
women role models, xiv
women rulers, xii, 207
women's agitations, 176
women's capacity building, 172
women's clubs and hospitals, 12
Women's Committee of the Rajya Sabha, 126, 167
Women's Coordinating Committee, 126
women's economic independence, 165
women's education and health, 12
women's empowerment, 3, 5, 41, 119, 169, 172, 177, 193
Women's History Month 2020: Sikandar Begum, Nawab of Bhopal, 13
women's issues, 5, 127, 164, 179
women's leadership, 180–81
women's market, 152
women's NGOs, 175
Women's participation in the freedom struggle, 41
women's representation, 173
women's rightful leadership roles, 127
women's schools and training institutes, 12
women's 'uplift', 41
women workers' demands, 58
working class, 57
working conditions, 57
working in the slums, 42
working with Narendra Modi, 122
working women, 32, 165
work life, xiii, 97, 149
workplace, 57, 59, 165
workplace policies, 165
World Bank, 145
World Plan of Action, 174
World Trade Centre, 140
World Trade Organization (WTO), 113, 193
World Wars, 21, 30
World Women's Forum at Harvard University, 173
wrongful arrest, 66

Yadav, Akhilesh, 120
Yadav, Lalu Prasad, 120
Yadav, Mulayam Singh, 119
Yadav, Shyamlal, 82
Yom Kippur, 76
Youth Congress, 41, 67, 86, 115
Yugoslavia, 43

Zainab, the niece of Sheikh Mohammad, 10
Zakaria, Dr Rafiq, 43, 67
Zakaria, Farid, 43
zardozi, 6
zari, 6
zero hour, 99
zero tolerance, 105
Zia-ul-Haq, Muhammed, then President of Pakistan, 77, 185
Zilla Parishad (District Council), 171–2
Zimbabwe, 179, 200
Zoroastrianism, 199
Zoroastrians, 144
Zubaida Canal, Mecca, 9